Philosophy and its Development in The Nikāyas and Abhidhamma

FUMIMARO WATANABE

MOTILAL BANARSIDASS
Delhi □ Varanasi □ Patna

Reprint : 1996
First Published in 1983

Head Office : Bungalow Road, Jawahar Nagar, Delhi-7
Branches : 1. Chowk, Varanasi-1 (U.P.)
2.Ashok Rajpath, Patna-4 (Bihar)

ISBN : 978-81-208-1181-2

Printed in India
By Shantilal Jain, at Shri Jainendra Press,
A-45, Phase-I, Naraina, New Delhi-110 028.
Published by Narendra Prakash Jain, for Motilal Banarsidass,
Delhi-110 007.

TABLE OF CONTENTS

FOREWORD

Professor Watanabe's main theme in this study is the development of logic, as a method of thinking or reasoning, in the Buddhist tradition. The discourses and especially dialogues attributed to the Buddha himself are full of arguments, partly informal and conversational but partly set out in a systematic way embodying logical principles. It should be noted here that, in order to establish whether the texts studied belong to the earliest accessible phase of the Buddhist tradition, Professor Watanabe has throughout collated the Pāli recension with the Chinese translations from other recensions. This collation should give us, in the case of agreement, texts as current before the schisms of the 3rd century B.C. which separated these recensions. In the subsequent period of the growth of the Abhidhamma in the various schools we find a new stage of strictly formalised arguments and debates, recorded especially in the Pāli *Kathāvatthu* and the Chinese translation of the Sabbatthivāda *Vijñānakāya*. These two texts of the 'Emptiness' Schools of the Theravāda group in fact seem to be based on records of the same debates against the 'Person' School which seceded, according to the tradition, in B.C. 286.

Professor Watanabe first seeks the meaning of the term *abhidhamma*, literally 'about the *dhamma*', since he rightly supposes that the earliest methods of argument and reasoning led directly into the systematic and formalised expression of the texts collected as *abhidhamma*. His initial conjecture is thus that this method called *abhidhamma* is itself the early logic of the Buddhists. This conjecture appears to be confirmed by the evidence of the earlier *Sutta* texts in which the origins of the method can be traced. But before investigating the meaning of the term *abhidhamma* it is first necessary to clarify the meaning of the simple term *dhamma* from which it was formed; thus *dhamma*, in which Professor Watanabe finds the four meanings 'truth', 'doctrine', 'morality' and 'principle', forms the actual starting point of this study.

The investigation shows that the dialogue form, or asking questions in order to elicit acceptable answers, is fundamental, a thread which runs through Buddhist philosophical analysis from the outset and through the whole period of the elaboration of *abhidhamma* texts.

Before studying the types of argument used in these dialogues in detail, Professor Watanabe takes note of a different element in the development of *abhidhamma*, namely the *mātikās*, 'matrices' or lists of topics which provided its content. He distinguishes two main types of *mātikā*: the 'practical' principles of meditation and the 'theoretical' principles which are the constituents of the 'world' and of 'man'. The former were studied synthetically by bringing together texts from the *suttas* bearing on the same topics. The latter were studied analytically by making dichotomies (on the basis of the principle of contradiction), trichotomies (of contraries and the neutral position between them) and various other classifications. The extant *abhidhamma* texts are shown to have been constructed by applying these methods of investigation.

After reviewing a selection of the somewhat informal methods of argument found in the *suttas*, Professor Watanabe in Chapter 11 takes up the strictly formalised debates of the *Kathāvatthu* and *Vijñānakāya*. Here a truly 'formal logic' is first found in the Buddhist tradition. The partial agreement of these two texts, of schools which separated during the reign of the Emperor Aśoka, appears to confirm the 3rd century B.C. as the period of the origin of a formal logic out of the practice of a formal debate with strict rules of procedure. The most valuable part of Professor Watanabe's study is his full account of the *Vijñānakāya* version of the debates against the 'Person' (Vajjiputtaka or Vātsīputrīya) School, which had not so far been adequately analysed and compared with the *Kathāvatthu* record.

Professor Watanabe arrives at the logically stimulating conclusion that the Buddha's philosophy is based on the mode of negation, is an avoidance of dogmatism, characterised by 'completely negative thinking'. This, he argues, is the mode or way which leads to freedom and humanism. It has been a pleasure to work with Professor Watanabe on these problems and we look forward to many more fruits of his negative thinking.

February 1982 A. K. Warder

PREFACE

It is said that ten years is an epoch. I tacitly understand this as a warning that at least during ten years something remarkable must be done with respect to learning. It is almost a decade since I completed the doctoral courses of the Department of Sanskrit and Indian Studies at the University of Toronto. In the meantime, I made slow progress in my study on account of my heart valves' operation in July, 1973. For me, fifteen or twenty years may be needed in order to make an epoch in learning. Or no matter how sufficient time is, it might be impossible for me to make it. But I think it is important to spend a lifetime in learning.

On reflection, it was Professor E. Mayeda of Aichi Gakuin University in Nagoya, Japan who first introduced to Japan Professor A. K. Warder's fascinating as well as extremely valuable study of the metres in the Pāli Canon, entitled *Pāli Metre*—A Contribution to the History of Indian Literature, and afterwards my uncle, S. Hanayama, Professor Emeritus of Tokyo University informed me that Professor A. K. Warder teaches at the University of Toronto and afforded me the occasion to go abroad for study. Then I became his student there because of my wish to carry on researches under him. It was 1965. I note, in passing, that in the spring of 1966 Professor E. Mayeda was first invited as a visiting professor from Japan to the University of Toronto by Professor A. K. Warder. I am deeply grateful to both Professor E. Mayeda and Emeritus Professor S. Hanayama for cultivating the opportunity to meet Professor A. K. Warder.

As a graduate student of the University of Toronto, I was much influenced by Professor A. K. Warder's lectures on linguistics, philosophy and literature, especially on selections from the Pāli Canon and on *Abhidhamma* philosophy, since I was very interested in such subject matters when enrolled as a graduate student at Ryukoku University in Kyoto, Japan. I therefore decided to make a special study of the *Nikāyas* and *Abhidhamma*, and after obtaining the M.A. degree and going on to the Ph.D. courses of the Department of Sanskrit and Indian Studies at the University of Toronto, I worked through the literature on the subjects under him for very long. Here I wish to express my deepest obligations to Professor A. K. Warder for critically reading my thesis and tirelessly making invaluable suggestions.

I was also given much useful information and helpful advice in their classes and in informal discussions by my other teachers: Professor T. Venkatacharya of the University of Toronto, Dr. H. Saddhatissa of the British Mahabodhi Society, who was a visiting professor of the University of Toronto at that time, Dr. J. W. Crichton who was then a professor of the Department of Philosophy at the University of Toronto, Professor H. G. Herzberger of the University of Toronto, Professor. B. K. Matilal of the University of Toronto, Professor J. D. Dhirasekera who is now the Editor-in-Chief of the Encyclopedia of Buddhism in Colombo, and many other professors. They are versed respectively in Sanskrit, Pāli, Modern Logic, Philosophy of Language, Indian Logic, Indian Philosophy, and other various fields of learning. To all of them I acknowledge with thanks my indebtedness.

My cordial thanks are likewise due to my colleague and able instructor Professor C. D. C. Priestley of the University of Toronto for giving me his good opinions and helping me improve my English style.

Nowadays I realize the weight of the words '*kalyāṇa mitta*', which literally mean 'good friend'. For me, he is sometimes a good adviser and a good teacher, by whom I am always brought up in many ways in my life. When I learn the fact that throughout the whole of Buddhism, to meet a good friend or to have good friends is very important in seeking the truth and in living the best life, I am very glad to have met many good teachers and friends, by whom so far I have been brought up in various respects. It is in fact the kind help of my teachers, colleagues, and friends which has enabled me to present my book in its present form.

Finally, I would like to add a word of grateful acknowledgement to my wife for her constant encouragement. I believe that my late parents and the eldest son protect me with blessings of the Triple Gem.

Kinki University
Higashi Osaka
January 1979

F. Watanabe

ABBREVIATIONS

A.	*Aṅguttara nikāya.*
AA.	*Aṅguttara Aṭṭhakathā* (Commentary, in Pāli) : *Manorathapūraṇī.*
adj.	adjective.
D.	*Dīgha nikāya.*
DAWB.	Deutschen Akademie der Wissenschaften zu Berlin.
Dh.	*Dhammapada.*
Dhs.	*Dhammasaṅgaṇī.*
Dpvs.	*Dīpavaṃsa.*
esp.	especially
GWG.	Gesellschaft der Wissenschaften in Göttingen.
IHQ.	*Indian Historical Quarterly*, Calcutta.
Itv.	*Itivuttaka.*
JPTS.	*Journal of the Pāli Text Society*, London.
JRAS.	*Journal of the Royal Asiatic Society*, London.
Kv.	*Kathāvatthu.*
lit.	literally.
M.	*Majjhima nikāya.*
MA.	*Majjhima Aṭṭhakathā* (Commentary, in Pāli) : *Papañcasūdanī.*
Miln.	*Milindapañha.*
Miln. T.	*Milinda-Ṭīkā.*
Nd(1)	*Mahāniddesa.*
Nd(2)	*Cūḷaniddesa.*
or g.	originally.
P.	Pāli.
Pṭm.	*Paṭisambhidāmagga.*
PTS.	Pāli Text Society.
RA	Royal Asiatic Society.

S.	*Saṁyutta nikāya.*
SA.	*Saṁyutta Aṭṭhakathā* (Commentary, in Pāli) : *Sāratthappakāsinī*
Samanta.	*Samantapāsādikā.*
SBB.	Sacred Books of the Buddhists.
Skt.	Sanskrit.
Sn.	*Suttanipāta.*
T.	*The Taisho Edition of the Chinese Tripiṭaka* (Taisho Shinshu Daizokyo).
Ud.	*Udāna.*
Vbh.	*Vibhaṅga.*
Vin.	*Vinaya*
ZDMG.	*Zeitschrift der Deutschen Morgenländischen Gesellschaft.*

PART I

THE ORIGIN OF ABHIDHAMMA PHILOSOPHY

1

INTRODUCTION

1.1 It was a *samaṇa* (striver) philosopher who claimed to have discovered the Four Truths. He founded his teachings on them. He was, therefore, called the Buddha, which is a title, meaning the 'enlightened'. To his disciples, his teachings were spiritual food. And even today, they are fresh gold in our cultural melting pot. After his enlightenment (531 B.C.),[1] he preached various doctrines to people of different spiritual and intellectual capacities, just as a doctor gives each patient a different type of medicine according to the nature of the illness. This is the manifestation of his *paññā* (understanding) and his *karuṇā* (compassion). This fact can also be realized from his last discourse in the *Mahāparinibbānasutta*, which is the work describing the scene before and after his final extinction (*parinibbāna*) :[2]

> Monks, the *dhammas* (doctrines[3]) which I have discovered and taught should be well learned by you, and practised,

---

1. We provisionally adopt 566 B.C. as a date for the birth. 537 B.C. for the renunciation, 531 B.C. for the enlightenment and 486 B.C. for the final extinction of the Buddha, because there is a certain doubt concerning the life of the Buddha. On this, see A. K. Warder, *Indian Buddhism* (1st edition), p. 44.

2. D.II, 119-20. This is available to us in several recensions. Refer to T. 1, 11a-30 b, 160b-175 c, 176 a-191 a, 191 b-207 c, T. 24,127 b-128 b and the Skt. text published by E. Waldschmidt in 1939, 1950 and 1951.

3. One of the meanings of the word *dhamma*, 'doctrine' or 'teaching' is generally accepted in Buddhism as the first of its senses. But, as we shall see in chapter 2, the word *dhamma* in this context could also be understood as meaning 'principle'.

developed and cultivated, so that this best life (*brahmacariya*) should be enduring and last long for the benefit and happiness of many people, for the world, for the welfare, benefit and happiness of men and gods. And which are the *dhammas*? They are:

1. four bases of self-possession,
2. four right exertions,
3. four bases of power,
4. five faculties,
5. five strengths,
6. seven factors of enlightenment,
7. eight factors of the way.

These are called the thirty-seven *bodhipakkhiyā dhammā* (doctrines or principles pertaining to enlightenment), which are widely used as the summary of the Buddha's teachings in Buddhist texts. Later on, these thirty-seven *dhammas* (which can also be called a set of seven headings) underlie the development of *Abhidhamma* philosophy.

1.2 After the Buddha's *parinibbāna*, a great number of *dhammas* (principles) taught by him and his chief disciples were compiled and came to be known as the *Sutta Piṭaka*, the collection of *suttas*.[1] At the same time; the constitution of the Buddhist communities was codified as the *Vinaya Piṭaka*, the collection of the discipline. In addition to these two *Piṭakas*, many doctrinal topics (*mātikā*) were gathered as the *Abhidhamma Piṭaka* (which could also be expressed as *Mātikā Piṭaka*, as we shall see in chapter 4). As a result, these *Piṭakas* came to be known as the *Tipiṭaka*, three kinds of collection.

About a century after the Buddha's *parinibbāna*, the Buddhists began to split up into separate schools. They seem each to

---

1. It is known in general that *sutta* is a sacred book (or scripture) beginning with the words *evam me sutam* (thus I have heard). But originally *sutta* meant 'dialogue' in Buddhist texts. This original meaning can also be discerned from those characteristics of *Sutta* reckoned as one of the nine *aṅgas* (types) of scripture (*navaṅga sāsanas*, see chapter **2.1**), e.g. those characterized by being divided into two parts : the explained and the explaining. On this, see E. Mayeda, *A History of the Formation of Original Buddhist Texts*, pp. 21-24.

have had its own recension of the *Tipiṭaka*. According to the Sthaviravāda school, the *Sutta Piṭaka* was arranged by the name of the "five *Nikāyas*" (collections) in the Pāli language (*bhāsā*),[1] preserved intact in Ceylon, Burma, Cambodia and Siam. According to the Chinese renderings, these collections are called the four (or five) *Āgamas* (traditions). The *Nikāyas* and *Āgamas* available to us are as follows:

	Pāli	Chinese renderings
1.	*Dīgha Nikāya*	*Ch'ang ah hsien* (*Dīrgha Āgama*)
2.	*Majjhima Nikāya*	*Chung ah hsien* (*Madhyama Āgama*)
3.	*Saṁyutta Nikāya*	*Sheng yü to ah hsien* (*Saṃyukta Āgama*)
4.	*Aṅguttara Nikāya*	*Yang chüeh to lo ah hsien* (*Ekottara Āgama*)
5.	*Khuddaka Nikāya*[2]	

The above five *Nikāyas* belong to the Sthaviravāda school. On the other hand, the four *Āgamas* belong to more than one school. The *Dīrgha* conjecturally belongs to the Dharmaguptaka school. The *Madhyama* and *Saṃyukta* seem to belong to the Sarvāstivāda school. There is another *Saṃyukta* which is incomplete. This is ascribed to the Kāśyapīya school. And the *Ekottara* is said to be a Dharmaguptaka text.[3]

As to the *Vinaya Piṭaka* now extant, we can mainly see the following texts, which belong to various schools:

1. The *Vinaya Piṭaka* of the Sthaviravāda school. (Pāli)
2. The *Shih-sung-lü* of the Sarvāstivāda school (sixty-one fascicles).
3. The *Ssu-fen-lü* of the Dharmagupta school (sixty fascicles).

---

1. It is pointed out that by Pāli is understood the language in which is composed the *Tipiṭaka*, ...The word *Pāli* however signifies only "(sacred) text." If we used this word to designate the language, it is merely a convenient abbreviation for *pālibhāsā*. On this, see W. Geiger, *Pāli Literature and Language*, p. 1.

2. As the fifth *Āgama*, we see the name of *Chu t'o chia ah hsien* (*Kṣudraka*) corresponding to *Khuddaka* in which twelve *sūtras* are reckoned. On this, see A. K. Warder, *Indian Buddhism* (1st edition), pp. 202-4.

3. Ibid, pp. 8-9.

4. The *Mo-ho-sêng-chih-lü* of the Mahāsaṃghika school (forty fascicles).
5. The *five-division-Vinaya* of the Mahīśāsaka school (thirty fascicles).
6. The *Kên-pên-shuo-i-ch'ieh-yu-pu-p'i-nai-yeh* of the Mūlasarvāstivāda school (fifty fascicles). (incomplete work)

We also have the Mūlasarvāstivāda *Piṭaka* from Tibet in the Tibetan language, and some Sanskrit fragmentary texts of the *Sūtra* and *Vinaya Piṭakas*.

1.3 We cannot deny the fact that the *Nikāyas* and *Āgamas* at our disposal include a number of late additions. But they are the oldest among all the Buddhist texts, so that we may grasp from them the Buddha's words and thought content directly; we might find out from them the best treasure (*dhanagga*) in Buddhism in common between the Mahāyāna and the old schools. Which are then the words he really spoke? It is certainly difficult to determine this point. Only one thing we can say here is that it may be possible to do so by examining the *Nikāyas* and *Āgamas* from all viewpoints. Fortunately, in order to determine which parts of the *Nikāyas* are likely to be the most original, so far some text-critical works have been carried out by certain scholars (e.g. A. K. Warder, *Pāli Metre* and *Indian Buddhism*). Therefore, on the basis of their works, we can start our study.

1.4 Under the title *Philosophy and its Development in the Nikāyas and Abhidhamma*, we intend to trace the development of the philosophical, and especially the logical aspects of Buddhist thought from the *Nikāyas* down to the systematic texts of the *Abhidhamma* class, finding certain embryonic anticipations of formal logical procedures.

This book is composed of twelve chapters, which can be divided into two Parts. The title of Part One is the Origin of *Abhidhamma* Philosophy, in which a brief survey of *Mātikās* (doctrinal topics) in the *Sutta* and *Abhidhamma* texts is given with the explanation of the thirty-seven *dhammas* as the summary of the Buddha's teachings, because it seems that in the earliest period the *Abhidhamma Piṭaka* consisted simply of some set of

Mātikās, originating from the *Nikāyas* and *Āgamas*. The title of Part Two is the Development of the Dialogue Form, where the characteristics of the style of argument used by the early Buddhists are clarified from a logical point of view.

In fact, it is impossible to read the *Nikāya* texts without constantly coming across important words such as *dhamma* and *abhidhamma*, which have multiple meanings. It is impossible to understand how the philosophical study of *dhammas* (principles) was made without noticing the conception of *abhidhamma* and its characteristics. Without clarifying the relationship between *Abhidhamma* and *Mātikā*, it is impossible to know the origin of *Abhidhamma* philosophy. Thus we shall examine these subjects in chapters 2, 3, 4, and 5.

Seeing that signs of fairly well advanced dialogue form are shown in the *Nikāyas* and *Āgamas*, it will be necessary first of all to discuss how the dialogue on *dhammas* (doctrines) was conducted and to see the characteristic of the four *pañhabyākaraṇas* (methods of answering questions) ; moreover, we cannot overlook the fact that the methods of Sañjaya's answer (in the time of the Buddha the teacher Sañjaya was known as the leader of the Agnostics) have something in common with the fourfold formulation or tetralemma, which is connected closely with the Buddha's way of thinking. These points are therefore discussed in chapters 6 and 7.

In the sense that certain words occupy a significant position in the evolution of thought, the relationship between *takka* and *dhammatakka*, both meaning logic, is discussed, especially from a semantical point of view, in chapter 8.

The logical analysis of *suttas* in the *Nikāyas* teaches us many important points in making clear the forms of argument used by the early Buddhists. In this sense, forms of reasoning and argument appearing in the *Nikāyas* are examined in chapter 9, and logical arguments in the dialogues (*suttas*) are clarified in chapter 10.

In order to trace the development of forms of questions and answers from the *Nikāyas* into the *Abhidhamma* texts, we take up the *puggalakathā* chapter in both the *Kathāvatthu* and the *Vijñānakāya*, and examine how questions and answers are treated in it in chapter 11.

It goes without saying that in our study, we need a comparison of the *Nikāyas* with the *Āgamas*, and so we refer to the Chinese versions according to the need. Where there is not much correspondence between the *Nikāyas* and *Āgamas*, it will be indicated in this book.

As a rule, Buddhist terms are given in their Pāli forms, because Pāli, though probably not the language of the Buddha, is close to it than Sanskrit. References are to the *Taisho Edition of the Chinese Tripiṭaka* and to the Pāli Text Society's edition of Pāli texts. Previous translations of some texts into English have been used, and quoted, but in many cases the technical terms have been retranslated to provide consistency with our discussions. For this reason, in quoting Chinese texts in English, their terms will be restored not into Sanskrit, but into Pāli, except for terms in the *Vijñānakāya* of the Sarvāstivāda school. Even Sarvāstivādin *Abhidhamma* terms have usually been given in Pāli for purposes of comparison, although these texts are believed to have been composed in Sanskrit. Titles of texts in Chinese and names of schools in Buddhism are by convention given in Sanskrit.

2

ON THE POLYSEMY OF THE WORD 'DHAMMA'

2.1 It is said that the first Buddhist council was held at Rājagaha under the leadership of Mahākassapa immediately after the Buddha had passed away. It is also said that the *Dhamma* (doctrine) and the *Vinaya* (discipline) taught by the Buddha were collected at this time.[1] It is, however, recorded in other texts that the teachings called *Abhidhamma* were collected with *Dhamma* and *Vinaya*,[2] or that the nine types of scripture (*navaṅga sāsanas*)[3] were assembled also at this time.[4]

Nowadays, Buddhist scholars recognize that *Dhamma* and *Vinaya* were compiled at the first Buddhist council on the basis of oral tradition. Now, how does the word *dhamma* differ from the word *abhidhamma*? It is necessary for us to clarify this point in making a study of philosophy and its development in the *Nikāyas* and *Abhidhamma*. But, prior to doing this, we need to define the word *dhamma* itself, because it has many meanings. In fact, it is no exaggeration to say that in the history of Indian philosophy the examination of various usages of the word *dhamma* may be one of the main subjects for

1. Vin. II, 285. The Mahīśāsaka Vin. (T.22, 190 b-c). The Mahāsaṃghika Vin. (T. 22, 491 c-492 a).

2. The Sarvāstivāda Vin. (T.23, 445 b). The Dharmagupta Vin. (T.22, 968 b).

3. They are known as *Sutta, Geyya, Veyyākaraṇa, Gāthā, Udāna, Itivuttaka, Jātaka, Abbhutadhamma* and *Vedalla.*

4. Dpvs. p. 31.

study. Even the concept of *dhamma* used in the *Nikāyas* is very complicated, and later on, among different schools of Buddhism (e.g. the Sthaviravāda school, the Sarvāstivāda school, etc.) great diversity of understanding exists as to what *dhamma* means in itself.

2.2 The purpose of this chapter is, however, to make clear the many meanings of *dhamma* in the *Nikāyas*, not to make reference to the different interpretations of *dhamma* maintained by Buddhist schools. Therefore, it is of crucial importance to determine the meanings of the word *dhamma* by judging the contexts in the *Nikāyas* in which the word *dhamma* occurs.

Apart from the etymological explanation of *dhamma* which can be derived from the verb *dhṛ* meaning 'to hold', 'to bear', 'to wear', 'to have', 'to support', etc., as far as the *Nikāyas* are concerned, our attention should be directed first towards the work of A. K. Warder, who indicates the basic meaning of the word *dhamma* to be approximately **'nature'**, and its usages divided into seven categories:[1]

1. (true, natural) doctrine;
2. natural phenomenon (including bad as well as good), natural element, natural substance, natural principle, phenomenon, element;
3. custom, way, law of nature, justice;
4. world, nature;
5. mental object, mental phenomenon, mental state, idea;
6. good mental object, good mental phenomenon, good idea (when opposed to bad: *adhamma*);
7. quality.

Afterwards, A. K. Warder tried to condense the above seven categories into five, like the following, because Nos. 5 and 6 of the seven are to be included in the same category as Nos. 2 and 3:[2]

1. doctrine.
2. phenomenon.

---

1. *Introduction to Pāli*, pp. 398-9.
2. *Indian Buddhism* (1st edition), pp. 97-100, pp. 162-5, p. 304, p. 443, esp. refer to pp. 578-9.

3. custom or justice.
4. nature (which occurs at the end of a compound).
5. quality or predicate (as a logical term).

The definition of the term *dhamma* (Skt. *dharma*) formulated by him is an exhaustive one.

Moreover, he published an article on "Dharmas and Data,"[1] in which he points out that a general notion of *dhamma* can be derived from the usages of the term in the Veda, in the pre-philosophical and proto-philosophical discourses, meaning something like 'maintaining', and further, that *dhamma* meaning an 'element' (as used by Th. Stcherbatsky[2]) and 'phenomenon' is not quite satisfactory at least in the old *Nikāyas*; instead, 'principle' seems to be a closer equivalent for *dhamma*. Except for *dhamma* signifying 'virtue' or 'justice' and the prominent usage of *dhamma* meaning 'doctrine' which could be derived from the idea of "the way things are," there is an interrelation between all other *dhammas* (e.g. *khandhas* 'aggregates' or 'groups', *āyatanas* 'spheres', *dhātus* 'elements', etc.). Also, some of them reduce to others and some are included in others. Thus, if these *dhammas* are taken as 'elements', the idea of 'elementary' must be distorted too much to accommodate them. They present more complexity than elements as an account of what there is. As far as we can see in the *Nikāyas*, there are ideas about the nature of all *dhammas*, as impermanent, empty, without soul, being stations or bases (*dhātus*) for other *dhammas*, etc.; there are attempts to establish the regularity of *dhammas* as determined by dependent origination; and there is a tendency to consider the *dhammas* as realities under the proper conditions; these *dhammas* are not merely 'elements' but 'principles'. Thus he states: "The term principle raises no expectation of a 'substance' or the like for it to inhere in. It also suggests something real and a cause or source, as well as regularity and truth... It may even be flexible enough to allow of the overlapping

1. *Journal of Indian Philosophy*, Vol. I, No. 3, November 1971, pp. 272-95.

2. He elucidates the Buddhistic technical *dhammas*, namely : *khandhas*, *āyatanas*, *dhātus*, and so forth, and regards the meaning of *dhamma* (*s*) as the element (s) of existence of matter and mind. On this see *The Central Conception of Buddhism and the Meaning of the Word "Dharma"*, p. 3.

or inclusion of *dhammas* which we find in the *Nikāyas*." (pp. 290-91)

It can be realized from the above that since 'principle' is closer to the import of the term *dhamma* in the *Nikāyas* and can cover more meanings, it is appropriate to substitute 'principle' for 'element' and 'phenomenon'.

Recently, A. K. Warder has also brought out a second edition of his book *Indian Buddhism*,[1] where he makes a considerable revision of the meanings of *dhamma* and concisely expresses the meanings of Nos. 2, 3 and 4 defined in a first edition of *Indian Buddhism* as 'principle'. Therefore, the meanings are :

1. doctrine.
2. principle.
3. quality or predicate (in the later logic).

This decidedly shows the way to the simplification from the complexity of the *dhamma*-meanings, picking up the essence of the meaning underlying a wide range of occurrences of the term.

As compared with the philological approach made by Magdalene and Wilhelm Geiger, who collect the usages of the word *dhamma* through Pāli canonical literature and elucidate more than sixty different meanings of it,[2] the above authentic studies made by A. K. Warder give us clear information of the meanings of *dhamma* as a philosophical concept, continuing the research of Th. Stcherbatsky. On the basis of A. K. Warder's studies, therefore, we would like to look at how the meanings of *dhamma* work in their respective contexts. For the sake of precision we would like to classify the differences in the meaning of *dhamma* into four types, because we will make use of the term frequently in our studies hereinafter. Since only one of them normally fits into a given context, let us see each case.

2.3 The Dhamma as the Truth. Although the generally accepted meaning of the word *dhamma* in Buddhism in the first of its senses as noted above is 'doctrine', it can also be understood as signifying 'truth'. For the Buddha's *dhamma* manifests

1. Published in 1980.
2. *Pāli Dhamma*.

the 'truth' which is naturally derived from his doctrine (s) or teaching (s), so that 'doctrine' and 'truth' may be in a certain sense inseparable. It would however be expedient to subdivide the Buddha's *dhamma* into two meanings: 'truth' and 'doctrine'. The former may be used as a narrow meaning and the latter, as a wide meaning.

As is generally known, that which the Buddha realized, the *dhamma,* was the order of law of the universe. And the Buddha was not a creator, but a discoverer of this order of the universe, in which the rational and the ethical elements are fused into one. This *dhamma* as discovered by the Buddha is synonymous with "the truth." And the Buddha is called "the Perfected One" or "one who is truly enlightened" (*sammā-sambuddha*). Therefore, the following statements, which express the essence of Buddhism, are recorded in the *Nikāyas* and *Āgamas* :

(1) *Yo kho dhammaṁ passati so maṃ passati; yo maṃ passati so dhammaṁ passati.*[1]

(2) *Yo paṭiccasamuppādaṁ passati so dhammaṁ passati; yo dhammaṁ passati so paṭiccasamuppādaṁ passati.*[2]

Especially, the first quotation suggests that the Buddha and the truth that he discovered are identical.

2.4 The Dhamma as Doctrine. The universal truth discovered by the Buddha is represented by the doctrine of the Four Truths (*saccas*), namely: (1) unhappiness (*dukkha*), (2) its origination (*samudaya*), (3) its cessation (*nirodha*) and (4) the way leading to this cessation (*magga*). It goes without saying that this *dhamma* was respected highly among a great many disciples of the Buddha as the doctrine leading to *bodhi* (enlightenment). However, because the Buddha preached his doctrine according to the mental and spiritual capacities of his disciples, a great number of doctrines (*dhammas*) were produced. Above all, the principles called "thirty-seven *bodhipakkhiyā*

---

1. He who sees the truth sees me (the Buddha); he who sees me (the Buddha) sees the truth. On this, see S. III, 120, T. 2, 652 c.

2. He who sees dependent origination sees the truth; he who sees the truth sees dependent origination. On this, see M. I. 190-1, T.1, 467 a.

dhammā" were esteemed greatly as the *dhammas* of practice which lead to calm, to insight, to enlightenment, to extinction (*nibbāna*, —of *bhava* 'existence'). The thirty-seven *bodhipakkhiyā dhammā*, we will call "thirty-seven *dhammas*" or "thirty-seven practical *dhammas*" below.

On the other hand, there are many doctrines which lead to enlightenment by understanding the Buddha's teachings logically or philosophically. For instance, the theory of dependent origination (*paṭiccasamuppāda*): "This being, this is (*imasmiṁ sati idaṁ hoti*); from the arising of this, this arises (*imassuppādā idaṁ uppajjati*). This not being, this is not (*imasmiṁ asati idaṁ na hoti*); from the cessation of this, this ceases (*imassa nirodhā idaṁ nirujjhati*)."[1] Or the doctrine of the twelve-linked chain of dependent origination (*dvādasa paṭiccasamuppādaṅgas*); these (namely, the theory of the dependent origination, the doctrine of the twelve-linked chain of dependent origination, and the like) would be called "theoretical doctrines (*dhammas*)."

Strictly speaking, the element of practice is included in any theoretical doctrine—for example, under the tree *Bodhi-duma*, the Buddha is said to have realized the chain of causation in direct and reverse orders by having given himself over to deep meditation (*jhāna*). In this case, the doctrine of the chain of causation would be the theoretical *dhamma* and the *jhāna* (or the four *jhānas*) would be the practical *dhamma*. Therefore, the practical and the theoretical *dhammas* may or may not be separable. But, in what we regard as theoretical *dhammas*, there are doctrines such as the five *khandhas*, six *āyatanas* and eighteen *dhātus*, which became the subject of study as the principles of matter (*rūpa*) and sentience (*nāma*) especially in *Abhidhamma* Buddhism, so that we would like to distinguish between the practical and the theoretical *dhammas* hereinafter.

2.5 The Dhamma as Morality. In order to demonstrate that the word *dhamma* means morality, Buddhaghosa (in the 5th century A.D.) quoted the following verse from the *Theragāthā* (No. 304):

1. M. II, 32, S. II, 28, T.2, 98 b, 100 a, etc.

> *Na hi dhammo adhammo ca ubho samavipākino; adhammo nirayaṁ neti dhammo pāreti suggatiṁ.*[1]

Thus, we see that the term *dhamma* meaning 'morality', 'merit' and the like is sometimes used with the term *adhamma* which means 'immorality', 'demerit' and the like. To take one more illustration, the point is:[2]

> The class of brahmans (*brāhmaṇas*: priests) is not always the highest . . . It must be decided by virtue of merit (*dhamma*), without demerit (*adhamma*).

Moreover, we see the word *adhamma-rāga*,[3] which means 'unlawful passion' or 'non-customary'.

The morality in Buddhism which is expressed by the term *dhamma* probably means "moral consciousness" of man rather than "discipline" (*vinaya*) and "virtue" (*sīla*) in the Buddhist communities. In other words, moral law of itself does not apply physical restraint to the body, but by the high development of his moral consciousness a man approaches enlightenment. Such an idea about moral consciousness seems to have accelerated studies of *kilesas* (defilements), and to have been seen as causing the element of *kusala* (the good), *akusala* (the bad) and *avyākata* (the undetermined). The high development of one's moral consciousness, or good quality, or merit is called *dhamma.*

In this context, we find the words *kusalā dhammā* or *akusalā dhammā* in the *Nikāyas*. The *dhammā* in *kusalā dhammā* (or *akusalā dhammā*) are not 'morality'. They are whatever principles are 'good' (or 'bad') and this has nothing to do with *dhamma* in the sense of morality.

2.6 Dhammas as the Principles of Matter and Sentience. The Buddha is said to have taught the five disciples as well as many other disciples that *khandhas*, *āyatanas*,

---

1. For *dhamma* (merit) and *adhamma* (demerit) do not both bear results that are equal; demerit leads to an unhappy state, merit, to a happy state. On this, see the *Atthasālinī*, p. 38.

2. D. III, 83, T.1, 37 a. In the latter, there is no word corresponding to 'without demerit'.

3. D. III, 70, T.1,40 a.

etc. are impermanent, painful and egoless.[1] However, these *dhammas*, in course of time, particularly in *Abhidhamma* Buddhism, came to be regarded as the principles of a sentient body, which is called *nāmarūpa*, a compound of *rūpa* (matter) and *nāma* (sentience).

In the twelve *āyatanas* which consist of six *indriya* (faculty)—*āyatanas* (1. *cakkhu* 'eye', 2. *sota* 'ear', 3. *ghāna* 'nose', 4. *jivhā* 'tongue', 5. *kāya* 'body', 6. *mano* 'mind') and six *visaya* (object)—*āyatanas* (1. *rūpa* 'sight' or 'visible object', 2. *sadda* 'sound', 3. *gandha* 'odour', 4. *rasa* 'taste', 5. *phoṭṭhabba* 'tangible object', 6. *dhamma*), *mano* deals with *dhamma* as *cakkhu* deals with *rūpa* (visible object). In other words, the six *visaya-āyatanas* are the objects of six *indriya-āyatanas*. In this case, how should we translate the word *dhamma* into English ? As pointed out by T. W. and C. A. F. Rhys Davids, it is difficult to make any English term coincide with either *dhamma* or *dhammā*.[2] Nevertheless, they do translate the word *dhamma* as 'mental object' or 'state of mind' or 'idea'. According to Th. Stcherbatsky, the word *dhamma* treated in the sixth *āyatana* is translated as 'non-sensuous object'.[3] According to Nyanatiloka, it is translated as 'mind-object'.[4] But, as we have seen in chapter **2.2**, following the lead of A. K. Warder, we prefer 'principle' to 'mental object', 'non-sensuous object', 'mind-object', etc. which were translated by some Buddhist scholars, as far as the *Nikāyas* are concerned. The point is that the mind is able to perceive all the principles which can be known in Buddhist philosophy.

In the same category as the term *dhamma* as one of the six *āyatanas*, the following words can be found :

dhammesu dhammānupassī viharati.

This is one of the four *satipaṭṭhānas* (bases of self-possession) and runs 'to live with reference to *dhammas* observing *dhammas*'. In this case, we also prefer to translate the above word *dhamma*

1. Vin. I, 13-4.
2. *Dialogues of the Buddha*, vol. 2, p. 325.
3. *The Central Conception of Buddhism and the Meaning of the Word "Dharma"*, p. 8.
4. *Buddhist Dictionary*, p. 25.

as 'principle', because the term principle has a wide meaning, as compared with what was translated by the above scholars.

The first *khandha*, *rūpa*, comprises four elements (*mahābhūtas* 'great existents': 1. *paṭhavī* 'earth', 2. *āpo* 'water', 3. *tejo* 'heat', and 4. *vāyo* 'air'). Except for the first *khandha*, the others were distributed among the four mental classes. Except for the fifth *khandha*, the three mental classes are called "mental *dhammas*," though we can see many other mental *dhammas* in the *Dhammasaṅgaṇī* (Enumeration of Principles), one of the *Abhidhamma* texts of the Sthaviravâda school. The fifth *khandha*, *viññāṇa*, 'consciousness', includes eighty-nine types of thought (*citta*) in the *Abhidhamma* Buddhism of the Sthaviravāda school. In this case, we call them "eighty-nine *cittas*." But, even in the early Buddhism, it seems that there was a tendency that not only the five *khandhas*, but also the six *dhātus*, the twelve *āyatanas*, the eighteen *dhātus* and so forth were to be regarded as the principles of matter and mind. In this case, these principles are also called *dhammas*.

2.7 We have learned that the term *dhamma* includes various meanings, and the sense of it depends on the context within which it appears. Apart from the term quality or predicate, as indicated in chapter **2.2**, which is used as a logical term in the later period, on referring to the meanings of the word *dhamma* shown by A. K. Warder, we may sum up the meanings of *dhamma* and divide them into the following four categories:

2.3 truth, perfect enlightenment, dependent origination, universal law.

2.4 doctrine, teaching, theory, discourse.

2.5 morality, merit, good quality, virtue, discipline.

2.6 principle.

However, when coming across the term *abhidhamma* in the *Nikāyas* and *Āgamas*, we cannot have a disregard for the semantical relationships between *dhamma* and *abhidhamma*. In order to clarify the complexity of them, we would like to discuss the difference between *dhamma* and *abhidhamma* and to find an important clue to the origin of *Abhidhamma* philosophy.

3

THE CONCEPTION OF *ABHIDHAMMA* AND ITS CHARACTERISTICS

3.1 Sometimes in the *Nikāyas*, *Āgamas* and *Vinayas* the term *abhidhamma* seems to refer to an *Abhidhamma Piṭaka.*[1] Sometimes, however, the term seems to refer only to certain types of discussion (*kathā*), out of which *Abhidhamma Piṭakas* were subsequently elaborated. It will be important first of all to examine the meaning of the term *abhidhamma* and then to make clear its characteristics in relation to the term *dhamma.*

3.2 Let us begin with instancing examples in which the term *abhidhamma* (with *abhivinaya*) is used :

1. A monk (*bhikkhu*) loves the Buddha's doctrine, the utterance of it is dear to him, he finds exceeding joy (*pāmujja*) in *abhidhamma* and *abhivinaya.*[2]

1. For example, in the *Āgamas* there is the word *abhidhamma* together with the words *sutta* and *vinaya* which can be regarded as the *Abhidhamma Piṭaka*: T.1,606 a, 857 a, which correspond partly to A. IV, 274-9; T. 2, 195 c; T.2, 552 b; T.2,652 b, which corresponds in part to A. II, 168; T.2, 673 b, which corresponds partly to S. II, 203-5. But, in the Pāli *suttas* shown above, there is no word *abhidhamma.* Also, in Vin. IV, 144 the words *suttanta, gāthā, abhidhamma* and *vinaya* can be found; in Vin. IV, 344 the words *suttanta, vinaya* and *abhidhamma* are shown. Incidentally, the word *gāthā* in Vin. IV, 144 seems important in the sense that in the same way as the three *Piṭakas* were gradually formed from *suttanta, vinaya* and *abhidhamma,* one more *Piṭaka* might have been elaborated as the *Khuddaka Piṭaka* from *gāthā,* which is of course presumably included in the *suttanta* now, but is known as the *Khuddaka Nikāya* of the Sthaviravāda school. But we need not complicate our discussion here.

2. D. III, 267.

2. Concentration (*yoga*) on *abhidhamma* and *abhivinaya* should be made by a monk who is living in the forest (*āraññaka*).[1]

Although, as we shall see below, there is a bewildering multiplicity of interpretations concerning the prefix *abhi* and the term *abhidhamma*, we should give attention especially to three points which have been attempted so far by modern scholars:

1. An attempt to interpret *abhi-dhamma* as a prepositional compound.
2. An attempt to interpret the prefix *abhi* as an adjective modifying the noun *dhamma*.
3. An attempt to use both items 1 and 2 properly in the contexts.

Item 1 is based merely on a philological point of view, so that as W. and M. Geiger point out,[2] there is not a philosophical meaning in the word *abhidhamma* itself. They turn their attention to the fact that the terms *abhidhamma* and *abhivinaya* are always expressed in the locative case, and interpret *abhidhamma* as meaning 'über den *Dhamma*'. Since the prefix *abhi* means 'towards', 'about', and the like,[3] we cannot deny the fact that the philological meaning of *abhidhamma* is 'about the doctrine'. Their interpretation is even to this day accepted by scholars. For example, A. K. Warder points out that the word *abhidhamma* meant originally 'concerning the doctrine'.[4] As far as only the *Nikāyas* are concerned, W. and M. Geiger's viewpoint is correct that the term *abhidhamma* as well as *abhivinaya* is always expressed in the locative case. But we must notice that the term *abhidhamma* appearing in the *Āgamas* (when it does not mean the *Abhidhamma Piṭaka*) is not always expressed in the

1. M. I, 472.
2. *Pāli Dhamma*, p. 118-9.
3. A. K. Warder, *Introduction to Pāli*, p. 388. The prefix *abhi* is also permissible in Pāli poetry to elevate the tone of a passage (Ibid., pp. 355, 362).
4. *Indian Buddhism*, p. 10. But he points out that the term afterwards was used for a systematic study of doctrine.

locative case, but is expressed in the accusative case in some instances: "The Buddha realized that the monk Rāhula had not been released to perfection and had not been capable of receiving *abhidhamma* from the Buddha."[1]

According to the *Pāli-English Dictionary*, the word *abhidhamma* means 'special *Dhamma*'. In this case, the prefix *abhi* functions as an adjective, meaning 'special'. It seems that the translators from Pāli into English follow this meaning: T. W. and C. A. F. Rhys Davids put the term *abhidhamma* and *abhivinaya* in the *Nikāyas* into "(in) the advanced teaching of both Doctrine and Discipline,"[2] F. L. Woodward, into "(a question about) extra doctrine or extra discipline"[3] or "(in) further *dhamma* and further discipline,"[4] and E. M. Hare translates *abhidhamma* as "(on) More-*Dhamma*."[5] All these translators recognize that *abhidhamma* mentioned above is not the so-called *Abhidhamma Piṭaka*, nevertheless, that there must be a difference between *dhamma* and *abhidhamma*. In this sense, we can assent to their views.

In deciding what the term *abhidhamma* means, it is important for certainty to refer to the whole context in which the term is used. I. B. Horner stresses this point. She collects the usages of *abhidhamma* and *abhivinaya* from the *Sutta* and *Vinaya Piṭakas* and examines them minutely,[6] and as a result, she uses the expression "(in) Further-*Dhamma*, (in) Further-Discipline" in some cases,[7] and the expression "(in) what pertains to *dhamma*, (in) what pertains to discipline" in some cases.[8] We see that she takes the best care of translating various terms in Pāli into English. It is certain that the meaning of the term *abhidhamma* is debatable, since this term must have gone through several

1. T. 2, 51 a.
2. *Dialogues of the Buddha*, vol. 3, p. 246.
3. *The Book of the Gradual Sayings*, vol. 1, p. 267.
4. Ibid., vol. 5, p. 19, p. 139, p. 217, etc.
5. Ibid., vol. 3, p. 85.
6. "*Abhidhamma, Abhivinaya* in the First Two *Piṭakas* of the Pāli Canon," IHQ, Vol. XVII, No. 3 (Sept. 1941), pp. 219-310.
7. *The Middle Length Sayings*, vol. 2, p. 145.
8. *The Book of the Discipline*, vol. 4, pp. 83-4, in which she states : the term *abhidhamma* in this case clearly has the *Abhidhamma Piṭaka* in mind.

fluctuations before coming to stand as the title of the *Abhidhamma Piṭaka.* Thus, according to her,[1] the particular meaning ascribed to this term in any one context must depend largely on the sense, linguistic style and terminology of that whole context, which should therefore be considered on its own merits. However, her dual interpretations are so flexible that it is difficult to grasp the conception of *abhidhamma* common in the *Nikāyas* and *Āgamas.*

3.3 The reason why certain scholars regarded *abhidhamma* as meaning "extra doctrine," "further *dhamma*", "More-*Dhamma*", and the like lies in the fact that they followed Buddhaghosa's commentary on the interpretations of the prefix *abhi* and the definitions of the *abhidhamma.* According to the *Samantapāsādikā* written by him, *abhi* shows the five different meanings, namely:

1. *Vuddhi* (increase).
2. *Salakkhaṇa* (characteristic).
3. *Pūjitā* (respect).
4. *Paricchinnā* (distinguishing, defining).
5. *Adhikā* (excellence).

Furthermore, the examples of *abhi* are given as follows:

> The term *abhi* in such a case as, "much pain attacks (*abhikkamanti*) me, and does not step backwards, etc." means 'comes to increase (*vuddhiya*)'; such *abhi* as "it is distinguished (*abhiññātā*) and marked (*abhilakkhita*) night, etc." is used in the sense of 'characteristic (*salakkhaṇa*)'; *abhi* like "a great king (*abhirājā*), or a lord of men, etc." is the meaning of 'revered (*pūjita*)'; *abhi* like "complete training in *abhidhamma* and *abhivinaya*, etc." is used in the sense of 'distinguished (or defined: *paricchinna*)'. It is said that this is for the sake of getting rid of confusion between *dhamma* and *vinaya*; *abhi* indicating "with a beautiful (*abhikkanta*) colour, etc." is in the meaning of 'excellent (*abhika*)'.[2]

In another work by Buddhaghosa, we can also see the explanation of the term *abhi* as follows:[3]

---

1. *The Book of the Discipline*, vol. 3, p. x.
2. See *Samanta*, p. 20.
3. The *Atthasālinī*, p. 2, pp. 19-20.

> Herein what is meant by *Abhidhamma*? That which exceeds and is distinguished from the *Dhamma* (the *Sutta*). The prefix *abhi*, like *ati*, is used in the sense of preponderance and distinction, as in such passages as, "severe pains overwhelm (*abhikkamanti*) me, brother; and do not abate"; and "of eminent (*abhikkanta*) beauty." Again: Hence when many sunshades and flags are uplifted, the sunshade which excels the rest in size and is of distinguished colour and form is called *atichattaṃ*, "the pre-eminent sunshade," and the flag which is the largest and is replete with various distinguished paints and colours is called *atidhaja*, "the pre-eminent flag." And when many princes and gods are gathered together, the prince who is specially distinguished and surpasses others in birth, property, pomp, dominion, and other attainments is called *atirājakumāra*, "the prince par excellence"; and the god who is specially distinguished and surpasses others in age, beauty, dominion, pomp, and other attainments is called *atideva* or *abhideva*, "the peerless god." Similarly Brahmā is called *Atibrahmā*, "the supreme Brahmā." Even so this *dhamma* is called *abhidhamma*, because it excels and is distinguished by several qualities from the other *dhamma*.[1]

In addition to the above explanations, we see the following definitions concerning *abhidhamma* (***kathā***) : *uttama-dhamma* 'the highest doctrine';[2] *abhivisiṭṭha-dhamma* 'very distinguished doctrine'.[3] For a certainty, Buddhaghosa's explanations are very helpful in considering the conception of *abhidhamma* in the *Nikāyas*. Before being inclined towards Pāli commentaries, however, we would like to turn our eyes to the explanations of *abhidhamma* in Chinese versions.

3.4 In the Chinese version of the *Samantapāsādikā*, the explanations of *abhi* and *dhamma* are described as follows:[4]

> The term *abhi* means 'mindful', 'conscious', 'praiseworthy', 'distinctive', 'excessive', 'wide', 'large', and 'unsurpassed'. . .

1. See *The Expositor*, tr. Pe Maung Tin, vol 1, pp. 3-4.
2. AA. III, 271.
3. MA. IV, 29.
4. T. 24, 676 b-c.

> And *dhamma* means 'attainment' (attain to *nibbāna*), 'drawing power' (draw in the path of virtue), and 'defence' (defend a man from an evil way).

It is not easy to find out the explanations in common between the *Samantapāsādikā* and its Chinese version. Nevertheless, we see that the term *abhi* is used in the sense of 'distinctive' or 'distinguishing', and that there are therefore distinctive (or distinguishing) characteristics in what is called *abhidhamma.*

In the *Abhidharmamahāvibhāṣāśāstra* (translated in Chinese by Hsuan-chuang between 656A.D. and 659 A.D.), and another incomplete *Abhidharmamahāvibhāṣāśāstra* (translated by Buddhavarman in 437A.D.), various explanations of *abhi* and *abhidhamma* which many scholars and schools tried are shown. We see in the former:[1]

> According to a certain grammarian, *a* means 'eliminable', and *bhi*, 'penetrative'. For, by the teaching called *Abhidhamma,* one eliminates the lusts such as *gantha* (fetter), *anusaya* (tendency), *upakkilesa* (corruption), and *pariyuṭṭhāna* (prepossession); one penetrates the true *dhammas* such as *khandhas*, *dhātus*, *āyatanas*, *paṭiccasamuppāda*, *saccas*, *āhāra* (food), *sāmañña* (profession of asceticism), and *bojjhaṅgas* (factors of enlightenment). In the opinion of Buddharakṣita, *abhi* means 'revealable'. For, by *abhidhamma* involving all *kusaladhammā* (good principles), one reveals enlightenment. In the opinion of Buddhadeva, *abhi* means 'undue'. For one who makes an undue estimate of oneself is called *abhimāna* (self-conceit or undue estimate of oneself); one who is free from lusts is called *adhimutta* (of firm resolve or determination) and the like.
>
> According to Vāmalabdha, *abhi* means 'respecting'. For that which shows respect for everything is called *abhivādana* (salutation).

And we see in the latter as follows:[2]

> In the opinion of Vasumitra, the reason why *Abhidhamma* is called *abhidhamma* is that it treats the analysis of the twelve

1. T. 27,4 b-c.
2. T. 28, 3 c-4 a.

types of scripture; the explanation of the twelve-linked chain of dependent origination (*dvādasa paṭiccasamuppādaṅgas*), and so on.

In the opinion of Mahābhadanta, the reason why *Abhidhamma* is called *abhidhamma* is that it treats of the collection and the analytical explanation of the *dhammas* such as *kilesas*, *ganthas*, *vimokkha* (freedom), *nibbāna*, and so forth.

In the opinion of Ghosa, the reason why *Abhidhamma* is called *abhidhamma* is that it analyzes all teachings of the Buddha just as "this is the noble truth of unhappiness"; "this is the noble truth of the origination of unhappiness"; "this is the noble truth of the cessation of unhappiness"; "this is the noble truth of the way leading to the cessation of unhappiness"; and so on.

In the opinion of Pārśva, the reason why *Abhidhamma* is called *abhidhamma* is that it treats of *ñāṇas* (knowledges) which express the enlightenment.

In the opinion of Abhidhammavādin (one who disputes or preaches some doctrine), the reason why *Abhidhamma* is called *abhidhamma* is that it deals with the real nature of profound (*gambhīra*) *dhammas* . . . and it treats of the *salakkhaṇa* (own characteristic) and *sāmaññalakkhaṇa* (universal characteristic) of each *dhamma* from the standpoint of understanding, and so on.

According to the Mahīśāsaka school, *Abhidhamma* is just like the brightest lamp, which means the highest knowledge.

According to the Dharmagupta school, *abhidhamma* means 'increase', and 'understanding which is the best one of all *dhammas*'.

In the opinion of Avadānavādin, *nibbāna* is the highest of all the *dhammas* and *Abhidhamma* comes second.

From these various interpretations of *abhi* and *abhidhamma* (or *Abhidhamma*, that is, the texts which contain *abhidhamma*), it is very difficult to choose what interpretation expresses the true meaning of *abhi*, because all *Abhidhamma* texts now extant (of the Sthaviravāda, the Sarvāstivāda, the Dharmaguptaka, the Saṃmitīya and the Bahuśrutīya schools) seem to include some elements which were interpreted above. But, judging from what has been interpreted above in various ways, the most general sense of *abhidhamma* seems to be making distinctions, defining *dhammas*. An *abhidhamma* text will thus be a book of definitions. In order to ascertain this point further, we would like to pay attention to the usages of *abhidhamma* (and also, *abhivinaya*) in the *Nikāyas* and *Āgamas* and to try to grasp firmly the conception of *abhidhamma*.

3.5 Let us begin with introducing *abhidhamma* and *abhivinaya* appearing in the *Gulissānisutta* which has its Chinese version.

(1) Abhidhamma and Abhivinaya in the Gulissāni-sutta. This *sutta* preached by Sāriputta presents the Buddhist manners in a Buddhist community (*saṅgha*) by taking those of a monk, Gulissāni as an example.[1] Above all, discussions on *abhidhamma* and *abhivinaya* are considered important practices:[2]

> Sir, concentration (*yoga*) on *abhidhamma* and *abhivinaya* should be made by a monk who is living in the forest (*āraññaka*). There are those who will question a monk who is living in the forest concerning *abhidhamma* and *abhivinaya*. If a monk who is living in the forest, on being asked a question on *abhidhamma* and *abhivinaya*, cannot explain, there will be those who speak about him and say: What is the good of this venerable one who is living alone in the forest doing as he pleases, but who, on being asked a question on *abhidhamma* and *abhivinaya*, cannot explain. Therefore, concentration on *abhidhamma* and *abhivinaya* should be made by a monk who is living in the forest.

A Chinese version of the above *sutta* runs as follows:[3]

> Monks, when a monk living in a forest joins a Buddhist community, he must study to treat of *abhivinaya* and *abhi-dhamma*. Why ? Because, when joining the Buddhist community, somebody will come up to treat of *abhivinaya* and *abhidhamma* with him. Monks, if he cannot treat of them in

1. M. I, 469-73, T. 1, 454 c-456 a.
2. See M. I, 472.
3. T. 1, 455 c.

> the Buddhist community, he will be called to account by them like this: In spite of the fact that he cannot treat of *abhivinaya* and *abhidhamma*, why does he join the Buddhist community? It is clear that he will be called to account, if not treating of *abhivinaya* and *abhidhamma*. Therefore, monks, when a monk living in a forest joins the Buddhist community, he must study to treat of these doctrines.

The term *abhidhamma* is to be distinguished from *dhamma* and the term *abhivinaya* is likewise to be distinguished from *vinaya*. Both the latter are general terms for teachings and disciplines taught by the Buddha. In other words, we might say that the above *abhidhamma* and *abhivinaya* show specific *dhamma* and *vinaya* respectively, which disciples of the Buddha must practice by all means. The teaching consists of *dhamma* (doctrine) and *vinaya* (discipline); the thorough study of each of these will be its *abhi-*. *Abhivinaya* might actually refer to the *Suttavibhaṅga* or *Vinayavibhaṅga*, the old commentary on the *Pātimokkhasutta* which is incorporated in the *Vinaya* text (just as the *Abhidhammavibhaṅga* explains the *dhamma*).

(2) Abhidhamma and Abhivinaya in the Dialogue of the Buddha with a Disciple, Subhūti.

> Again, Subhūti, a monk delights in *dhamma* (teaching), the utterance of it is dear to him, he delights exceedingly in *abhidhamma* and *abhivinaya*. Insofar as a monk is such, Subhūti, this also is the harvest of belief (*saddhāpadāna*) in a believer.[1]

From the above, it is hard to understand completely the differences between *dhamma* and *abhidhamma*. But, in this case, it is clear that "delight in *dhamma*" (*dhammakāma*) and "exceeding delight in *abhidhamma* and *abhivinaya*" (*abhidhamme abhivinaye uḷārapāmujja*) are respectively not identical. In this respect, case (2) is similar to case (1).

(3) Abhidhamma in the Mahāgosiṅgasutta. At one time, in order to listen to the discourse (*dhamma*) of the

1. A. V, 339

venerable Sāriputta, then staying in a grove in the Gosiṅga *sāl*-wood (*sālavana*), many famous disciples (ranking as elders), such as Ven. Moggallāna, Ven. Kassapa, Ven. Anuruddha, Ven. Revata, Ven. Ānanda approached Ven. Sāriputta. Ven. Sāriputta asked Ven. Moggallāna: "Delightful is the Gosiṅga *sāl*-wood; it is a clear moonlight night; the *sāl*-trees are in full blossom; by what type of monk would the Gosiṅga *sāl*-wood be illuminated ?" Then, Ven. Moggallāna answered as follows:[1]

> In this connection, Ven. Sāriputta, two monks are talking on *abhidhamma*; they question one another; in answering one another's questions they respond and do not fail; and their talk on *dhamma* goes forward. By a monk of such a type, Ven. Sāriputta, would the Gosiṅga *sāl*-wood be illuminated.

On the other hand, in the Chinese text of the *Mahāgosiṅgasutta*, the questioner is Ven. Sāriputta and the answerer is Ven. Kaccāyana. Ven. Kaccāyana's answer corresponds with the Pāli text. Especially, a noteworthy point in the Chinese text is that the word *gambhīra* (profound) is added before the word *abhidhamma*.[2] From this fact, it is understood that what is called *abhidhamma* means to talk on *dhammas* (they may be specific doctrines) in the form of questions and answers, and that it is to derive the intrinsic value or the profound theory from talks on *dhammas*. To demonstrate this point further, let us observe another *sutta*.

(4) Abhidhamma in the Kintisutta. In this, the Buddha lays down rules on the treatment of monks who discuss the meaning and letter of the doctrine:[3]

> Therefore, monks, those *dhammas* (doctrines or principles) taught to you by me out of insight, that is to say the four bases of self-possession (*satipaṭṭhānas*), the four right exertions (*sammappadhānas*), the four bases of power (*iddhipādas*), the five faculties (*indriyas*), the five strengths (*balas*), the seven factors

1. M. I. 212-9, T. 1,726 c-729 b.
2. Such a word can be found widely in Chinese texts, e.g. T. 1, 450 a. 634 c, 688 c, 728 c, etc.
3. M. II, 238-43.

> of enlightenment (*bojjhaṅgas*), the excellent eight factors of the way (*maggaṅgas*)—all together, in harmony (*samagga*), in agreement (*sammodamāna*) and without contention (*avivādamāna*), you should train yourselves in all of these. But when you, monks, all together, in harmony, in agreement and without contention train yourselves in these, there might be two monks speaking differently about *abhidhamma*. If it occurs to you concerning this: "Between these venerable ones there is a difference concerning the meaning (*attha*) and the letter (*byañjana*)," then, approaching that monk whose speech you think better, you should speak thus to him: "Between these venerable ones there is a difference concerning the meaning and the letter, on account of which they should know that there is a difference concerning the meaning and the letter. Don't let the venerable ones fall into contention." After that, approaching a monk of another group whose speech you think better, you should speak thus to him: "Between these venerable ones there is a difference concerning the meaning and the letter, on account of which they should know that there is a difference concerning the meaning and the letter. Don't let the venerable ones fall into contention."

This exists in Pāli only. But, as can be realized from the above, where two monks differ in opinion on *abhidhamma*, other monks suggest restraint on the part of the one monk who speaks better. It is to be understood that the differences in opinion between two monks were an outgrowth of the heated discussion on *abhidhamma*. Therefore, we might say that the purpose of the discussion between monks was to derive the intrinsic value or the profound theory from *dhammas* (principles) taught by the Buddha or by some great disciple of his. The problem of what *abhidhamma* originally meant will also be solved by looking at the context within which the words *dhammakathā* and *abhidhamma-kathā* appear.

3.6 The words *dhamma-kathā* mean 'a talk on *dhamma*', though the meaning of the word *kathā* is, according to the *Pāli-English Dictionary*, classified into six categories: 1. talk (ing), conversation, 2. speech, sermon, discourse, lecture, 3. a (long) story, 4. word(s), advice, 5. explanation, exposition, and

6. discussion. As far as the word *kathā* is concerned in the *Nikāyas* and *Āgamas*, however, it is not a word used only for a philosophical discussion; rather the usage varies, for we see the words *gāma-kathā* meaning 'gossip about village-affairs', which is regarded as low (*hina*) and vulgar (*gammā*) talks, also called *tiracchānakathā* (lit. 'talk on animals or childish talk'). The Buddha and his great disciples admonish many disciples not to talk *tiracchānakathā*, because such a talk is not concerned with true profit; is not the essentials of life; does not conduce to dispassion, to cessation, to tranquillity, to full understanding, and to complete enlightenment. Therefore, first in importance is the content of *kathā*, that is, to carry out talks on *dhamma* or *abhidhamma*.

In the *Rathavinitasutta*,[1] after the Buddha has instructed, roused, incited, delighted Mantāṇiputta with *dhammakathā*, who is known as a monk wanting little for himself and at the same time, as a monk who talks to others on wanting little; as a monk who is content for himself and who also talks to others on contentment, etc., Sāriputta meets Mantāṇiputta and discusses the Buddha's teachings warmly with him. Mantāṇiputta characterizes the *dhammakathā* by explaining to Sāriputta that the best life (*brahmacariya*) under the Master (*bhagavant*: a title of the Buddha) is lived neither for the purity of virtue (*sīlavisuddhatta*), nor for the purity of thought (*cittavisuddhatta*), nor for the purity of view (*diṭṭhivisuddhatta*), but for the attainment of liberation from existence (*parinibbāna*) without attachment (*anupādā*), and that the liberation can be attained finally by means of the purity of virtue, thought, view, etc., just as King Pasenadi of Kosala reaches the palace-gate at Sāketa at last by changing chariots seven times. A noteworthy point in this discussion is that the words *gambhira gambhira pañhā* are indicated: Mantāṇiputta says, "it is wonderful that the very profound questions were asked step by step by the venerable Sāriputta who knows the Master's instruction." But these words do not always suggest the words *gambhira abhidhamma*, rather they mean that a talk on *dhammas* taught by the Buddha was zealously carried out.

---

1. M. I, 145-151, T. 1,429 c-431 c, T. 2, 733 c-735 b.

In the discourse named *Cūḷahatthipadopamasutta*,[1] where the monk Pilotika explains to the brahman Jāṇussoṇi about the greatness of the Buddha by way of the four similes of the elephant's footprint, we see the following expression in which *dhammakathā* is used:

> Such and such adversaries hear : Undoubtedly the recluse Gotama will visit some village or little town (*nigama*). They prepare a question, thinking: Having approached the recluse Gotama, we will ask him this question of ours. If, on being asked by us thus, he answers thus, we will refute him in this manner; and if, on being asked by us thus, he answers thus, we will refute him in that manner. They heard: It is certain that the recluse Gotama is visiting the village or the little town. So they approached the recluse Gotama. He instructed, roused, incited, delighted them with *dhammakathā*. Those who were instructed (*sandassita*), roused (*samādapita*), incited (*samuttejita*), and delighted (*sampahaṁsita*) by the recluse Gotama with *dhammakathā*, did not ask him the question at all. How could they refute him? On the contrary, they became disciples of the recluse Gotama.

It is clear that the purpose of the above-mentioned is to describe the capacity of the Buddha who excelled in *dhammakathā*. At this point, we can quote another passage from the *Ariyapariyesanasutta*, which corresponds exactly with the Chinese version:[2]

> The Buddha approached the hermitage of the brahman Rammaka. At that time, a number of monks happened to be sitting down and talking about *dhamma* (*dhammakathā*) in the hermitage of the brahman Rammaka. Then the Buddha stood outside the gateway and waited for the talk to finish. Then the Buddha, knowing that the talk had finished, coughed and knocked on the bar of the door; those monks opened the door to the Buddha. Then the Buddha, having entered the hermitage of the brahman Rammaka, sat down on the appointed seat. Having sat down, the Buddha said to the

1. M. I, 176, T. 1,656 b.
2. M. I, 161, T. 1, 775 c-776 a.

monks: As you were sitting down just now, what was your talk about, monks? What was your talk that was interrupted? Buddha, our *dhammakathā* that was interrupted was about the Buddha himself; then he arrived.

Then the Buddha teaches his disciples that there are two things to be done: either talk about *dhamma* or the noble silence (*ariya tuṇhibhāva*).

Besides the word *dhammakathā*, we can find the word *dhammasākacchā* in the *Nikāyas*.[1] The meaning of the word *sākacchā* is 'conversation', 'talking over', 'discussing'. Therefore, it is regarded as having the same meaning as the word *kathā*. Apart from the strict usage of *kathā* and *sākacchā*, it is true that the word *kathā* rather than the word *sākacchā* was widely used, because in addition to the word *dhammakathā*, we see the word *abhidhammakathā* and also, the word *vinayakathā* in a *Vinaya* text.[2]

As far as we can tell of *dhammakathā*, it seems to be used in general as a talk on *dhammas* taught by the Buddha, which were then elaborated as ten *kathās* (discussions): 1. on wanting little (*appiccha*), 2. on contentment (*santuṭṭhi*), 3. on seclusion (*paviveka*), 4. on avoiding society (*asaṁsagga*), 5. on putting forth energy (*viriyārambha*), 6. on moral practice (*sīla*), 7. on concentration of mind (*samādhi*), 8. on understanding (*paññā*), 9. on liberation (*vimutti*), and 10. on knowledge and insight of liberation (*vimuttiñāṇadassana*),[3] and to be used as a discussion to conduce to complete enlightenment opposite to *tiracchānakathā*.

3.7 Compared with *dhammakathā*, the word *abhidhammakathā* is seldom used in the *Nikāyas* and *Āgamas*. But *abhidhammakathā* seems to indicate an advanced discussion on *dhamma*:[4]

1. For example, see Sn. 266.
2. Vin. II, 168.
3. M. III, 113, 115, A. III, 117, 118, IV, 357, V. 67, Ud. 36. etc. In Chinese Texts (e.g. T. 1,492 b, 739 b, etc.), there are 15 items including all those in the Pāli : 1. on austere penance (*sallekha*), 2. on self-abnegation (*nekkhammasaṅkappa*), 3. on cessation (*nirodha*), 4. on dependent origination (*paṭiccasamuppāda*), 5. on charity (*dāna*).
4. A. III, 107.

(1) Monks, in the long road of the future, there will be monks who have not practiced the subduing of this body (unpracticed in body), not made virtue a habit, not brought thought into order, and not made insight into guidance. Monks who have not achieved this "becoming" will not be fully awake to the meaning, but will enter on a state of darkness, when giving a talk on *abhidhamma* (*abhidhammakathaṃ*) or on *vedalla* (*vedallakathaṃ*).[1] Thus verily, monks, from the pollution of *dhamma* (doctrine) comes that of *vinaya*; from the pollution of *vinaya* comes that of *dhamma*.

The above suggests that monks who do not devote themselves to Buddhist practice should not give a talk on *abhidhamma* or on *vedalla*. In other words, only monks who earnestly try to achieve Buddhist practice are qualified for giving a talk on *abhidhamma*. Moreover, the following statement is worth noticing:

(2) Ven. Sāriputta, two monks give a talk on *abhidhamma* (*abhidhammakathaṃ kathenti*); they ask one another (*aññamañña*) questions; in answering one another's questions they respond (*vissajjati*) and do not fail (*saṁsidati*), and their talk on *dhamma* goes forward (*pavattati*). Ven. Sāriputta, by a monk of such a type the Gosiṅga *sāl*-wood would be illumined.[2]

As we have already seen in chapter **3.3**, commenting on *abhidhammakathā*, Buddhaghosa says : it is *uttamadhammakathaṁ*, which means 'a talk on the highest doctrine'. But it seems to import essentially 'an illuminating or a philosophical talk on doctrine'. This point may be clearly demonstrated by the following words :[3]

(3) At one time, when the Buddha dwelt near Benares in the Deer Park at Isipatana, a number of elder monks who had returned from alms-gathering sat together in the round hall (*maṇḍalamāla*) and spoke on *abhidhamma*. From time to time, Ven. Citta Hatthisāriputta interrupted their talk. And Ven.

1. Although *vedalla* is regarded as one of the nine types of scripture, originally it probably means 'style based on questions and answers'.
2. M. I, 214.
3. A. III, 392.

Mahākoṭṭhita said to him: let not Ven. Hatthisāriputta constantly interrupt when the elders talk on *abhidhamma*; Ven. Hatthisāriputta should wait until the talk is over.

From the above, it can readily be imagined that this talk on *dhamma* by elder monks (*therā bhikkhū*) must have had depth, because they had learned much of the doctrines of the Buddha, were leaders of young monks, and had given discourses for the Buddha at times. Therefore, the above words teach us that novices or young monks were not permitted to interrupt when their elders talked on *abhidhamma*.

Judging from the usages of *dhammakathā* and *abhidhammakathā*, the latter has some element which distinguishes it from the former. That is to say, it seems that the word *abhidhammakathā* means 'understanding a certain profound meaning or a philosophical meaning of *dhamma* by the medium of questions and answers'. We see that it sometimes happened that the difference of opinion as to the meaning or the expression of *dhammas* was discussed among disciples of the Buddha, and that in such a case, they had to think to the utmost extent of the reason why there was the difference and to cultivate a better understanding by asking it of the Buddha or his elder monks.

3.8 In connection with the usages of *abhidhamma* and *abhivinaya* mentioned in chapter **3.5**, it must be noted that three stereotyped expressions are discovered throughout the *Nikāyas* and *Vinayas*:

(a) *Dhammakāmo hoti piyasamudāhāro abhidhamme abhivinaye uḷārapāmujjo.*[1]

(b) *Abhidhamme kho pana abhivinaye pañhaṃ puttho saṃsādeti no vissajjeti.*[2]

---

1. A monk loves the Buddha's doctrine, the utterance of it is dear to him, he finds exceeding joy in *abhidhamma* and *abhivinaya*. See D. III, 267, A. V, 24, 27, 90, 201. 339, 341, etc.

2. On being asked a question on *abhidhamma* and *abhivinaya*, he falters and cannot explain. See A. I, 288, 290, 291, IV, 398, 399, 400, etc. Also, we can find the following passage: ***Abhidhamme abhivinaye*** *pañhaṁ pucchitāro*. See M. I, 472.

(c) *Aparehi pi bhikkhave pañcah' aṅgehi sammannāgatena bhikkhunā na upasampādetabbaṃ na nissayo dātabbo na sāmaṇero upaṭṭhāpetabbo: na paṭibalo hoti . . . abhidhamme vinetuṃ, abhivinaye vinetuṃ.*[1]

We see even from these three stereotyped expressions that there is a distinct difference between *dhamma* and *abhidhamma*, and between *vinaya* and *abhivinaya.*

To sum up the arguments which have been given about *abhidhamma*(*kathā*) and *abhivinaya* appearing in the *Nikāyas* and *Āgamas*, it may be said that whilst *dhamma* and *vinaya* are words to express teaching and discipline generally, *abhidhamma* as well as *abhivinaya* seems to be used to develop *dhamma*(doctrine) and to define *dhammas* (principles) and *vinaya* (*s*) in the forest (which seems to indicate 'by oneself', 'alone', see example (1) of chapter **3.5**) or in question and answer form (see examples (3) and (4) of chapter **3.5** and examples (1), (2) and (3) of chapter **3.7**), and also the discussion on *abhidhamma* is to understand a certain profound meaning of *dhamma* and to understand the relations of a *dhamma* to other *dhammas.* Therefore, the Buddha and his disciples seem to have already formed a philosophical conception in the term *abhidhamma* (also in *abhivinaya*) itself; otherwise, we cannot realize the following aspects: only monks who have been released to perfection are capable of receiving *abhidhamma* from the Buddha or his great disciples;[2] those who rank as elders (like Ānanda) are capable of expounding in detail (*vitthārena*) the meaning of the teaching made in brief (*sankhittena*) by the Buddha;[3] they must study to treat of *abhivinaya* and *abhidhamma*;[4] elder monks can talk on *gambhīra abhidhamma*;[5] the Buddha lays down rules on the treatment of monks who discuss the meaning and letter of the doctrine;[6]

1. If a monk is possessed of five qualities, he should not ordain. These qualities are namely, if a monk is not adequate to lead a disciple in the fundamentals of conduct;...to lead him in *abhidhamma*; to lead him in *abhivinaya.* See Vin. I, 64, V. 181, etc.
2. See quotation in chapter **3.2**.
3. S. IV, 93.
4. See example (1) of chapter **3.5**.
5. See example (3) of chapter **3.5** and example (3) of chapter **3.7**.
6. See example (4) of chapter **3.5**.

only monks who earnestly try to achieve Buddhist practice are qualified for giving a talk on *abhidhamma*,[1] and so forth.

In addition, we must notice that further discussion came to be held among the disciples, sometimes in the presence of the Buddha, to analyze the thirty-seven *dhammas*, to expound dependent origination, to formulate the theory of *anicca*, *dukkha*, *anattan*, and to classify many other *dhammas* into different types, such as the practical, the theoretical, etc. (*vibhaṅga*: lit. 'division') by being free from taking narrow views (by *vitthāra*: lit. 'breadth'). In this connection, we see that as to all *dhammas* taught by the Buddha, his disciples gave attention to two points, namely: *dhammaṃ vibhajati* and (*Gotamassa bhāsitassa*) *atthaṃ vibhajati*. The verb *vibhajati* (3rd person, singular of the root *vi-bhaj*, lit. 'divide') is translated as meaning 'analyze', 'explain', 'expound', etc.[2] But it seems that the former originally means to divide *dhamma* (or *dhammas*) into certain groups or classes or categories, and that the latter, to explain or expound the meaning (*attha*) of their respective *dhammas* divided first. As far as we can tell of the *Nikāyas*, both *dhammaṃ vibhajati* and *atthaṃ vibhajati* are not always indicated simultaneously, but there is a sharp distinction between the two.[3] In the *sutta* named *Vibhaṅga*, the Buddha divides the doctrine of dependent origination into the twelve *paccayākāras* (the aspects of condition), and then expounds on their respective items.[4] Also, certain *suttas* called *Vibhaṅga* must be noted, in which a detailed analysis of dependent origination, the eight factors of the way, the four *satipaṭṭhānas*, the five *indriyas*, etc. are dealt with.[5]

We can also see that apart from the doctrinal items of the *Aṅguttaranikāya* and the *Ekottarāgama* which are classified according to the numerical order from ones up to elevens, there is an elaborated *sutta* named *Saṅgitisutta* (as well as the *Dasuttarasutta*) of the *Dighanikāya* (also, the *Dirghāgama*), in which numerous

---

1. See example (2) of chapter 3.7.
2. For example, see *The Book of the Kindred Sayings*, vol. 2, p. 2, 59, *The Middle Length Sayings*, vol. 2, p. 27, etc.
3. The former : S. II, 2, M. I, 364, etc. The latter : S. IV, 93, 97, M. III, 203, 223, etc.
4. S. II, 2, T. 2,85 a. Cf S. III, 73-4, T. 2, 4 b.
5. M. III, 187—257, T. 1,690 a—708 c.

principles (*dhammas*) are classified and expounded by Sāriputta systematically from ones up to tens.[1] This scheme is a kind of index to the doctrine scattered through the *Nikāyas* and *Āgamas*.

3.9 Thus we cannot deny the fact that the word *abhidhamma* means etymologically 'concerning *dhamma*'. But, when we trace the origin of *Abhidhamma* philosophy back to the *Nikāyas* and *Āgamas*, we come to know that the term *abhidhamma* was used for a study of the doctrine in which a philosophical conception has already been formed in the sense that the Buddha and his disciples attempted:

1. defining *dhamma*(*s*),
2. seizing the relations of a *dhamma* to other *dhammas*,
3. analyzing *dhammas*,
4. classifying *dhammas* into different types,
5. arranging *dhammas* in numerical order.

In this sense, we may define the term *abhidhamma* in the *Nikāyas* and *Āgamas* as 'an elementary philosophical study of *dhammas*'. (For the sake of convenience, the expression '*abhidhamma* study' will be used below according to the need.) In the five different meanings of *abhi* which Buddhaghosa explained, item 2 (see chapter **3.3**), namely, *salakkhaṇa* meaning 'characteristic' is similar to the meaning of *abhi* used widely in the *Nikāyas* and *Āgamas*, because some characteristic element would be included in what is called "specific *dhamma*," i.e. *abhidhamma*, stated in the *Pāli-English Dictionary*. Item 4 also (especially) seems relevant: 'distinguishing', 'defining'; and further, *abhi* seems to be analysis of, theory of, discussion of or about, so that we might prefer the views of Mahābhadanta, Ghosa and the Abhidhammavādin. The meaning of *abhi* should not be limited to some scholars' opinion that *abhi* shows 'excellent' or 'increasing'. And among the various interpretations of *abhidhamma* (which were recorded in the *Abhidharmamahāvibhāṣāśāstra*), the explanation presented by Abhidhammavādin seems to be similar to the original meaning of *abhidhamma* (see chapter **3.4**).

1. D. III, 207-271, T. 1, 49 b-52 c.

4

ABHIDHAMMA AND MATIKĀ

4.1 It has become clear that the Buddha's disciples formed the conception of *abhidhamma* as an elementary philosophical study of *dhammas* and carried on this study. Such a study was made: (1) in the form of questions and answers, or (2) in the way of minute explanation by one monk to others, or (3) by one monk alone (see example (1) of chapter **3.5** and chapter **3.8**). Apart from item 3, items 1 and 2 should be discussed from a different point of view, because item 1 is vitally concerned with the problem of dialogue form, which will therefore be examined in another Part.

As we have seen in chapter **3.6**, the word *kathā* used in the *Nikāyas* has no other meaning than 'talk', 'discussion', and it is not a word used only for a philosophical discussion. Therefore, *abhidhammakathā* means that (the Buddha and his disciples) discuss *abhidhamma* or talk on *abhidhamma.* What is then the original (or simple) form of the *Abhidhamma Piṭaka* ? Before examining this point, let us look at how the *abhidhamma* study was advanced.

4.2 In chapter **3.9**, we have learned that the disciples' attempts at the elementary philosophical study of *dhammas* consisted of five points. If we discuss especially the first (defining *dhammas*) and fifth points (arranging *dhammas* in numerical order) of the five by adducing examples, the embryonic element of *Abhidhamma* philosophy may be brought to light. The first point will of course be related directly or indirectly to the second, third and the fourth points.

In illustration of the first point, we may take the examples of a series of *Vibhaṅgasuttas*, of which the *Uddesavibhaṅgasutta* (Discourse on a Summarized Description and Analysis) consists of both the Buddha's brief statement and Mahā-Kaccāna's detailed explanation of it,[1] whilst in the other *Vibhaṅgasuttas* the Buddha's brief statement is given first and then explained in detail by the Buddha himself in most cases. To say more precisely, the *Uddesavibhaṅgasutta* is characterized by an elaborate method: The Buddha left his seat without having explained the meaning in detail of a summarized description which was taught in brief by him first, in spite of the fact that he says, "I will teach you, monks, a summarized description and (its) analysis," and then Mahā-Kaccāna defined in detail the *dhammas* taught first by the Buddha such as the consciousness which is not externally diffused (*visaṭa*) and the consciousness which is not internally set (*saṇṭhita*), and finally the Buḍdha concluded: "Mahā-Kaccāna is, monks, learned, of great underṣtanding. If you had questioned me as to this meaning, I too would have explained it precisely as he did. This is indeed the exact meaning of that, and thus you should hold it." In this *sutta* Mahā-Kaccāna alone continues to explain minutely the teaching made in brief by the Buddha and from start to finish, a large audience listen to him without asking any questions. This teaches us two matters: (1) that Mahā-Kaccāna has a full understanding of *abhidhamma* and (2) that he knows completely the way that the *abhidhamma* study should be.

It seems that the Buddha encouraged his disciples to preach the *dhamma* (discourse) which is possessed of the meaning and to investigate the meaning of *dhamma* (doctrine). This fact is more explicit in the following two different statements :

1. Monks, preach the *dhamma* (discourse) which is beautiful in the beginning, in the middle and in the end; and which is possessed of the meaning (*sāttha*) and expression (*savyañjana*).[2]

---

1. M. III, 223-9, T. 1, 694 b-696 b.

2. S. IV, 315, A. II, 147, III, 113, D. I, 62, T. 1, 438 b, 727 a, 2, 58 c, etc. F. L. Woodward regards this paragraph as the Buddha's epithets, so that he translates it into English by referring not to *dhamma* itself but to the

2. It is important to listen to the Buddha's teachings and to investigate the meaning of them (*atthupaparikkhati*) by reflecting on them (*anuvitakketi*), pondering on them (*anuvicāreti*) and poring over them (*anupekkhati*).[1]

Item 1 can be regarded as one's attitude to discourse, and item 2 is important for the disciples (especially, for the novices) in trying to define *dhammas*. It can therefore be understood that from the very beginning, the way to define *dhammas* was probably held among the disciples, and that in the course of time, it was established as the way that the *abhidhamma* study should be. To define or expound in detail the meaning of the teaching made in brief by the Buddha is closely connected with both *dhammaṃ vibhajati* and *atthaṃ vibhajati* (see chapter **3.8**). Both of them are also related to the Buddha's admonishment: "Show the true meaning of *dhammas*, expound on it, open it up, make it clear,"[2] "Don't speak of the false meaning by concealing it when one asks the true meaning,"[3] "Give pure or clear expression (*parisuddha vohāra*),"[4] etc.

In connection with the definition of *dhammas* taught by the Buddha, there are two types of statement which must be noticed. Since the Buddha sometimes speaks in conventional everyday terms, such as 'being' (*satta*), 'reborn' (*upapad*), 'universe' (*loka*), as if accepting the opinion that there is some kind of permanent soul, which he elsewhere rejects, there rather appears to be some obscurity or inconsistency in his doctrine. To resolve this difficulty we must recognize that two types of statement have to be distinguished in the *Nikāyas*: those consisting of popular terms and those consisting of terms of strict truth. The former belongs to everyday language, literally 'concealing' (*sammuti*), and the latter, to philosophical language, 'ultimate' (*paramattha*). The philosophical language is called

---

time of life, namely: "He is one who teaches *dhamma*, lovely in youth, lovely in middle age, lovely at the end of life, both in the spirit and the letter." See *The Book of the Gradual Sayings*, vol. 2, pp. 151 and 221.

1. A. III, 381-3, T. 2, 266 c.
2. S. IV, 93, V, 262, etc.
3. Sn. 126.
4. A. II, 188.

'having the meaning drawn out' (*nitattha*), i.e. to be taken as it stands, as an explicit and definitive statement, while everyday language is called 'having the meaning requiring to be drawn out' (*neyyattha*), i.e. that which requires restating so as to relate it to the philosophical standpoint of ultimate truth.[1] In this context, we can see the following words:[2]

> These two slander the thus-gone (*tathāgata*). Which two? He who elucidates a dialogue (*suttanta*) whose meaning requires to be drawn out as one whose meaning is drawn out; and he who elucidates a dialogue whose meaning is drawn out as one whose meaning requires to be drawn out.

This implies immediately that there were two types of statement: the everyday and the philosophical. This can also be understood as implying the rule of definition (or interpretation) which must be observed by the disciples. Thus we see that the Buddha instructed the proper relation between questions and answers: instead of posing meaningless problems such as "Who desires?" or "Who is conscious?" or "Is he who acts the same as he who experiences the result of the action?", one must substitute the proper questions "Through what condition is there consciousness?" or "Through what condition does such and such a result occur?", and as a result, one will obtain the proper answers: "A is the cause of B," or "Conditioned by B, there is A."[3]

The fact that the definition of *dhammas* was formulated by the chief disciples (or by the Buddha himself in some cases) marks clearly the first stage of helping the growth of *Abhidhamma* philosophy, in which the analytical study of the five *khandhas*, the twelve *āyatanas*, etc. is established, i.e. to divide and classify these *dhammas* into the principles of matter and mind, or to expound on them from a philosophical and psychological point of view. The *Vibhaṅga* and *Dhammasaṅgaṇi* of the Sthaviravāda school are, though they must have gone through several

1. On this see A. K. Warder, *Indian Buddhism*, pp. 150-51.
2. A. I, 60.
3. S. II, 13, T. 2, 102 a. Also, on this see A. K. Warder, "The Concept of a Concept," *Journal of Indian Philosophy*, vol. 1, No. 2, pp. 181-82.

fluctuations before coming to stand as the *Abhidhamma* texts, in fact the most representative of the *Abhidhamma* texts in which many *dhammas* are set forth systematically from the standpoint of both *dhammaṃ vibhajati* and *atthaṃ vibhajati.*

4.3 In illustration of the fifth point (arranging *dhammas* in numerical order), we may take the examples of the *Saṅgītisutta* and the *Dasuttarasutta* (also, their Chinese versions), as we have mentioned briefly in chapter **3.8**. In the beginning of the *Saṅgītisutta,*[1] it is recorded that after the death of Nigaṇṭha Nāthaputta, the Nigaṇṭhas (lit. meaning 'free from bonds', followers of Nāthaputta here) became disunited and divided into two parties by disputing with one another as to their doctrine (*dhamma*) and discipline (*vinaya*)—this record can also be seen in the *Pāsādikasutta.*[2] Therefore, in order to avoid such a dispute in the Buddhist community, in this *sutta* Sāriputta tries to collect various doctrinal principles (*dhammas*) which were well set forth and imparted by the Buddha and to arrange them in numerical order. It seems that this *sutta* shows Sāriputta's study on concentration of *abhidhamma.*

It was probably important at the time of the Buddha to collect *dhammas* taught by him and to distinguish them from what was not taught by him. This will be understood from the following statement:[3]

> If there is a person who explains as the utterance of the *tathāgata* what he has never talked or uttered, and who does not explain as his utterance what has been talked or uttered by the *tathāgata*, he is a slanderer of him.

What was not taught by the Buddha, this is in fact to be understood as metaphysical subjects such as the eternity or non-eternity of the world, the existence or non-existence of the *tathāgata* after death, etc. (which will be discussed in another

---

1. D. III, 209-10, T. 1, 49 c, and the Skt. text : E. Waldschmidt, "Die Einleitung des Saṅgītisūtra" (ZDMG 1956), p. 301, and also see: *Das Saṅgītisūtra und Kommentar Saṅgītiparyāya*, ed. Valentina Stache-Rosen (*Dogmatische Begriffsreihen im älteren Buddhismus*, II, Berlin, DAWB, 1968), Teil 1, p. 44.
2. D. III, 117-8, T. 1, 72 c.
3. A. I, 60.

chapter). To the question "Was it taught by the Buddha ?" his disciples had to answer immediately in the affirmative in some cases or in the negative in other cases, as we see, for example, in the *Cūla-Māluṅkya-sutta*, where the Buddha points out to Māluṅkyaputta that metaphysical speculations are not conducive to enlightenment, asking the questions of Māluṅkyaputta.

> Did I speak ever thus to you: "the world is eternal ?" "the *tathāgata* exists after death ?"
> No, reverend sir.[1]

Such questions and answers are most important in checking whether or not his disciples draw a clear distinction between *dhammas* taught by the Buddha and what does not belong to the *dhammas*. In addition to these question and answer forms, which play also a major role in the development of *Abhidhamma* philosophy, to distinguish *dhammas* taught by the Buddha from what was not taught by him and to arrange them in numerical order show clearly a step in the progress of *Abhidhamma* philosophy. The *Saṅgitiparyāya* of the Sarvāstivāda school is made up in this manner. The *Saṅgitiparyāya* is an *Abhidhamma* text, but it is based on the *Saṅgitisūtra* of the Sarvāstivāda school. In fact the *Saṅgitiparyāya* is simply a kind of commentary on the *Saṅgitisūtra*, each *dhamma* mentioned being explained by quotations from other *suttas* and by other discussions. The method is like some parts of the *Dharmaskandha* of the Sarvāstivāda school or the *Vibhaṅga* of the Sthaviravāda school.

4.4 Through the medium of the special study of *dhammas* such as defining *dhammas* and arranging them in numerical order, the Buddha's disciples established a sound foundation of the *Abhidhamma Piṭaka*, and called these *dhammas* which were defined and arranged *Mātikā*. The word *mātikā* means 'matrix' or list of topics. We can see from the *Nikāyas* and *Āgamas* that what was called *Mātikā* was rehearsed (probably in "*abhidhamma* study"), though it is difficult to decide what kinds of doctrinal

---

1. M. I, 428, T. 1, 804 b-c.

topics it meant. In the *Mahāparinibbānasutta* the following statement can be seen:[1]

> In such and such a dwelling-place many elder monks live, having much learning (*bahussuta*) as handed down by tradition (*āgatāgama*), versed in the doctrine (*dhammadhara*), versed in the discipline (*vinayadhara*), versed in the doctrinal topics (*mātikādhara*).

And also, we see in another text:[2]

> Monks, there is a monk who frequents the monks, having much learning as handed down by tradition, versed in the doctrine, versed in the discipline, versed in the doctrinal topics (*mātikādhara*). He inquires (*paripucchati*) of them and questions (*paripañhati*) thus: "How is this, reverend sir? What is the meaning of this?" They then open up (*vivarati*) to him what was unopened (*avivaṭa*), make clear (*uttāni karoti*) what was obscure (*anuttānikata*), and as to diverse doubtful points of doctrine (*kankhāṭṭhāniya dhamma*), they dispel (*paṭivinodeti*) his doubts. This is how he finds his strength (*nissayasampanna*).

The word *mātikā* can also be found in the *Vinaya Piṭaka*, where it appears with the word *vibhaṅga* (indicating the *Suttavibhaṅga* or *Vinayavibhaṅga*) and the word *khandhaka* (indicating the *Khandhakas*).[3] Therefore, it is also a word used for a special study of *vinaya* (*abhivinaya*: probably studying the *Pātimokkhasutta*, see example(1)of chapter **3.5** and chapter **3.8**). However, it seems that the word *mātikā* came to be used as a special word for *abhidhamma*.

In Chinese *Vinaya* texts such as the *Kên-pen-shuo-i-ch'ieh-yu-pu-p'i-nai-yeh* of the Mūlasarvāstivāda school[4] and the *Mo-ho-sêng-*

---

1. D. II, 125, T. 1, 17 c. T. 1, 182 c, in which the word 'doctrine' can be seen.
2. A. I, 117, III, 179, 361, V, 15-16, M. I, 221. T. 2, 343 a, in which the word '*abhidhamma*' is used.
3. Vin. V, 86.
4. T. 24, 408 b.

chih-lü of the Mahāsaṁghika school,[1] and also in "A Story of the King Aśoka" (*Aśokāvadāna*),[2] the word *mātikā* is used as a synonym for the word *abhidhamma*, and is regarded as the *Abhidhamma Piṭaka*, one of the three *Piṭakas*. However, *Mātikā* cannot be regarded as the *Abhidhamma Piṭaka* now extant, but can be considered to be the simple form of the *Abhidhamma Piṭaka*. In fact such *Mātikās* are served as the kernel of the respective *Abhidhamma* texts (particularly the seven well known texts of the Sthaviravāda and the Sarvāstivāda schools). On this point, A. K. Warder's opinion is worthy of note: It seems very probable that in the earliest period this third section of the *Tripiṭaka* consisted simply of some set of *Mātṛkā* headings, possibly propounded by the Buddha himself when giving systematic instruction to his followers, and that this was only later fully elaborated into *Abhidharma* expositions.[3]

What are then the original *Mātikās*? It is difficult to draw them exactly from the *Nikāyas* and *Āgamas*. The Mūlasarvāstivāda *Vinaya* states that *Mātikās* are:[4]

1. 4 *satipaṭṭhānas* (bases of self-possession),
2. 4 *sammappadhānas* (right exertions),
3. 4 *iddhipādas* (bases of power),
4. 5 *indriyas* (faculties),
5. 5 *balas* (strengths),
6. 7 *bojjhaṅgas* (factors of enlightenment),
7. 8 *maggaṅgas* (factors of the way),
8. 4 *vesārajjas*,(bases of self-confidence),
9. 4 *paṭisambhidās* (bases of comprehension),
10. 4 *sāmmaññaphalas* (fruits of striverhood),
11. 4 *dhammapadas* (bases of the doctrine),
12. *araṇadhamma* (?) (peacefulness),
13. *pantasamādhi* (?) (mental concentration),
14. 3 *samādhis* (bases of concentration),
15. *samādhibhāvanā* (?) (development of concentration),
16. *abhisamaya* (insight),

1. T. 22, 334 c.
2. T. 50, 113c.
3. *Indian Buddhism*, p 10
4. T. 24, 408 b.

17. *sammutiñāṇa* (?) (common knowledge),
18. *samathavipassanā* (tranquillity and insight),
19. *dhammasaṅgaṇi* (enumeration of principles),
20. *dhammakkhandhas* (groups of principles).

It is understood that these *Mātikās* do not indicate *Abhidhamma Piṭaka* books except for the last two, which actually show the titles of *Abhidhamma* texts of the Sthaviravāda and the Sarvāstivāda schools, but doctrinal topics or list of topics, a set of notes giving just the headings of a body of doctrine. Accordingly, we could justifiably say that in the earliest period *Mātikās* like the above were rehearsed in an *abhidhamma* study. The various *Mātikās* mentioned above neither cover all the topics in the *Abhidhamma* texts, nor include the universal ones in early Buddhism. In the *Nikāyas* and *Āgamas*, there are many *suttas* (dialogues) which collected the varied topics of *dhammas* without using the word *mātikā*. And it is certain that these topics helped the growth of *Abhidhammamātikās*. Above all, the most representative topics are thirty-seven practical *dhammas* or a set of seven headings. Therefore, this point should be discussed in the following chapter.

5

THE SYSTEMATIZATION OF MĀTIKĀS

5.1 It is doubtful whether any *Abhidhamma* texts were recited at the time of the Buddha, though we could say that by comparing the available *Abhidhamma* texts, a substantial development took place within the first two centuries after the Buddha's *parinibbāna*, and in great part before the First Schism (not earlier than a hundred and thirty-seven years after the *parinibbāna*: placing the event in B.C. 349[1]). However, we have learned that *Mātikās* had already existed in the earliest period (see chapter **4.4**). We would say that since the Buddha's disciples showed an attitude of analyzing ***dhammas*** taught by the Buddha clearly and of organizing them synthetically in an *abhidhamma* study, they maintained the same attitude in dealing with *Mātikās*.

Not only various *Mātikās* in the *Saṅgītiparyāya*,[2] which are classified and expounded in the order of ones, twos, threes, etc. up to tens, but also *Mātikās* in the other *Abhidhamma* texts have served as headings of a body of doctrine. We have already indicated some of the available *Abhidhamma* texts in previous

---

1. On this see A. K. Warder, *Indian Buddhism*, pp. 13-4, 214, 218.

2. In *Das Saṅgītisūtra und sein Kommentar Saṅgītiparyāya*, a comparison of *Mātṛkās* in the *Saṅgītisūtra* in Skt., Pāli and Chinese with those in the *Saṅgītiparyāya* is made (Berlin, DAWB, 1968, Teil 1, pp. 213-7), and also in the *Vinaya* section of a Japanese translation of the Chinese *Tripiṭaka* (Kokuyaku Issaikyo), a comparison of *Mātṛkās* in the *Saṅgītiparyāya* with those in the *Saṅgītisuttanta* and its Chinese version is made (vol. 1, pp. 7-29).

pages. But, at this point, let us introduce the seven well known *Abhidhamma* texts of the Sthaviravāda and the Sarvāstivāda schools. The seven well known *Abhidhamma* texts of the Sthaviravāda school are:[1]

1. *Dhammasaṅgaṇi*,
2. *Vibhaṅga*,
3. *Dhātukathā*,
4. *Puggalapaññatti*,
5. *Kathāvatthu*,
6. *Yamaka*,
7. *Paṭṭhāna*.

On the other hand, the *Abhidharma* texts of the Sarvāstivāda school, preserved in its Chinese version, also comprise seven treatises. They are as follows:[2]

1. *Jñānaprasthāna* of Ārya Kātyāyanīputra,
2. *Saṅgītiparyāya* of Mahākauṣṭhila,
3. *Prakaraṇapāda* of Sthavira Vasumitra,
4. *Vijñānakāya* of Sthavira Devaśarman,
5. *Dhātukāya* of Pūrṇa,
6. *Dharmaskandha* of Ārya Śāriputra,
7. *Prajñaptiśāstra* of Ārya Maudgalyāyana.

In addition to the above texts of the two different schools, we cannot overlook the *Śāriputrābhidharmaśāstra*, probably of the Dharmaguptaka school, which seems to cover the whole field of *Abhidhamma*.[3] That is to say, the *Śāriputrābhidharmaśāstra* itself includes the subject matter of the *Dharmaskandha*, *Vibhaṅga*, *Puggalapaññatti* (Concept of 'Person'), and so on. How were then various *Mātikās* in these *Abhidhamma* texts worked up?

5.2 According to A. K. Warder, the seven *Abhidhamma* texts of the Sthaviravāda school are based on three primary and

---

1. For details, see Nyanatiloka Mahathera, *Guide Through the Abhidhamma-Piṭaka*.

2. For details, see A. C. Banerjee, *Sarvāstivāda Literature*.

3. On this see A. Bareau, "Les origines du *Śāriputrābhidharmaśāstra*," Museon, t. LXIII, 1-2, pp. 69-95, and A. K. Warder, *Indian Buddhism*, p. 220.

separate lists of topics, worked up in a variety of ways. They are seen in the following order:[1]

(1) The list of twenty-two *tikas* (triplets) and 100 *dukas* (couplets), to which a list of a further forty-two *Suttantika dukas* is sometimes appended. This *Mātikā*, which is set out at the beginning of the *Dhammasaṅgaṇi*, is the basis of that book and also of the *Paṭṭhāna*. Besides, we can see that the *Pañhapucchaka* sections in the *Vibhaṅga* (pp. 12-61) analyze the *dhammas* according to these *tikas* and *dukas*, and the *Dhātukathā* simply adds the twenty-two *tikas* and 100 *dukas* to the *khandhas* (groups), *āyatanas* (spheres), *dhātus* (elements), etc. The *Puggalapaññatti* also adds its own *mātikās* of *puggala samayavimutta* (one who is emancipated in season), *puggala asamayavimutta* (one who is emancipated out of season), etc., culled from the *Sutta* texts. **But this is placed under No. 2.**

(2) The groups of *dhammas* such as the *khandhas*, *āyatanas*, *dhātus*, etc. The list of such groups is very variable, but it forms the basis of the *Vibhaṅga*, *Dhātukathā*, *Puggalapaññatti* and *Yamaka*. The *dhammas* (*phassa*: touch, *vedanā*: sensation, *saññā*: perception, etc.) of the *Dhammasaṅgaṇi* seem to be connected with this.

(3) The list of controversial topics in the *Kathāvatthu*.

We have no objection to the above. So we would like to examine each of the three different types.

5.3 On Tikas and Dukas. For us, it is unnecessary here to make a full list of twenty-two *tikas* and 100 *dukas* in the *Dhammasaṅgaṇi* and *Paṭṭhāna*. The most important is to know the reason why such *mātikās* were produced. It is said that the *Dhātukathā* adding the twenty-two *tikas* and 100 *dukas* to the *khandhas*, *āyatanas*, etc. is a mere exercise in classifying all these *dhammas* by *khandhas*, *āyatanas*, and *dhātus*.[2] This exercise is, however, important in the case of analysis and systematic study of *dhammas* taught by the Buddha. That is, from the very beginning the Buddha's disciples had to understand his teachings analytically and systematically. In this case, what was

1. Ed. A. P. Buddhadatta and A. K. Warder, *Mohavicchedanī*, p. xix.
2. See *Mohavicchedanī*, p. xix.

always required of his disciples is to grasp the contrary concept of words or to see contradictory terms. Generally speaking, Indian languages (including Pāli) have various prefixes (*upasaggas*) expressing the negative, such as *a*, *an(a)*, *ni(s)*, *vi*, etc., and also use indeclinable particles (*nipātas*) for negation, such as *na*, *no*, *mā*, *alam*, *halam*, and so on. For example, in a list of *cūḷantaraduka* (the short intermediate set of couplets), the following *dukas* are given:[1]

1. *Sa(p)paccayadhamma*; *a-(p)paccaya dhamma* (principles that are causally related; not causally related).
2. *Saṅkhata dhamma*; *a-saṅkhata dhamma* (principles that are activated; unactivated).
3. *Sanidassana dhamma*; *a-nidassana dhamma* (principles that are visible; invisible).
4. *Sa-(p)paṭighadhamma*; *a-(p)paṭigha dhamma* (principles that are reactions; not reactions).
5. *Rūpi dhamma*; *arūpi dhamma* (principles that have visible object; that have invisible object).
6. *Lokiya dhamma*; *lokuttara dhamma* (principles that are mundane; supramundane).
7. *Viññeyya dhamma*; *na viññeyya dhamma* (principles that may be cognized in a given way; that may not be cognized in that given way).

These *dukas* are shown clearly by using both *upasaggas* and *nipātas* expressing negation (except for No. 6) and are contradictory to each other. To say that the *upasaggas* and *nipātas* were already used in the time of the Buddha is no more than to say that they were part of the language. (Of course the *way* in which he used them may well have been new.) For instance, the *Saṁyuttanikāya* deals with varieties of synonym denoting the concept for *nibbāna* (extinction) in which there are negative expressions:[2]

1. *An-āsava* : non-influence.
2. *A-jajjara* : unfading.
3. *Nis-papañca* : non-differentiation.

---

1. Dhs. pp. 2-3.
2. S. IV, 368-73, T. 2, 224 a.

4. *A-mata* : deathlessness.
5. *An-ālaya* : non-attachment.

Also, the word 'falsity' that is contrary to 'truth' (*bhūta*) is expressed by the words *a-bhūta*, the word 'bad' that is contrary to 'good' (*kusala*) is expressed by the words *a-kusala* and so forth. Thus, we cannot overlook the fact that the practical use of negative prefixes accelerated the development of *Mātikās* of *tikas* and *dukas*. This may be clarified further from a logical point of view.

5.4 As can be realized from the above, the words *sappaccaya dhamma* are contradictory to the words *appaccaya dhamma*, and the former is the contradictory term of the latter. For the sake of convenience, let us put the capital letter *B* for *sappacca dhamma* and put -*B* (expressing the denial of B)[1] for *appaccaya dhamma*. At this point, we should not fall into the fallacy that *duka-Mātikās* consist, like the following, of two propositions :

(1) Everything is *B*.
(2) Everything is not *B*.

If so, item (1) is A form and item (2), E form according to traditional Aristotelian logic, which we will refer to more or less in another chapter. Four ways of joining terms pairwise into statements have been treated as fundamental throughout the logical tradition stemming from Aristotle: 'All *F* are *G*', 'No *F* are *G*', 'Some *F* are *G*', and 'Some *F* are not *G*'. Statements of these four forms were called *categorical*. The four forms were distinguished by special nomenclature and by code '**A**', '**E**', '**I**', and '**O**', as follows :

A (Universal affirmative) : All *F* are *G*.
E (Universal negative) : No *F* are *G*.
I (Particular affirmative) : Some *F* are *G*.
O (Particular negative) : Some *F* are not *G*.

Apart from the explanation of the four forms,[2] a matter of great importance concerning the *duka* is the relationship between

1. On this see W. V. Quine, *Elementary Logic*, p. 11.
2. For details, see W. V. Quine, *Methods of Logic*, pp. 66-9.

B and not *B*. Specifically, the relation of the two can be expressed through what is called *alternation*, which corresponds to the connective "or," or "either . . . or . . .": Either *B* or not *B*. The components connected by "or" or "either . . . or . . ." are called *alternants* and there may be two or more of them.[1] The components may be interchanged in position without affecting the meaning (unlike components in conditionals), and they may be categorical, non-categorical, compound, or any other kind of proposition.

Now, the relation of *duka*, namely: *sappaccaya dhamma* and *appaccaya dhamma* becomes:

(3) Anything is *B* or not *B*.

It does not become:

(4) Everything is *B* or everything is not *B*.

Although "anything" includes case *a*, case *b*, case *c*, . . . case *x*, which can be viewed as "everything," items (3) and (4) are not the same. If we replace the term 'everything' by the universal quantifier '(x)', (3) becomes:

$(x)\ [(x \text{ is } B) \text{ or } -(x \text{ is } B)]$

And (4) becomes with the false proposition, which contains (1) and (2) :

$(x)\ (x \text{ is } B) \text{ or } (x) - (x \text{ is } B)$

Thus most of the *duka-Mātikās* are based on contradictory terms, which can be expressed by item (3) above. It seems that various *Mātikās* of *dukas* were produced with the object of clarifying the fundamental standpoint of Buddhism, of clearing

1. In ordinary speech the words "either...or..." are taken in two different senses. One sense may be called the "inclusive sense" of alternative propositions. (In this case, "v" of the word *vel* in Latin is used.) In this sense a statement of the form : "Either *p* or *q*" would be considered true if (a) *p* were true, (b) *q* were true, or (c) *p* and *q* were both true; it would be considered false only in case *p* was false and *q* was false also. The other sense may be called the "exclusive sense". (In this case, the connective *or* is used in modern logic.) Ordinary speech sometimes treats "either...or..." as implying that one alternant or the other must be true exclusively, and thus that "Either *p* or *q*" would be false if both *p* and *q* were true at the same time. This second sense of "either...or..." is called the "exclusive sense". On this, see Richard B. Angell *Reasoning and Logic*, p. 145.

up doubts, and of comparing what one knows with the knowledge of others. In view of the fact that Buddhists had a good command of *upasaggas* and *nipātas* expressing negation, it was linguistically not difficult for them to understand contradictory terms. And by doing so, they could carry on the further analysis and systematic study of *dhammas*.

5.5 *Tika-Mātikās* can be produced from the concept of contrary terms. As one of the most representative *tikas*, we see the words *sukha* (happiness), *dukkha* (unhappiness) and '*adukkhamasukha*' (neither unhappiness nor happiness). Both *sukha* and *dukkha* are contrary to each other, from which the "neutral" can be drawn: *adukkhamasukha*. A certain *sutta* text states:[1]

> There are three feelings (or sensations, *vedanā*) : (1) happy feeling (*sukha vedanā*), (2) unhappy feeling (*dukkha vedanā*), and (3) feeling that is neither unhappy nor happy (*adukkhamasukha vedanā*). What is item (1)? That which is experienced, whether by body or mind, and is happy and sweet (*sāta*), this is a happy feeling. What is item (2)? That which is experienced, whether by body or mind, and is unhappy and unsweet (*asāta*), this is an unhappy feeling. What is item (3)? That which is experienced, whether by body or mind, and is neither sweet nor unsweet, this is a feeling that is neither unhappy nor happy.

And in another place, the following statement can be seen:[2]

> Whenever one feels item (1), one feels neither item (2) nor item (3).
> Whenever one feels item (2), one feels neither item (1) nor item (3).
> Whenever one feels item (3), one feels neither item (1) nor item (2).

Therefore, this expression would be "All men feel either happiness or unhappiness or neither-happiness-nor-unhappiness." This is schematized by:

1. M. I, 302-303.
2. M. I, 500, D. II, 66, T. 1, 61 c, 2, 249 c, 449 b, etc.

$(x)\ [x \text{ is a man} \supset ((x \text{ is } a) \text{ or } (x \text{ is } b) \text{ or} - (x \text{ is } a \vee x \text{ is b}))]$

After this fashion, in the *Dhammasaṅgaṇi*, all *dhammas* (principles) are systematized according to the criteria of *kusala* (good), *akusala* (bad) and *avyākata* (neither-good-nor-bad), because Buddhists came to the conclusion that the root of one's mind was not always *avijjā* (ignorance), and there was the element of *kusala*, *akusala* and *avyākata*. Although the words *a-kusala* are philologically contradictory to *kusala*, the former is not always equivalent to that which is expressed by the negative of the latter, namely: *a-kusala* meaning 'not good'.[1] In other words, *a-kusala* should be regarded as meaning 'bad' which is contrary to 'good' (*kusala*). From the contradictory of the two, the neutral *avyākata* can be produced. Therefore, we can see the expression "The root of one's mind is either good or bad or neither-good-nor-bad." Since "one's mind" here can be viewed as "anyone's mind," the schematization becomes:

$(x)\ [(x \text{ is } a) \text{ or } (x \text{ is } b) \text{ or} - (x \text{ is } a \vee x \text{ is } b)]$

From the preceding discussions, we are led to the conclusion that by understanding a certain profound meaning of *tikas* and *dukas*,[2] Buddhists attempted the analysis and systematic study of such doctrinal topics, and at the same time, that through the contradictory concept of terms and the concept of contrary terms, they tried to realize a view of life and the world in Buddhism.

5.6 On Khandhāyatanadhātuyo, etc. About the groups of *dhammas* such as the *khandhas*, *āyatanas*, *dhātus*, etc., there is little need to talk at length. Our main task is to survey how the doctrinal topics or *Mātikās* which form the basis of *Abhidhamma* philosophy developed from the *Nikāyas* and *Āgamas*, and how the *Mātikās* were classified in the *Abhidhamma* texts.

For Buddhists, one of the chief tasks in developing the Buddha's doctrines as the *Abhidhamma* texts must have been the

---

1. We see from this that logic is not given by the language, which uses negative prefixes inconsistently (for both contradictories and contraries). Logic had to be imposed on the natural language by philosophers.

2. On these detailed explanations of *tikas* and *dukas*, translated into English, see C. A. F. Rhys Davids, *A Buddhist Manual of Psychological Ethics*, pp. cv-cxii.

selection and the arrangement of *Mātikās*; e.g. the 18 topics reckoned in the *Vibhaṅga* of the Sthaviravāda school, the 21 topics in the *Dharmaskandha* of the Sarvāstivāda school, the first 21 topics in the *Śāriputrābhidharmaśāstra* of the Dharmaguptaka school (probably) and the like, because some groups or aggregates of doctrinal topics (*dhammakkhandhas*) can be found in the *Nikāyas* and *Āgamas*. In this case, these do not always mean the *Sutta* texts which collect topics numerically such as *Saṅgitisutta*, *Dasuttarasutta* and so on. For instance, the *Chachakkasutta* (M. III, 280-87) and its Chinese version (T. 1, 562 a-566 a); the *Cūḷavedallasutta* (M. I, 299-305) and its Chinese version (T. 1, 788 a-790 b); the *Mahāvedallasutta* (M. I, 292-98) and its Chinese version (T. 1, 790 b-792 b) are the typical texts which involve some aggregates of doctrinal topics. Above all, many topics in the Chinese rendering of the *Chachakkasutta* correspond to chapters in the *Dharmaskandha*, one of the seven well known *Abhidhamma* texts of the Sarvāstivāda school (T. 26, 453 b-514 a). The former seems to be the original text of the latter:

Topics in the *Chachakkasutta*	Chapters in the *Dharmaskandha*
5 *khandhas* (groups)	19th *vagga* (chapter).
6 *ajjhattikāyatanas* (internal spheres) 6 *bāhirāyatanas* (external spheres)	18th *vagga*.
6 *viññāṇakāyas* (bodies of consciousness)	
6 *phassakāyas* (bodies of touch)	
6 *vedanākāyas* (bodies of sensation)	
6 *saññākāyas* (bodies of perception)	
6 *sañcetanākāyas* (bodies of thought)	
6 *taṇhākāyas* (bodies of thirst)	
6 *dhātus* (elements)	20th *vagga*.
12 *paṭiccasamuppādas* (dependent originations)	21st *vagga*.
4 *satipaṭṭhānas* (bases of self-possession)	9th *vagga*.
4 *sammappadhānas* (right exertions)	7th *vagga*.
4 *iddhipādas* (bases of power)	8th *vagga*.
4 *jhānas* (meditations)	11th *vagga*.
4 *saccas* (truths).	10th *vagga*.
4 *saññās* (perception)	
4 *appamaññās* (boundlessness).	12th *vagga*.
4 *arūpas* (invisible object).	13th *vagga*.

4 *ariyavaṁsas* (noble lineages) . . . . 6th *vagga.*
4 *samaṇas* (strivers) . . . . 4th *vagga.*
5 *vimuttāyatanas* (liberation from spheres)
5 *indriyas* (faculties) . . . . 17th *vagga.*
5 *balas* (strengths)
5 *nissaraṇadhātus* (liberation from elements)
7 *dhanas* (treasures)
7 *balas* (strengths)
7 *bojjhaṅgas* (factors of enlightenment) . . . 15th *vagga.*
8 *maggaṅgas* (factors of the way) . . . . . 10th *vagga.*
4 *lakkhaṇas* (characteristics)

The above *Mātikās* are arranged at random. The most elaborated *Mātikās* in the *Nikāyas* and *Āgamas* are the thirty-seven practical *dhammas* (or a set of seven headings for them). According to the *Mahāparinibbānasutta*, when in Vesāli on his way to Kusinārā, the Buddha convened his monks and explained that his doctrine should be the 'refuge' (*saraṇa*) for his monks, and later he says it will be the teacher after he has gone. At that time, as a summary of his teachings, the thirty-seven *dhammas* are indicated.[1] This summary seems to have been common to all schools of Buddhism. Apart from the versions of the *Mahāparinibbānasutta* which give it such prominence, we find the same list of seven headings, from the four bases of self-possession (*satipaṭṭhānas*) to the noble eightfold way (or eight factors of the way), in many other texts of all known schools.[2]

We would say that the thirty-seven practical *dhammas* given by the Buddha at Vesāli gave rise to the idea of a set of *mātikas* and in due course to the various elaborations of it as *Abhidhamma* philosophy, and at the same time, that the four *saccas*, together with the nine or twelve *paṭiccasamuppādas* as the theory of causation, which is really an expansion of the second truth of the four *saccas*, came to be classified as the *mātikās* for

1. D. II, 119-20.
2. In the *Parinibbānasutta* translated by Fu-to-yeh-she and Chu Fu-nien (T. 1, 16 c) as well as in the *Sutta* translated by an anonymous person (T. 1, 181 b), forty-one *dhammas* (with the four *jhānas* added to the 37 *dhammas*) are given.

study of *paññā* (understanding) and the Buddhist analysis of life and eventually of the universe.

5.7 Such a tendency is displayed clearly in the case of *khandhāyatanadhātuyo*, which are a group of *dhammas* composed of the five *khandhas*, twelve (or six) *āyatanas*, and eighteen *dhātus* —also we find six *dhātus* which are the principles constituting matter and mind. These are collected in both the *Saṁyutta-nikāya* and ***Saṃyuktāgama***. They contain sections called "*khandha saṁyutta*,"[1] "*saḷāyatana saṁyutta*,"[2] and "*dhātu saṁyutta*."[3] Also, in the Pāli *Vinaya*, we can see a discourse on the five *khandhas* which was given to five monks by the Buddha:[4]

> Matter (*rūpa* as physical principles) is non-ego. If matter were ego, it would not be involved in sickness, and one could say of matter: "Thus let it be. Thus let it not be." But, inasmuch as matter is non-ego, that is why matter is involved in sickness, one cannot say of matter: "Thus let it be. Thus let it not be." Sensation (*vedanā*) is non-ego . . . "Thus let it be. Thus let it not be." Perception (*saññā*) is non-ego . . . "Thus let it be. Thus let it not be." Forces (*saṅkhāra*) are non-ego. . . "Thus let them be. Thus let them not be." Consciousness (*viññāṇa*) is non-ego . . . "Thus let it be. Thus let it not be."

From the above, we can understand that the five *khandhas* (as well as six *āyatanas*) preached by the Buddha were the *dhammas* (doctrines) which would lead to the realization of *anicca*, *dukkha*, and *anattan* in this phenomenal world. Also, the Buddha always said, "*Sabba* (everything) in the world is *anicca*, *dukkha* and *anattan*."[5] In this case, *sabba*, of course, involves the five *khandhas* or six *āyatanas*. However, in course of time, the five *khandhas* or six *āyatanas* were regarded as the principles composing the human being, and became the subject of an analytical study. Because the list of eighteen *dhātus* was created

1. S. III, 1-188, T. 2, 1 a-22 b, 29 c-37 b, 64 b-72 b.
2. S. IV, 1-204, T. 2,49 b-79 a, 86 c-93 b, 310 b-317 b.
3. S. II, 140-77, T. 2, 114 c-119 a.
4. Vin. I, 10-4. T. 22, 789 a, Also, see T. 22, 105 a, 24, 128 b-c, etc.
5. S. IV, 15, T. 2, 91 a-b.

by adding six kinds of consciousness to the twelve *āyatanas* (which are composed of six sense-organs and their objects), a group of *dhammas* consisting of the five *khandhas*, twelve *āyatanas*, and eighteen *dhātus* came to develop in the direction of an analytical study of man. As a result, the *Abhidhamma* texts presented the topics of *khandhāyatanadhātuyo*, in which many *dhammas* (principles) were linked with one another. We cannot see yet the study of the components of man in the *Nikāyas* and *Āgamas*, but there is no denying the fact that many *Sutta* texts which have reference to the eighteen *dhātus* have a great influence on the study of the classification of man.

5.8 As can be realized from the discussions in chapter **5.6** and **7**, there is a distinct difference between the group of the thirty-seven *dhammas* and that of *khandhāyatanadhātuyo*, etc. The former gives a consistent and orderly exposition of the striving of the early Buddhists, and the latter, the Buddhist analysis of life with its constituent principles, and the theory of causation. The analysis of principles and of causation belongs to the field of insight rather than of striving and meditation, but its understanding was doubtless considered to be dependent on the training of Buddhists. In this sense, we can agree with A. K. Warder's view that a comparison of the Pāli tradition with the Sarvāstivāda *Abhidhamma* and with the lists of *mātikā* in the *Aśokāvadāna* (A Story of the King Aśoka) and in the Mūlasarvāstivāda *Vinaya* suggests an early system of twenty-one groups:[1]

1. 4 *satipaṭṭhānas*: 4 bases of self-possession.
2. 4 *sammappadhānas*: 4 right exertions.
3. 4 *iddhipādas*: 4 bases of power.
4. 5 *indriyas*: 5 faculties.
5. 5 *balas*: 5 strengths.
6. 7 *bojjhaṅgas*: 7 factors of enlightenment.
7. 8 *maggaṅgas*: 8 factors of the way.

---

1. See *Mohavicchedanī*, pp. xxii. A. K. Warder has recently stated that an early system of twenty-one groups may be revised in the light of additional evidence, e.g. *Śāriputrābhidharmaśāstra*, etc.

8. 5 (orig. 4 ?) *sikkhāpadas*: 5 precepts.
9. 4 *sāmaññaphalas*: 4 fruits of striverhood.
10. 4 *ariyavaṁsas*: 4 noble lineages.
11. 4 *paṭisambhidās*: 4 comprehensions.
12. 4 *jhānas*: 4 stages of meditation.
13. 4 *appamaññās*: 4 kinds of boundlessness.
14. 6 (orig. 4 ?) *abhiññās*: 6 kinds of insight.

15. 5 *khandhas*: 5 groups.
16. 12 *āyatanas*: 12 spheres.
17. 18 *dhātus*: 18 elements.
18. 22 (?) *indriyas* (? or *paññās*) : 22 faculties (or understandings).
19. ? *puggalas* or *ekottaras* : persons or one up.
20. 4 *saccas*: 4 truths.
21. 12 *paṭiccasamuppādas*: twelve-linked chain of dependent origination.

The first seven topics are very constant, even in internal order, in the several sources, and seem to have constituted the whole *mātikā* at first. As mentioned in chapter **5.6**, these are identical with the list of the thirty-seven *dhammas* attributed to the Buddha in the ***Mahāparinibbānasutta*** (D. II, 120) as a summary of his teachings, elsewhere called *bodhipakkhiyā dhammā* or simply *saddhammo* (true doctrine).[1] The middle seven topics list the stages of the Buddhist life and especially of *samādhi* (concentration). The last seven topics are what we have called theoretical *dhammas* (see chapter **2.4**) or the Buddhist analysis of life (see chapter **5.6**).

For a certainty, the topics in the *Abhidhamma* texts are presented by arranging the *Mātikās* as displayed above. That is to say, the 18 topics in the *Vibhaṅga*, the 21 topics in the *Dharmaskandha* and the first twenty-one topics in the *Śāriputrābhidharmaśāstra* are related to one another. But the arrangement of the topics differs greatly in the three texts. This indicates the different sectarian characteristics of these three texts and the different stages of the development of the study of *Abhidhamma*. At this point, let us collate the topics in the three texts :

1. Vbh. p. 372.

	Vibhaṅga	*Dharmaskandha*	*Śāriputrābhidharma*
1.	*khandha* (group)	*sikkhāpada*	*āyatana*
2.	*āyatana* (sphere)	*sotāpattiyaṅga* (factor of obtaining the stream)	*dhātu*
3.	*dhātu* (element)	*aveccappasāda* (complete confidence)	*khandha*
4.	*sacca* (truth)	*sāmañña* (profession of asceticism)	*sacca*
5.	*indriya* (faculty)	*abhiññāpatipadā* (way of knowledge)	*indriya*
6.	*paccayākāra* (aspect of condition)	*ariyavaṁsa* (noble lineage)	*bojjhaṅga*
7.	*satipaṭṭhāna* (base of self-possession)	*sammappadhāna*	*akusala-mūla* (bad root)
8.	*sammappadhāna* (right exertion)	*iddhipāda*	*kusala-mūla* (good root)
9.	*iddhipāda* (base of power)	*satipaṭṭhāna*	*mahā-bhūta* (great existent)
10.	*bojjhaṅga* (factor of enlightenment)	*sacca*	*upāsaka* (lay disciple)
11.	*magga* (way)	*jhāna*	*dhātu*
12.	*jhāna* (meditation)	*appamaññā*	*kamma* (action)
13.	*appamaññā* (boundlessness)	*āruppā* (invisible object)	*puggala* (person)
14.	*sikkhāpada* (precept)	*bhāvanā* (development)	*ñāṇa*
15.	*paṭisambhidā* (comprehension)	*bojjhaṅga*	*paccayākāra*
16.	*ñāṇa* (knowledge)	*khuddakavatthu*	*satipaṭṭhāna*

17.	*khuddakavatthu* (minor ground)	*indriya*	*sammappadhāna*
18.	*dhammahadaya* (heart of the teaching)	*āyatana*	*iddhipāda*
19.		*khandha*	*jhāna*
20.		*dhātu*	*magga*
21.		*paccayākāra*	*kilesa* (defilement)

5.9 The first fifteen chapters of the *Dharmaskandha* deal with moral and practical *dhammas* pertaining to enlightenment, and the remaining chapters deal with the theoretical *dhammas* belonging rather to the field of insight. The main topics of the *Dharmaskandha* appear to be in the first fifteen chapters. To speak more precisely, the first, second and the third chapters include a great many *dhammas* (teachings) which the laymen and the novices of the Buddha ought to study. The fourth, fifth and the sixth chapters explain the methodology of studying Buddhism. The last nine chapters (from the seventh to the fifteenth) expatiate upon the thirty-seven *dhammas* and other paths of practice. Therefore, the purpose of the *Dharmaskandha* was to arrange a series of *dhammas* (doctrines) according to a certain definite system. For example, although the internal order of the thirty-seven practical *dhammas* is free and not in the regular order, namely :

5th chapter deals with 5 *indriyas* and 5 *balas*,
7th chapter deals with 4 *sammappadhānas*,
8th chapter deals with 4 *iddhipādas*,
9th chapter deals with 4 *satipaṭṭhānas*,
10th chapter deals with 8 *maggaṅgas*,
15th chapter deals with 7 *bojjhaṅgas*,

yet the thirty *dhammas* are systematized by the seven *bojjhaṅgas*. In other words, the main topic in the thirty-seven *dhammas* is the seven *bojjhaṅgas*.

The arrangement of the twelve chapters in *mahāvagga* of the *Saṁyuttanikāya* is also free :[1]

1. S. V, 1-473.

46th chapter deals with 7 *bojjhaṅgas*,
47th chapter deals with 4 *satipaṭṭhānas*,
48th chapter deals with 5 *indriyas*,
49th chapter deals with 4 *sammappadhānas*,
50th chapter deals with 5 *balas*,
51st chapter deals with 4 *iddhipādas*,
56th chapter deals with 8 *maggaṅgas*.

And the arrangement of the nine chapters in the *maggavagga* of the *Saṃyuktāgama* is free too :[1]

1st chapter deals with 4 *satipaṭṭhānas*,
2nd chapter deals with 5 *indriyas*,
3rd chapter deals with 5 *balas*,
4th chapter deals with 7 *bojjhaṅgas*,
5th chapter deals with 8 *maggaṅgas*;
9th chapter deals with 4 *sammappadhānas*.

So we might say that the *Dharmaskandha* follows in succession the way of the *Nikāyas* and *Āgamas*. But it is also true that there is a basic difference between them. In the *Nikāyas* and *Āgamas*, there is apparently not any system of arrangement among all the *dhammas*. On the other hand, the *dhammas* in the *Dharmaskandha* tend to be systematized according to the *Abhidhammic* explanation. For example, we can see the relationship between the four *satipaṭṭhānas* and the five *khandhas* as follows :

1. *Kāya*———————1. *Rūpa*
2. *Vedanā*———————2. *Vedanā*
3. *Citta*———————3. *Viññāṇa*
4. *Dhamma*——————[4. *Saññā*, 5. *Saṁkhāra*]

In view of the fact that according to A. K. Warder,[2] the old *Nikāyas* anticipate in some ways the classification of *dhammas* worked out in the *Abhidhamma*, where some *dhammas* are

1. T. 2, 170 c-205 c and 219 b-226 a.
2. "Dharmas and Data," *Journal of Indian Philosophy*, Vol. I, No. 3, November, 1971, p. 287.

included in others, it might be recognized in the *Nikāyas* and *Āgamas* that the fourth *dhamma* of the four *satipaṭṭhānas* includes all five *khandhas* as mental object. However, the *Dharmaskandha* seems to be intended to emphasize especially the relation of the fourth *dhamma* of the four *satipaṭṭhānas* to both *saññā* and *saṁkhāra*.

The eleventh and the twelfth chapters in the *Dharmaskandha* are devoted to the exposition of the four *jhānas* (meditations) and the four *appamaññās* (boundlessness). There are eight stages of meditation. It is from the four *jhānas* that one starts the lowest meditation, and the highest meditation is included in the four *appamaññās*. The purpose of this arrangement is to systematize both of these *dhammas*. The last six chapters deal with the five *khandhas*, twelve *āyatanas*, eighteen *dhātus* and the like, but the arrangement of these chapters is not systematic. Regardless of the fact that the first three chapters of the *Vibhaṅga* are arranged according to the regular order of the *dhammas* : *khandhāyatanadhātuyo*, chapter eighteen, nineteen and twenty in the *Dharmaskandha* deal with these *dhammas* irregularly: *āyatana* ——>*khandha*——>*dhātu*. On the whole, the last six chapters are not arranged in any system, whereas fifteen chapters are organized into mutual relationship. It seems that the last six chapters were added to the first fifteen chapters which were compiled earlier. But these six chapters help the growth of *Abhidhamma* philosophy in the later period.

5.10 The *Vibhaṅga* expatiates upon the important doctrines of Buddhism. The first six chapters explain the Buddhist epistemology; view of the world and psychology. From the seventh to the eleventh chapter, the thirty-seven *dhammas* are treated. The twelfth, thirteenth, fourteenth, fifteenth, and the sixteenth chapters deal with the three types of learning, namely: (1) *sila* (virtue), (2) *samādhi* (concentration), and (3) *paññā* (understanding); and the last two chapters explain mental *dhammas* and the occasion of them in detail from the standpoint of Buddhism. And also, in each chapter there are three types of explanation, namely, the *suttanta-bhājaniya* (analysis according to the teaching), the *abhidhamma-bhājaniya* (analysis according to *Abhidhamma*), and the *pañhāpuccha* (interrogation). The characteristic of the *Vibhaṅga* is that the regular arrangement of *khandhāyatanadhātuyo* is adopted in the first three chapters. The treatment of the *paṭisambhidhā* (comprehension), *ñāṇa* (knowledge) and the *dhammahadaya* (the heart of the teaching) is found in the later half of the eighteen chapters, and the theoretical *dhammas* seem to be systematized, such as the five *khandhas*, the twelve *āyatanas*, the eighteen *dhātus* and so forth. Therefore, the chapters dealing with the moral and practical *dhammas* such as the four *satipaṭṭhānas*, the *sammappadhānas* and the like are found in the middle, and moreover, there is no chapter teaching the five *indriyas* and the five *balas* in the *Vibhaṅga*. In this sense, we might say that the compilation of the *Vibhaṅga* seems to have been designed to systematize the theoretical *dhammas* by way of questions and answers.

Incidentally, the categories of *khandhāyatanadhātuyo* form the subjects of the second, third and fourth chapters of the *Yamaka* (Pair), which lists a large number of propositions with their converses, enquiring whether both are true : 1. Is all S P ? and 2. Is all P S ? And many of the passages in the *Vibhaṅga* are also found in the *Paṭisambhidāmagga* (Way of Comprehension), which is in content a supplement to the *Vibhaṅga* and consists of thirty discussions (*kathās*). Both the *Vibhaṅga* and the *Paṭisambhidāmagga* are often referred to and quoted in the *Visuddhimagga* (Path of Purification), written by Buddhaghosa.

5.11 The *Śāriputrābhidharma* is a work in four divisions consisting of thirty-three chapters, called (1) *Sapraśnaka* (with questions), (2) *Apraśnaka* (without questions), (3) *Saṃgraha-Saṃyoga* (inclusion and conjunction) and (4) *Prasthāna* (basis); and it has more pages than the other two treatises. This work contains materials which belong to the middle and the late *Abhidhamma* texts such as the *Prakaraṇapāda*, the *Dhātukāya* and the like. The first division deals with *āyatanas*, *dhātus*, *khandhas* and so on. The second division deals with *dhātus*, *kammas* (actions), *puggalas* (persons) and so on. Especially, the thirteenth chapter in this division describing *puggalas* is generally similar to the *Puggalapaññatti*,[1] which collects most of the

1. See T. Kimura, *A Study of Abhidharma Texts*, pp. 118-25.

statements about many types of persons made in the *Sutta* texts. The third division deals with only two chapters, namely : inclusion and conjunction, i.e. principles occurring together and inclusion in classes as two basic kinds of relation between principles.[1] This division is the subject of the *Dhātukathā* and the *Dhātukāya*, though these are compiled as separate *Abhidhamma* texts in the Sthaviravāda and Sarvāstivāda schools. The last division explains the ten *paccayas* (conditions), ten *hetus* (causes) and others in detail. But this work is generally simple and primitive.

The purpose of the *Śāriputrābhidharma* as well as the *Vibhaṅga* was to systematize theoretical *dhammas*. It is one of the characteristics of the *Śāriputrābhidharma* that the twelve *āyatanas*, the eighteen *dhātus* and the five *khandhas* are adopted in the first three chapters; and the explanations of a great many *kilesas* (defilements) are given in the following four chapters: *akusala-mūla* (root of the bad), *kusala-mūla* (root of the good), *kamma* and *kilesa*. The main subject of the *Śāriputrābhidharma* is the study of the mental *dhammas* of man rather than that of the practical *dhammas* such as the thirty-seven *dhammas*. However, this does not always mean that the practical *dhammas* are treated briefly. The thirteenth chapter especially deals with seventy-five kinds of *puggalas* and tries to explain the meaning of each *puggala*. Also, the fourteenth chapter deals with many *ñāṇas*. In short, the contents of the *Śāriputrābhidharma* and its ways of description are immature, even though it contains many pages.

5.12 From the above evidence, we are led to the conclusion that the doctrinal topics in the three *Abhidhamma* texts were mainly grouped by the respective schools with a definite purpose, that of :

1. Analyzing the thirty-seven *dhammas* before the summary of the Buddha's teachings.
2. Listing the stages of Buddhist life, and further expounding and elaborating the training of the thirty-seven *dhammas*.
3. Classifying the principles composing the human being and the universe.

---

1. See A. K. Warder, *Indian Buddhism*, p. 221.

4. Making a special study of the theory of causation and knowledge.

Items 3 and 4 were developed by the Sthaviravāda and Sarvāstivāda schools. Especially, the Sarvāstivāda later came to recognize a list of seventy-five *dhammas* indicating all principles of existence by adding certain groups of *saṁkhāras* (forces) to the topics (or categories) resulting from the investigation of items 3 and 4 (see the last seven topics of chapter **5.8**).[1]

5.13 On Disputable Topics It is mentioned in the *Mahāvedallasutta* that Mahākoṭṭhita asked a series of questions on disputable topics, e.g. understanding (*paññā*), consciousness (*viññāṇa*), sensation (*vedanā*), perception (*saññā*), mental consciousness (*manoviññāṇa*), etc. and Sāriputta answered his questions.[2] And the *Poṭṭhapādasutta* deals with a discussion between the Buddha and the wanderer Poṭṭhapāda in which a chain of controversial topics is indicated, such as perception, soul (*attan*), training (*sikkhā*), virtue (*sīla*) and acquisition of a personality (*atta-paṭilābha*).[3] Such topics are the topics which were hotly debated between Buddhist monks and other strivers, or among the Buddha's disciples, from the very beginning. These topics were naturally gathered by his disciples after his *parinibbāna*, and in the course of time compiled into the *Abhidhamma* texts.

The most important of these is the *Kathāvatthu* (Ground for Discussion). It consists of twenty-three chapters, and is a collection of 219 controversies and refutations of the views maintained by other schools of Buddhism (supposedly compiled in the 3rd century B.C. but undoubtedly added to after that date[4]). On the other hand, the *Vijñānakāya* (Body of consciousness) which can be regarded as similar to the *Kathāvatthu* contains six chapters. The first chapter records Maudgalyāyana's opinion about *pudgala* (person), *indriyas* (faculties), *cittas* (thoughts),

1. On this see Th. Stcherbatsky, *The Central Conception of Buddhism and the Meaning of the Word "Dharma"*, pp. 95-107.
2. M. I, 292-8. T. 1, 790 b-792 b, in which Mahākoṭṭhita answers Sāriputta's questions.
3. D. I, 178-203, T. 1, 109c-112 c.
4. See A. K. Warder, *Outline of Indian Philosophy*, p. 85.

kleśas (defilements) *vijñāna* (consciousness), etc., and refutes his views concerning the non-existence of past and future (principles or phenomena). The second chapter contains a refutation of the Vātsīputrīya doctrine of *pudgala*, very similar in its arguments to the first chapter in the *Kathāvatthu*. It has been said that this refutation was probably inherited from the older school as it was immediately after the personality schism.[1] The third and fourth chapters deal with the theory of conditions and analyzes the mental phenomena. The fifth and sixth chapters deal with the mental functions of a person under training and define the mental states of the *arhant* (perfected one, Pāli : *arahant*).

There will be no necessity for introducing the contents of these texts any further, for a noteworthy point here is that we see from the texts how controversial topics were discussed between the schools in order to argue the opponent down. In a word, the method applied in the discussions is in most cases a purely logical one, so that it is important to clarify the established logical techniques in them.[2]

5.14 We may, therefore, reasonably conclude that the three types of *mātikās* in the *Abhidhamma* texts (see chapter **5.3, 6** and **13**) were collected from the *Sutta* texts in the following stages :[3]

1. The synthetic study of the thirty-seven *bodhipakkhiyā dhammā* in seven groups.
2. The settling of stages of the Buddhist life, training and meditation.

---

1. See A. K. Warder, *Indian Buddhism*, p. 344.

2. This point will be discussed in another Part. We find that the *Tattvasiddhiśāstra* (T. 32, 293 a-373 b) by Harivarman (3rd century A.D.) of the Bahusrutīya school deals with the *abhidhamma* type of ten discussions (*kathās*)—T. 32, 253 c-260 c. Especially, the tenth *kathā* of the ten is the *anattan* (non-ego) chapter, in which Harivarman refutes the Vātsīputriya school's doctrine which maintains the existence of the *puggala* (person) or something like *attan* (ego) in the form of questions and answers (T. 32, 259 a-260 c). Such a form is similar to that in the *Kathāvatthu* and the *Vijñānakāya*. However, the *Kathāvatthu* and the *Vijñānakāya* deal with more logical arguments than the *Tattvasiddhiśāstra*.

3. On this, see *Mohavicchedanī*, p. xxvii.

3. The analysis and classification of the *khandhāyatanadhātuyo*, etc.
4. The collection and definition of disputable topics.
5. The analysis of the *tika* and *duka* topics.
6. The study of theory of causation and knowledge.

5.15 Briefly speaking, *Abhidhamma* philosophy may be said to have been established firmly by both the synthetic study of *dhammas* and the analytical study of *dhammas*. It goes without saying that the origin of such studies can be found in the *Nikāyas* and *Āgamas*, where there are attempts: (1) to define *dhammas*, (2) to seize the relations of a *dhamma* to other *dhammas*, (3) to analyze *dhammas*, (4) to classify *dhammas* into different types, and (5) to arrange *dhammas* in numerical order. Our study in Part One was therefore directed towards the examination of these points in relation to *Mātikās* which had already existed in the time of the Buddha. And it was suggested that the thirty-seven *dhammas* were the original *Mātikās*, and that the synthetic study of such practical *dhammas* and the analysis and classification of the theoretical *dhammas* such as *khandhāyatanadhātuyo*, etc. especially came to establish the basis of *Abhidhamma* philosophy.

PART II

THE DEVELOPMENT OF THE DIALOGUE FORM

6

THE METHOD OF PROGRESS OF A DIALOGUE AND THE FOUR *PAÑHABYĀKARAṆAS*

6.1 It has already been pointed out that from the very beginning, one of the *abhidhamma* studies was made in the form of questions and answers (see chapter **4.1**). How then was the dialogue on *dhammas* (doctrines) developed and what sort of logical techniques were established in the form of questions and answers? These points will be our main subject for study in Part Two.

6.2 The Buddha decided to preach his teachings (*dhammas*) to man. At first, he taught five old friends, known as strivers (*samaṇas*) including Assaji. After that, the Buddha preached his teachings to many persons until his *parinibbāna*. As the Buddha himself said, enlightenment in itself is beyond logic (*atakkāvacara*) :[1]

> This *dhamma* (truth) attained by me is profound, difficult to see, difficult to understand, peaceful, beyond logic, subtle, intelligible to the wise.

This means that the truths are facts to be experienced and verified personally by recluses. There is no question of believing

1. M· I, 167, II, 172, T. 2, 103 c, 786 c-787 a, etc. As we shall see later, 'beyond logic' in such a case means the well established conclusion which cannot be controverted.

anything simply on authority, not even on the authority of the Buddha himself. "The outlook is that of the making of a scientific discovery and announcing it to the world, whereupon others may investigate its truth for themselves."[1]

However, the Buddha did not make light of the expression and communication of his own thought by the use of words, though we are told that his mind did not incline to teaching *dhamma* (truth) soon after his enlightenment.[2] For example, we can see the following explanation:[3]

> Through discussion (*sākacchā*), you must learn understanding (*paññā*) . . . Hereupon, monks, a person by discussing with another knows thus: Judging from this reverend's approach to a question (*ummagga*), judging from his intention (*abhinihāra*), judging from his behaviour towards a question (*pañhasamudācāra*), he has understanding (*paññavant*), he is not weak in understanding (*duppañña*). What is the cause of that? In this case, this reverend utters the meaning and words (*atthapada*) which are profound, peaceful, excellent, beyond logic, subtle, intelligible to the wise. As to the *dhamma* (teaching) the reverend talks, he is competent both in brief and in detail, is competent to explain its meaning, to expound on it, to make it clear, to lay it down, to open it up, to analyze it and to make it plain. This reverend has understanding, he is not weak in understanding.

We can realize from the above that rigorous methods of argument were established. In the *Nikāyas* and *Āgamas*, the following representative forms of a dialogue can be found:

1. Where a questioner demands 'Yes' or 'No' from an answerer.
2. Where a questioner requests some explanation of an answerer.
3. Where an answerer returns a reply in the form of a new question.

---

1. A. K. Warder, *Outline of Indian Philosophy*, p. 49.
2. M. I, 168.
3. A. II, 187-9.

4. Where a questioner suggests some reply to an answerer (i.e. leading-question).

In entering upon the consideration of these forms of dialogue, it is fitting to note first of all how the dialogue on *dhammas* was conducted.

6.3 It is said that public debating was an ancient custom in India.[1] This can be also inferred from the following words used in the *Poṭṭhapādasutta*,[2] the *Samaṇamaṇḍikāsutta*,[3] etc.:

1. *Samayappavādaka*: hall for debating on different views.
2. *Samanuyuñjati*: to cross-question, to take up.
3. *Samanugāhati*: to ask for reasons, to cross-examine.
4. *Samanubhāsati*: to criticize, to refute.

And moreover, it can readily be imagined from the *Kosambiya-sutta*,[4] the *Sāmagāmasutta*, etc. that a discussion was very heated on occasion: some monks become quarrelsome (*bhaṇḍanajāta*), become contentious (*kalahajāta*), fall into dispute (*vivādāpanna*), and live attacking one another with piercing words.[5] But the Buddha did not encourage his disciples to argue for the sake of argument, though he did not make light of helpful discussion pertaining to enlightenment. It is therefore natural that the Buddha pointed out the wrong attitude towards holding a dialogue and taught the right method of progress of it. As the *Nikāyas* and *Āgamas* deal with one's attitude of mind in a dialogue and treat of what a debate should be, let us turn our eyes to them and learn how the dialogue on *dhammas* was conducted.

6.4 The *Aṅguttaranikāya* states that if any person practises any one of the following nine things, he is not fit for discussion:[6]

---

1. A. K. Warder, *Outline of Indian Philosophy*, p. 85.
2. D. I, 178, T. 1, 110 a.
3. M. II, 22, T. 1, 720 b.
4. M. I, 320, T. 2, 626 b.
5. M. II, 243, T. 1, 752 c.
6. A. I, 198. In the Chinese text, 15 things are indicated (T. 1, 609 a-b).

1. To evade the question by asking another irrelevantly (*aññenāññaṃ paṭicarati*).
2. To carry the discussion away from the point (*bahiddhā katham apanāmeti*).

3-5. To display ill-temper, aversion and mistrust (*kopañ ca dosañ ca appaccayañ ca pātukaroti*).

6. To blame (one's opponent) (*abhiharati*).
7. To beat down the questioner (*abhimaddati*).
8. To laugh the questioner to scorn (*anupajagghati*).
9. To catch the questioner up when he falters (*khalitaṃ ganhāti*).

Generally speaking, the aim of dialogue is to express methodically one's own opinions and to make a listener (or listeners) understand them. The dialogue is characterized by judging directly whether or not the listener understands completely what one has explained of his ideas or his opinions. In this sense, the dialogue is a very important way to help people understand the Buddhist teaching dealing with truth. Especially, when we learn that, as indicated above, public debating was an ancient custom in India, we can say that from the early days of Buddhism a great deal of discussion, including public debates, must have been of great importance, not only for discussions among Buddhists themselves, but for refuting the views of non-Buddhists (also in the *Abhidhamma* period, for refuting Buddhists belonging to different schools). Therefore, the correct attitude of carrying on a dialogue is clearly displayed in the *Nikāyas* and *Āgamas*.

6.5 In holding a discussion, the early Buddhists were required to hold the same idea consistently throughout the discussion. In other words, it was important that what they had spoken at the beginning was consistent with what they spoke at the end. As we have seen in chapter **4.2**, the Buddha encourages his disciples to preach the *dhamma* (discourse) which is beautiful in the beginning, in the middle and in the end. This suggests not only one's attitude to discourse, but also one's attitude for discussion. Such an attitude for discussion was maintained also in the discussions with non-Buddhists, whilst non-Buddhists talked ambiguously and gave equivocal answers, as we shall see in another chapter. We can learn from many discourses (e.g. *Cūḷahatthipadopamasutta*)[1] that non-Buddhists who were gifted with eloquence met the Buddha to confute his doctrine, and all of them were argued down by him; consequently, they became his disciples. This indicates definitely that the Buddha was an eloquent debater. Therefore, the Buddha is called "one who speaks at the proper time (*kāla-vādin*)," "one who speaks truth (*bhūta-vādin*)," "one who speaks what is significant (*attha-vādin*)," "one who speaks according to the doctrine (*dhamma-vādin*)," "one who speaks in accordance with the discipline (*vinaya-vādin*)"[2]; it is also said of him, "as he speaks, so he acts: as he acts, so he speaks (*yathā-vādin tathā-kārin, yathā-kārin tathā-vādin*)," etc.[3] And the disciple who follows the Buddha is called "a wise elder (*paṇḍita thera*)."[4] From the explanation of one's attitude for any discourse and many epithets of the Buddha, we come to know that he did not talk ambiguously, nor gave equivocal answers, but did hold the same idea consistently throughout discussion with his disciples and non-Buddhists.

As mentioned already in chapter **6.4**, in order not to evade the question by asking another irrelevantly and not to carry the discussion away from the point, the Buddha's disciples (especially, his novices) always have to listen to the Buddha's teachings and to bend their mind to the investigation of the meaning of them. And they have to advance their arguments with cogency. To build up a cogent argument, this can be in a sense drawn from right thinking or logical thinking. Now the question of the Buddha's and his disciples' way of thinking comes up. We would say in a word that his way of thinking is quite logical (this point will be discussed in another chapter), so that to become the Buddha's disciple is nothing other than to agree with the Buddha's ways of thinking and to maintain in dialogue the same attitude as the Buddha's. In this sense, to investigate the meaning of the Buddha's teachings by reflecting on them,

---

1. T. 1, 656 a-658 a, M. I, 175-84.
2. D. I, 4-5, 165, III, 175, A. II, 209, III, 205, T. 1, 89 a, 103 b, etc.
3. D. II, 224,229, Sn. 357, Itv. p. 122, T. 1, 31 a, etc.
4. A. II, 22.

pondering on them and poring over them (see chapter **4.2**), this was probably the best training for the disciples in having a controversy. When we examine the *Nikāyas* and *Āgamas*, most of them are scriptures in dialogue (*sutta*) form, in which it is recorded that not only the Buddha, but also his chief disciples had discussions with monks and non-Buddhists. There are, for instance, many *suttas* (dialogues) in the ***Saṃyuktāgama*** which refer to Sāriputta. They are broadly divisible into four groups as follows:

1. The *suttas* in which the Buddha questioned Sāriputta.
2. The *suttas* in which Sāriputta questioned *bhikkhus* (monks).
3. The *suttas* in which Sāriputta questioned some of the Buddha's disciples: a. Ānanda; b. Mahākoṭṭhita; c. Sona; d. Candimaputta; e. Anāthapiṇḍika; f. Nakula; g. Yamaka.
4. The *suttas* in which Sāriputta questioned non-Buddhists: a. Jambukkhādaka; b. Titthiyas (-yās).

It is recorded in the *Subhasutta* that the Buddha said to the Brahman youth Subha, Todeyya's son, "I am not a one-sided answerer (*ekaṁsavāda*), but I am an analytical answerer (*vibhajjavāda*)."[1] It is certain that both the terms *ekaṁsavāda* and *vibhajjavāda* do not mean an individual one of the four *pañhabyākaraṇas* (4 methods of answering questions), which will be discussed later. We should realize that the former signifies "a prejudiced answer arisen from a narrow view," and the latter, on the other hand, "knowing how to use the four *pañhabyākaraṇas* properly." We can learn from the *Nikāyas* and *Āgamas* the fact that the Buddha and his disciples made the dialogues on *dhammas* progress logically until they argued down many philosophers.

6.6 Another method of explanation very prominent in the *Nikāyas* and *Āgamas* is by using metaphors, similes and analogies. It goes without saying that the method of making one's opinion understood by a listener is to use figures of speech such as hyperbole, metaphor, metonymy, simile and so on. We could

1. M. II, 197.

say that 'simile' plays an important role in the *Nikāyas*. In the Pāli canon, the words '*upamā*', '*opamma*' and the like are used. And although the term *upamā* is translated in many cases into 'simile', in the *Nikāyas* it is not always used as a simple simile; sometimes it is used as an extended simile. We can learn that the Buddha tried to explain his teachings by adopting similes in them, and recommended his disciples to make use of simile in their explanations of Buddhism. The Buddha says:[1]

> Well then, Sandaka, I will make you a simile (*upamā*), for by a simile some intelligent persons (*viññū purisā*) here understood the meaning of what has been said.

And moreover, most *upamās* given in the *Nikāyas* and *Āgamas* are statements by analogy. The most representative *sutta* containing analogy is the *Pāyāsisutta* in which the existence of another world is argued for merely on the basis of analogy against a materialist.[2] In general, the application of analogy in the explanation of doctrinal points has been effective as a teaching method throughout the whole of the Buddhist canon. Certainly, among similes which are found widely in the Pāli canon, there are not a few unsuccessful ones.

However, it can be seen in the *Nikāyas* and *Āgamas* that many disciples put forth great efforts to give similes and applied them to their arguments. At this point, we would like to touch briefly upon the role of simile in the *Nikāyas* and *Āgamas*.

6.7 As stated above, both the words '*upamā*' and '*opamma*' could be understood as meaning simile, though the latter means in some cases 'comparison'. For instance, we see the following *suttas* (dialogues) in which numerous similes are given:

1. *Vattha-upamā*: The simile of the cloth (M.I,36-40).
2. *Kakaca-upamā*: The simile of the saw (M.I,122-29).
3. *Alagadda-upamā*: The simile of the water-snake (M.I,130-42).
4. *Hatthipada-upamā*: The simile of the elephant's footprint (Lesser and Greater, M.I, 175-84 and 184-91).
5. *Sāra-upamā*: The simile of the pith (Greater and Lesser. M.I, 192-97 and 198-205).

---

1. M. I, 523, A. V, 194, T. 2, 248 a, etc.
2. D. II, 316-58, T. 1, 42 b-47 a, 525 a-532 b, 831 a-835 c.

6. *Laṭukitā-upamā*: The simile of the quail (M.I, 447-56). The word '*adhivacana*' means 'designation' but is sometimes extended to a 'metaphor'. As pointed out by A. K. Warder,[1] in various texts of the *Nikāyas*, the word '*adhivacana*' as well as the words '*samaññā*' (agreed usage), '*nirutti*' (expression), '*saṃkhā*' (denomination), etc., appears approximately synonymous with the word '*paññatti*' (concept). To say nothing of the relation of *paññatti* to *adhivacana*, we see the following usages of *adhivacana*:[2]

a. The anthill (*vammika*), this is a designation (*adhivacana*) for the body made of the four great elements (*mahābhūtas*);

b. 'Brahman', this is a designation for the *tathāgata*, perfected one (*arahant*);

c. The wise (*sumedha*), this is a designation for a monk who is learning (*sekha*) and many other things.[3] However, when we examine figurative expressions with examples of simile and metaphor in the *Nikāyaṣ* and *Āgamas*, we see that passion (*rāga*) is expressed by the word '*acci*' (flame) or '*visa*' (poison) and that the Buddha's preaching is expressed by the word '*sihanāda*' (a lion's roar).[4] These are good examples of metaphor. In this sense, it might be possible to regard Brahman as a metaphorical expression (*adhivacana*) of the *tathāgata*. After this fashion, we see that there is the expression: "The bottomless pit (*pātāla*) is a metaphor (or metaphorical expression) of unhappy feeling (*dukkha vedanā*)".[5] Moreover, from the explanation of the '*pārāyana*' chapter in the *Suttanipāta*, which deals with the sixteen brief verse dialogues between the Buddha and brahmanas on the doctrine, mostly consisting of a bare question and answer, the word '*pārāyana*' (the way across) could be regarded as a metaphorical expression of the Buddha's teachings.[6]

Generally speaking, metaphor is a kind of transfer, by which the meaning or appearance of one thing is imaginatively ascribed

---

1. "The Concept of a Concept," *Journal of Indian Philosophy* 1 (1971) pp. 183-4.
2. M.I, 144.
3. Besides, see S. IV, 174.
4. *Mahā* (and *Cūḷa*)-*sīhanādasutta* (M.I, 63-68, 68-83).
5. S. IV, 206.
6. Sn. p. 218.

to some other thing, while simile is based on a comparison of subjects or objects that are basically different. But to the effect that rhetorical devices matter much to the way of thinking or the development of ideas, metaphor must be especially observed in consideration of simile and *vice versa*. Moreover, as we have mentioned in chapter **6.6**, some of them are in the form of an analogy. With regard to this, let us illustrate a few examples of similes as analogy.

6.8 Analogy is the means of reaching conclusions on the basis of comparison or similarity. If the analogy is weak, the argument will have little power to persuade, but in any of the arguments found in the *Nikāyas*, the analogy therein does not appear as a weak form.

It is also necessary to emphasize the fact that analogy never gives proof in the strict sense of the word, but in some dialogues (*suttas*) of the *Nikāyas* and *Āgamas* analogy is apparently advanced as actual proof, although we see no actually recognized distinction between analogy and strict inference.

1. The bundle of reeds (*nalakalūpi*) :[1]

> It is just as if (*seyyathāpi*) there stood two bundles of reeds one leaning against the other. Even so, conditioned by a sentient body is consciousness (*nāmarūpapaccayā viññāṇam*). Conditioned by consciousness is a sentient body (*viññāṇapaccayā nāmarūpaṃ*).
>
> If I were to pull towards me one of the bundles of reeds, the other would fall; If I were to pull towards me the other, the former would fall. Even so, from the cessation of a sentient body is the cessation of consciousness (*nāmarūpanirodhā viññāaṇa-nirodho*). From the cessation of consciousness is the cessation of a sentient body (*viññāṇanirodhā nāmarūpanirodho*).

To sum up the above statement:

"A (or B) exists through the condition of B (or A)"
is analogous to
"By leaning one against the other, two bundles of reeds stand."
"If there were no A (or B), there would be no B (or A)"
is analogous to

1. S. II, 114, T. 2, 81 b.

"If I were to pull towards me one of the bundles of reeds, the other would fall. If I were to pull towards me the other, the former would fall."

Thus we come to know that analogy helps us to understand the doctrine of the dependent origination.

2. The elephant's footprint:[1]

(a) As among all living beings that can walk their footprints (*padajātas*) are included in an elephant's footprint (*hatthipada*), and as the elephant's footprint in point of size is the chief among all kinds of footprints, (A) all good principles of mind are included among the four noble truths: 1. unhappiness, 2. its origination, 3. its cessation and 4. the way leading to this cessation.

It goes without saying that the Four Truths form the essentials of the content of the Buddha's enlightenment and are the basic doctrine of Buddhism, which is the knowledge of how the 'influences' (*āsava*: passion, desire for existence and ignorance) can be exhausted. Therefore, we can realize from the above that the small letter (a) analogously suggests the situation of the capital letter (A).

3. On fire:[2]

Just as a fire is blazing through its contact with firewood and grass, and is extinguished in the absence of such contact, the thus-gone (*tathāgata*) exists through his five *khandhas*. And just as one could not say in which direction the fire's flame will spread to after its extinction, one could not say the place where the thus-gone is reborn after his death.

We have simplified the original statement such as the above to clarify its meaning. It seems that in Indian philosophy the subject of the thus-gone was a matter of primary concern from the very beginning. Especially, for brahmans and strivers (*samaṇas*)

1. M.I, 184, T. 1,464 b, S.I,86, A.III,364.
2. See the *Aggi-Vacchagottasutta* (M.I,482-9, T.2,245 b-246 a).

the answer to the following questions (including the above subject) was a much debated point:[1]

Is the thus-gone reborn?
Is he not reborn?
Is he both reborn and not reborn?
Is he neither reborn nor not reborn?

Consequently, the Buddha attempted to make himself understood by illustrating the example of fire which is in the form of an analogy.

On the whole, although it is difficult to distinguish between them, the analogies in the *Nikāyas* and *Āgamas* are of two types, namely: the logical analogy and the figurative analogy. It is, however, clear that the Buddha and his disciples used both of them to explore their ideas and to clarify or support their convictions or positions. The above three examples have the following characteristic in common with one anothor. That is, since analogy promotes understanding of similarities (as well as differences), the small letters (a), (b), ... (x) in the statement by analogy always suggests the situation of the capital letters (A), (B), (C), ... (X) in the statement of proof. If we consider the case of item 3 (titled "On fire") we see:

(A) Through his five groups,	(a) Through its contact with firewood and grass,
(B) the thus-gone exists.	(b) a fire is blazing (exists).

Thus the capital letter (B) based on the letter (A) is analogous to the small letter (b) based on the letter (a), and the latter (b+a) can be regarded as an important way to persuade people that the former (B+A) is reasonable. In this sense, we would say that an analogy which agrees with the statement of proof is an analogy based on the method of agreement.

6.9 From the preceding discussions, we have found the following points concerning one's attitude of mind in a dialogue in early Buddhism:

---

1. For a further discussion of such questions, see *Brahmajālasutta* (D.I, 1-46, T. 1, 88 b-94 a. Esp. see D.I, 27).

1. One must try hard not to evade the question by asking another irrelevantly, not to carry the discussion away from the point, and so on.
2. Bending one's mind always to the investigation of the meaning of the Buddha's teachings, one must try to hold the same idea consistently throughout discussion.
3. One should use similes in explaining the *dhamma* (doctrine).

6.10 Now, another important problem is how the debate on *dhammas* was developed. We introduced very briefly in chapter **6.2** the representative forms of a dialogue in the *Nikāyas*. Let us examine again how the representative forms were explained in the *Nikāyas* and *Āgamas*. They would be clarified by showing "four *pañhabyākaraṇas*" and the meaning of them. They are:[1]

1. *Ekaṁsa-pañhabyākaraṇa*: to give a categorical reply to a question requiring it or to give a direct answer in the affirmative or in the negative.
2. *Vibhajja-pañhabyākaraṇa*: to give a discriminating reply to a question requiring it or to give an analytical answer.
3. *Paṭipucchā-pañhabyākaraṇa*: to reply by a counter-question to a question requiring such or to reply by a counter-question to ascertain what the question means.
4. *Ṭhapaniya-pañhabyākaraṇa* : to waive a question which should be waived or to keep silent.

The Buddha says that one who knows how to use the four *pañha-byākaraṇas* properly is competent to discuss the teaching of the Buddha and convince a listener of what one has said:

> The first is a direct answer in the affirmative or negative; the second, an analytical answer; the third, a counter-question; and the fourth, keeping silent. A monk who knows how to answer truly in conformity with the *dhamma* is called "skilled in the fourfold question." Such a monk is hard to overcome, hard to vanquish; profound and invincible. And he is skilled in discriminating between the true meaning and the false one;

---

1. See D.III, 229, A.I, 197, II,46, T. 1, 51 b, 609 a, etc.

he avoids the false and grasps the true. He is called "sage in the grasp of truth."

As far as the *Nikāyas* and *Āgamas* are concerned, the first one mentioned above means not only to give a direct answer in the affirmative, but also to give it in the negative in some cases, as indicated in chapter **4.3**. It might be possible that the earliest division was into (1) *ekaṁsa-vyākaraṇiya-pañha-*, and (2) *anekaṁsa-vyākaraṇiya-pañha-* corresponding to the two kinds of statements (*ekaṁsikā dhammā* and *anekaṁsikā dhammā*) mentioned in the *Poṭṭhapādasutta.*[1] The latter class was later subdivided into (a) *vibhajja-vyākaraṇiya-* and (b) *ṭhapaniya-*. Moreover, *paṭipucchā-vyākaraṇiya* is, in fact, a sub-class of *vibhajja-vyākaraṇiya.*[2] At any rate, we can learn from the *Nikāyas* that if a person on being asked these sorts of questions gives the proper reply, then he is competent to hold a dialogue.

6.11 Although most of the *suttas* are characterized by using some of the four *pañhabyākaraṇas* and they are listed in the *Nikāyas*, we cannot find explanations of them in the *Nikāyas.* In order to grasp their main characteristic, we would like here to turn our eyes to the *Milindapañha* (this work in its original form is considered to have been compiled between the 1st century B.C. and the 1st century A.D.), where they are explained; then these explanations have been transmitted by the Sthaviravāda school, especially by the Pāli tradition:[3]

1. To the question "Is matter impermanent (*rūpaṁ aniccan ti*)?," "Are feelings impermanent (*vedanā aniccā ti*)?," "Is perception impermanent (*saññā aniccā ti*)?," etc., the answer is "Yes, it is," or "Yes, they are." In this case, it is called *ekaṁsa-pañhabyākaraṇa.*
2. To the question "Is matter really impermanent (*aniccaṁ pana rūpan ti*)?," "Are feelings really impermanent (*anicccā pana vedanā ti*)?," etc., the answer is given analytically, in which the characteristic of *rūpa* is displayed. This is called *vibhajja-pañhabyākaraṇa*.

---

1. D. I, 191-2.
2. On this see K. N. Jayatilleke, *Early Buddhist Theory of Knowledge*, pp. 281-2.
3. Miln. pp. 144-5.

In other words, the questioner challenges the speaker and demands more than a categorical answer. Therefore, an explanation is required from the speaker.

3. To a questioner an answerer returns a reply in the form of a new question, or replies by a counter-question such as "What then? Does one perceive everything by the eye (*kin nu kho cakkhunā sabbaṃ vijānāti*)?"

The *Milindapañha* does not give a detailed explanation of this. On this point, the *Milindapañha-Ṭikā* states:[1]

> The question "Does one perceive everything by the eye?" is to ask whether man (*puggala*) perceives everything by the eye. From this question, two kinds of questions are also asked: "Does he perceive everything by either the eye of the *tathāgata* (*samantacakkhu*) or the physical eye (*maṃsacakkhu*)?" and "By the physical eye?" The answer to the former should be "No," and the answer to the latter should be "Yes." This is called *paṭipucchā-pañhabyākaraṇa*.

What is called *ṭhapanīya-pañhabyākaraṇa*, this is said in general to have been laid down for the questions involving metaphysical problems. For a certainty, the Buddha proclaims that there are two different types of *dhammas*: one belongs to *ekaṁsikā* (definite) *dhammā* and the other to *anekaṁsikā* (indefinite) *dhammā*, and that the latter are the subject of questions such as "Is the world (*loka*) eternal or not?," "Is it finite or not?," "Are the soul and the body the same or different?," "Does the thus-gone exist after death or not?," etc. (strictly speaking, they comprise four sets of questions and have four alternatives each, which will be listed in chapter 7). The reason why the Buddha waived these questions was that they are not connected with the meaning (*n' atthasaṁhita*), are not the starting point of the best life, and do not conduce to aversion from worldly life (*nibbidā*), to dispassion (*virāga*), to cessation (*nirodha*), to calm (*upasama*), to insight (*abhiññā*), to enlightenment (*sambodhi*), and to liberation from existence (*nibbāna*).[2]

1. Miln. T. p. 28.
2. M.I, 431. In the Chinese text, the words "These are not connected with *dhamma* (truth)" can be seen (T. 1,805 b).

However, we must note here what the Buddha states in the *Brahmajālasutta*: "The opinion of those strivers and brahmans who are eternalists (*sassatavādas*) and who in four ways maintain that the soul (*attan*) and the world (or universe: *loka*) are eternal (*sassata*) is neither known, nor seen, is based merely on sensation, on worry, on writhing, and is subject to craving."[1] And finally, he rejects all the sixty-two opinions (*diṭṭhis*) maintained by many strivers and brahmans at the time of the Buddha. We must also note the discussions on metaphysical subjects between the Buddha and the wanderer Vacchagotta in the *Aggi-Vacchagottasutta*, where the latter fires a hundred questions at the Buddha about the permanence of the world, the existence of the *tathāgata*, etc., and then, Vacchagotta asks: "Do you have any speculative opinion?" To his question, the Buddha answers: "No, I have already got rid of it."[2] And also, the Buddha says in the "*Anamatagga*" chapter that transmigration (*saṃsāra*: this world) is beginningless (*anamatagga*),[3] which could be regarded as 'infinite', but not in the sense of the eternalists — thus a distinction has been made. This is obviously a categorical reply.

What we want to emphasize here is that the Buddha seems to have denied all the speculations including the doctrines of the soul, the world, etc., regarded as an entity, which non-Buddhists maintained. For "to deny," "to disregard" could be substituted. The latter appears to have something in common with "silence." To the Buddha, "silence" seems to be a kind of negative expression. Metaphysical problems must be rejected in which dependent origination is disregarded and, in this sense, the objects maintained are not real, not existent. The Buddha keeps silent only when he feels it a waste of time to explain metaphysical problems. Consequently, in the process of a dialogue he replies to them by using any one of the four *pañha-byākaraṇas*, especially, two of them: *ekaṁsa* and *ṭhapaniya*. His disciples must follow the same procedure.

---

1. D.I, 1-46 (esp. 39-42), T. 1, 88 b-94 a.
2. M.I, 483-9 (esp. 486), T. 2, 245 b-264 a.
3. S.II, 178-93, T. 2,240 c-243 b.

6.12 It is likely that, in the later period, Buddhists attached importance to the four *pañhabyākaraṇas* and made a special study of them. The detailed explanations of the four *pañhabyākaraṇas* can be found in the Chinese *Tripiṭaka*. Among the Chinese texts, some explain the meaning of the four *pañhabyākaraṇas* individually; some explain them in relation to each other.[1] In the *Saṅgītiparyāya* the following explanation can be seen:[2]

Ques.: Teach me (mental) *dhammas*.

Ans.: There are various *dhammas*. What kinds of *dhammas* do you ask me about ?

In this case, if the answerer makes clear that there are *dhammas* in the past, present and future, this will be *vibhajja-pañhabyākaraṇa*.

Ques.: Teach me *dhammas* in the past.

Ans.: There are various *dhammas* in the past. What kinds of *dhammas* do you ask me about ?

In this case, if the answerer makes clear that there are good (*kusala*), and bad (*akusala*) and neither-good-nor-bad (*avyākata*) *dhammas* in the past, this will be *vibhajja-pañhabyākaraṇa*.

Ques.: Teach me *kusala dhammas*.

Ans. : There are various *kusala dhammas*. What kinds of *kusala dhammas* do you ask me about?

Such answers are called *paṭipucchā-pañhabyākaraṇa*.

6.13 For a certainty, the four *pañhabyākaraṇas* are considered to be a dialectical method. When trying to trace the development of Buddhism from *Nikāya* philosophy into *Abhidhamma*

---

1. Cf. *Mahāparinirvāṇasūtra* (T.12,571 a), *Mahāprajñāpāramitopadeśa* (T. 25, 222 c), *Daśabhūmivibhāśāśāstra* (T. 26, 80 c), *Buddhabhūmisūtraśāstra* (T. 26,320 c) *Abhidharmamahāvibhāṣāśāstra* (T. 27, 75 b), *Saṃyuktābhidharmahṛdayaśāstra* (T. 28, 874 c), *Abhidharmakoṣabhāṣya* (T. 29,103 a). *Ābhidharmanyāyānusāraśāstra* (T. 29, 618 c), etc.

2. T. 26, 401 c.

philosophy, we cannot overlook the examination of the forms of the dialogue on *dhammas*, which were based on the four *pañha-byākaraṇas*. Therefore, we have to examine the style of argument used by the early Buddhists—its characteristics. In this case, it may be important to start by making clear the ways of thinking of the Buddha and his disciples according to the evidence of the *Nikāyas* and *Āgamas*.

7

METAPHYSICAL QUESTIONS AND TETRALEMMAS

7.1 To four kinds of metaphysical subjects dealing with sixteen questions, Sañjaya Belaṭṭhiputta, one of the six heretical teachers at the time of the Buddha, known as the leader of the Agnostics, is said to have replied by means of four (or five) types of ambiguous answer. The sixteen questions are :[1]

I. 1. Does the other world exist (*Atthi paro loko*)?
   2. Does it not exist (*N'atthi paro loko*)?
   3. Does it both exist and not exist (*Atthi ca n'atthi ca paro loko*)?
   4. Does it neither exist nor not exist (*N'ev'atthi na n'atthi paro loko*)[2]

II. 5. Do beings reborn exist (*Atthi sattā opapātikā*)?
   6. Do they not exist?
   7. Do they both exist and not exist?
   8. Do they neither exist nor not exist?

III. 9. Does the result of good and bad karmas exist (*Atthi sukaṭadukkaṭānaṃ kammānaṃ phalaṃ vipāko*)?

---

1. D. I, 27, 58-9.

2. Concerning item I, we see the following Sanskrit expression : "*. . .asti paraloka iti . . . nāsti paralokaḥ asti ca nāsti ca naivāsti na nāsti paraloka . . .*" See *The Gilgit Manuscript of the Saṅghabhedavastu*—Being the 17th and Last Section of the Vinaya of the Mūlasarvāstivādin, Part II, ed. R. Gnoli with the Assistance of T. Venkatacharya, p. 226.

10. Does it not exist?
11. Does it both exist and not exist?
12. Does it neither exist nor not exist?

IV. 13. Does the thus-gone exist after death (*Hoti tathāgato param maraṇā*)?
14. Does he not exist after death (*Na hoti tathāgato param maraṇā*)?
15. Does he both exist and not exist after death (*Hoti ca na hoti ca tathāgato param maraṇā*)?
16. Does he neither exist nor not exist after death (*N'eva hoti na na hoti tathāgato param maraṇā*)?

The four (or five) types of ambiguous answers are :[1]

1. I do not do so (*Evam pi me no*).
2. I do not say it is true (*Tathā ti pi me no*).
3. I do not say it is otherwise (*Aññathā ti pi me no*).
4. I do not say it is not so (*No ti pi me no*).
5. I do not say it is not not so (*No no ti pi me no*).

Therefore, Sanjaya Belaṭṭhiputta was named "one who gets into equivocation, into eel-wriggling" (*vācāvikkhepaṁ āpajjati amarāvikkhepaṁ*). Or such a man may be called a skeptic. On the

1. D. I, 27, 59, M. I, 521, etc. Among scholars, there are two different opinions concerning these answers. The one is that which regards Sañjaya's answers as five answers. The other is that which regards his answers as four answers (from item 2 to 5). However, the commentator, Buddhaghosa interprets this point in both ways (see *Sumaṅgalavilāsinī*. pp. 115-6).

As for the English translation of these answers, see A. K. Warder, *Outline of Indian Philosophy*, p. 45.

In Chinese texts, we see the following expressions :

(I) 1. "此事如是", 2. "此事実" 3. "此事異", 4. "此事不異", 5. "此事非異非不異" (see T. 1, 91 c).

(II) 1. "此事如是", 2. "此事実", 3. "此事異", 4. "此事非異", 5. "(此事) 非不異" (see T. 1, 108 c). We cannot see in either of items I and II the words corresponding to *me no* in Pāli. Also, the meaning of No. 5 of item I is not the same as that of No. 5 of item II. The former could be translated into English : "Neither is it not, nor is it not not."

other hand, the Buddha kept silent on the metaphysical subjects involved in the following sixteen questions in some cases (see chapter **6.11**). Concerning them, there is a difference between the Pāli and Chinese texts. So let us compare them first.

7.2 In the *Dirghāgama*, four subjects dealing with sixteen questions are reckoned:[1]

I. 1. Are the soul and the world eternal?
2. Are they not eternal?
3. Are they both eternal and not eternal?
4. Are they neither eternal nor not eternal?

II. 5. Are the soul and the world finite?
6. Are they not finite?
7. Are they both finite and not finite?
8. Are they neither finite nor not finite?

III. 9. Are the soul and the body the same?
10. Are they different?
11. Are they both the same and different?
12. Are they neither the same nor differnt?

IV. 13. Does the thus-gone exist after death?
14. Does he not exist after death?
15. Does he both exist and not exist after death?
16. Does he neither exist nor not exist after death?

In the ***Saṃyuktāgama***,[2] fourteen questions are reckoned, namely: the above questions excluding Nos. 11 and 12. Also, in the first and second, only the subject of the world is dealt with, not the subject of the soul.

In the *Nikāyas*[3] and the *Madhyamāgama*,[4] ten questions are reckoned, namely : the above questions excluding Nos. 3, 4, 7, 8, 11 and 12. Also, in the first and second only the subject of the world is dealt with.

In the *Milindapañha*, twelve questions are reckoned.[5] But, as

1. T. 1. 111 a, 75 c-76 a, etc.
2. T. 2, 245 c, 246 a-b, etc.
3. S. III, 258, D. I, 189-90, M. I, 426, 484, etc.
4. T. 1, 803 c, 804 a-b, etc.
5. Miln. p. 145.

far as we can discover, the questions in the *Milindapañha* were introduced from ten questions in the *Cūḷamālunkyasutta* of the *Majjhimanikāya*—also, its Chinese version deals with ten questions; therefore, we cannot but think that two questions in the *Milindapañha*, namely: "Is the world both finite and not finite?" and "Is it neither finite nor not finite?"[1] were added in the later period. Similarly, we would say that the larger number of questions in the *Dīrghāgama* and in the *Saṃyuktāgama* developed from the ten questions in the *Nikāyas*. What we are here concerned with is not to examine the number of metaphysical questions, but to find out the ways of thinking of the early Buddhists by the use of pattern of questions.

7.3 We can learn that according to the metaphysical questions stated above, there are four kinds of pattern, namely:

1. *Atthi* (or *hoti*) *S*?[2]
2. *N'atthi S*?
3. *Atthi ca n'atthi ca S*?
4. *N'ev'atthi na n'atthi S*?

We can also learn that according to Sañjaya's replies, there are four or five types of answers. Although it is said that the Buddha avoided giving such answers as Sañjaya did, it seems to us that the ways of thinking of the Buddha were substantially the same as those of Sañjaya.

In the *Aggi-Vacchagottasutta*, the wanderer Vacchagotta cross-examined the Buddha on a metaphysical problem:[3]

Vaccha : My friend Gotama, where is a monk (whose thought is released—*vimuttacitta*) reborn?

Gotama: "Reborn," Vaccha, does not apply.

V. : Well then, my friend Gotama, is he not reborn?

G. : "Not reborn," Vaccha, does not apply.

---

1. Since these questions can be found in the *Brahmajālasutta* (D. I, 22-4), we cannot disregard it in taking up metaphysical subjects.

2. Here '*S*' means 'the subject' such as the soul, the world, the *tathāgata*, etc.

3. M. I, 486-7, T. 2, 245 a-b. Cf A. IV, 67-98.

V. : Well then, my frind Gotama, is he both reborn and not reborn?

G. : "Both reborn and not reborn," Vaccha, does not apply.

V. : Well then, my friend Gotama, is he neither reborn nor not reborn ?

G. : "Neither reborn nor not reborn," Vaccha, does not apply.

G. : Such a doctrine (*dhamma*), Vaccha, is profound (*gambhīra*), difficult to see (*duddasa*), difficult to understand (*duranubodha*), peaceful (*santa*), excellent (*paṇīta*), beyond logic (*atakkāvacara*), subtle (*nipuṇa*), intelligible to the wise (*paṇḍitavedanīya*); it is difficult for you who are of another view (*aññadiṭṭhika*), of another belief (*aññakhantika*), pleased with another (*aññarucika*), of another discipline (*āññatrayoga*) and of another teacher (*aññathācariyaka*).

Vaccha's question itself was that which should be waived or undecided (*avyākata*) from the standpoint of Buddhism, so that the Buddha did not meet it. If the Buddha, however, replied to Vaccha's question by applying four kinds of possible answer (Skt. *catuṣkoṭi*, 'tetralemma' or 'fourfold formulation'), namely: (1) It is, (2) It is not, (3) Both, and (4) Neither, the Buddha's answers would be the same as Sañjaya's, namely: (1) It is not so (*tathā ti pi me no*), (2) It is not otherwise (*aññathā ti pi me no*), (3) I do not say it is not (*no ti pi me no*), and (4) I do not say it is not not (*no no ti pi me no*). Why? Because we could express Sañjaya's answers in other words:

(1) The word '*tathā*' is contradictory to '*aññathā*'.

(2) The word '*aññathā*' is contradictory to '*tathā*'. Therefore, the relationship between them is: in case the one is "it is," the other is 'it is not."

(3) The words '*no ti*' are the negative proposition of each of items (1) and (2). That is, if the one is denied, it becomes "it is not." If the other is denied, it becomes "it is not not." And if the words '*no ti*' serve to negate simultaneously both of items (1) and (2), the relationship between the two can be regarded as "it neither is nor is not."

(4) The words '*no no ti*' are the negative proposition of item (3). Therefore, this is "it neither is not nor is not not."

Apart from item (4), it seems that Sañjaya's answers have something in common with the tetralemma, which is used widely in the *Nikāyas*. For example, we see: Sāriputta, one of the Buddha's chief disciples, is asked by another of his followers whether each condition in the sequence is made by oneself, by another, by both oneself and another, or neither oneself nor another.[1] This is the same mode of question as the tetralemma. According to A. L. Basham,[2] the Ājīvaka (meaning 'way of life') school (formed probably in B.C. 489 according to A. K. Warder)[3] maintained three sets of possible statements (Skt. *trairāśika*), namely: (1) It is, (2) It is not, and (3) Both it is and it is not. This may also be compared with the tetralemma.

From the four methods of asking, we can find out the ways of thinking of the early Buddhists to some extent, and there is no gainsaying the fact that the four kinds of possible answer influenced the development of Buddhist doctrines, especially the doctrine of voidness (*suññatā*) in Buddhism. So let us try to clarify further the ways of thinking of the early Buddhists.

---

1. S.II, 112-3, T. 2, 81 a.
2. *History and Doctrines of Ājīvakas*, pp. 175, 218, 274.
3. *Outline of Indian Philosophy*, p. 40.

8

TAKKA AND DHAMMATAKKA

8.1. We have to notice that certain words occupy a significant position in the evolution of thought, and as time goes by, changes in the meaning of the words came to produce changes in meaning in the text. In the history of Indian thought, the word '*takka*' is no exception to the rule. But the concept of the word '*takka*' is not always clear. And as far as the *Nikāyas* are concerned, it seems that instead of *takka*, the words '*dhammatakka*' are maintained by the Buddha and his disciples. In this chapter, we would like to trace the relationship between *takka* and *dhammatakka*, because both of them are important concepts in clarifying the ways of thinking of the early Buddhists.

8.2. In the later period, the word '*takka*' as well as *ñāya* came to be used with the meaning of 'logic'[1] (e.g. the *Tarkabhāṣā* : The Language of Logic, written by Mokṣākaragupta some time between 1050-1202 A. D.[2]). As is well known, Indian logic developed as the science of proof. For this reason, Indian logic, according to Dignāga (either in the 4th century A.D. or

1. Besides, we see the word '*hetuvidyā*' in the meaning of 'logic' or 'logical reasons'. *Hetuvidyā* seems to have been used mainly in Buddhist texts, and was translated into Chinese.

2. See Y. Kajiyama, "An Introduction to Buddhist Philosophy—An Annotated Translation of the *Tarkabhāṣā* of Mokṣākaragupta," *Memoirs of the Faculty of Letters*, No. 10, p. 1.

in the 5th century A.D.[1]), is characterized by inferring for oneself and inferring for others. In this case, in order to prove one's view validly it is naturally required that the proof be based on valid ways of thinking. As far as we can tell of the *Nikāyas*, logical principles as the basis of modes of thinking can be found in them. (This point will be discussed in Chapter 9.)

According to the *Pāli-English Dictionary*, the word '*takka*' means : a doubtful view, hairsplitting, reasoning, sophistry, etc.[2] Apart from the two different words '*takka*' and '*ñāya*', having the same meaning 'logic', we can see that the word '*takka*' has two or more different meanings. Let us examine the meanings of the word '*takka*'.

8.3. Generally speaking, "sophistry" and "a doubtful view," though there is a lack of clear-cut boundaries between the two, are considered to be "false reasoning." "False reasoning" is contradictory to "true reasoning."[3] Both "false reasoning" and "true reasoning" include "reasoning." Therefore, the sense of "reasoning" cannot be regarded in the same light as that of "a doubtful view" or that of "sophistry." This can be, in a sense, understood from the word and its associative field based on connection between the senses :

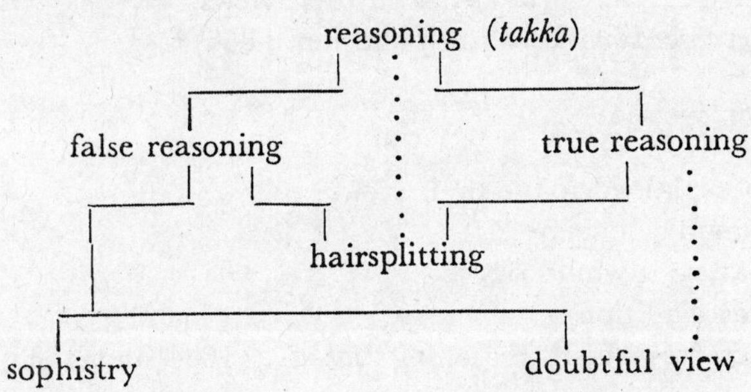

1. On this, see A. K. Warder, *Indian Buddhism*, pp. 444-46 (referring to Vasubandhu) and pp. 447-62 (referring to Dignāga).

2. As we shall see below, the meanings of *takka* in the *Pāli-English Dictionary* seem to be hardly authoritative.

3. As to the concepts 'true' and 'false', see R. Carnap, *The Logical Syntax of Language*, pp. 214-7.

This kind of diagram was presented by F. de Saussure,[1] and his disciple, C. Bally, introduced the useful concept of *associative fields*.[2] In the above diagram, bold-faced lines indicate direct relations and dotted lines indicate indirect relations. At this point, we would like to see statements using the word '*takka*' in order to learn the meaning from the context. The *Suttanipāta* runs :[3]

What some assert as very truth
Others assert as vanity and lies.
Thus, they indeed argue and dispute.
Why do not recluses agree in what they say ?(883)
There is only one truth, nor is there two.
Why do those who understand it dispute with each other ?
They praise the diverse truths as theirs,
Therefore, recluses do not agree in what they say. (884)
Why do they speak diverse truths
Those who bandy words by asserting their own truth ?
Do they hear many diverse truths from others ?
Or do they follow their own reasoning (*takka*) ? (885)
Indeed, there are not many diverse truths
Except for surmise on 'permanence' in the world.
Formulating reasoning (*takka*) from their views,
They assert two *dhammas* : truth and lies. (886)[4]

And moreover, we see:

Those who explained to me their views
Before Gotama's doctrine:
"It was that, so it would be."
All that was tradition.
All that increases (false) reasoning (*takka*). (1084 and 1135)

---

1. *Cours de linguistique générale*, p. 175.
2. "L' Arbitraire du signe," *Le Francais Moderne*, 8, pp. 193-206.
3. Also, see T. 4, 182 b. Cf. T. 25, 60 c.
4. In the Chinese text, *takka* is translated into "分別擇" (lit. meaning 'discriminating and choosing', but from the context, meaning '(one's own) judgement'.

8.4 Our words are never completely homogeneous: even the simplest and the most monolithic have a number of different facets depending on the context and situation in which they are used, and also on the personality of the speaker using them. Also, we must note that any word may acquire emotive overtones in a suitable context; conversely, even words with a strong emotional charge may on occasion be employed in a purely objective manner.[1] Therefore, as can be realized from Nos. 884 and 885 mentioned above, non-Buddhists thought of themselves as true reasoners. But, from the standpoint of Buddhism, the reasoning stated by a reasoner (*takkin*) was contrary to reason. Because he was addicted to reasoning for the sake of reasoning, he was also called sophist (*takkin*). With regard to this matter, the Buddha says as follows :

> He does not understand view (*diṭṭhi*), the cause of view, the extinction of view, and the ways of extinguishing view. For him view increases; and he is not released from birth, decay, death, grief (*soka*), lamentation (*parideva*), pain (*dukkha*), depression (*domanassa*), misery (*upāyāsa*); he is not released from unhappiness.[2]

After all, the paragraph "Formulating reasoning (*takka*) from their views" mentioned in the *Suttanipāta* becomes "Formulating *false* reasoning (*takka*) from their views." False reasoning is no other than the obsession of craving, of imagination (*maññita*), of differentiation (*papañcita*), of grasping (*upādānagata*) and is no other than a source of remorse (*vippaṭisāra*). As the Buddha points out also in the *Brahmajālasutta*, a so-called reasoner (*takkin*) or investigator (*vimaṁsaka*) is a philosopher who is possessed of false reasoning. The reason for this is that, being addicted to reasoning, he gives utterance to the following conclusion of his own (*sayaṁpaṭibhāna*), beaten out by his argumentations (*takkapariyāhata*) and followed by his investigation (*vimaṁ-*

1. On this, see S. Ullmann, *The Principles of Semantics*, pp. 96-105 and *Semantics*, p. 52.
2. A. IV, 68.

sānucarita) : "the soul is eternal," "the world is eternal" and so on.[1]

It is recorded in the *Vinaya* that, one day, Sañjaya's disciples, Sāriputta and Moggallāna, who were renowned as reasoners, listened to the theory of dependent origination introduced by Assaji who was a disciple of the Buddha; consequently, they became Buddhist monks. At that time, Assaji introduced to these two the following verse:

Principles (*dhammas*) proceed from a cause,
This cause the thus-gone has told,
And also its cessation;
The great recluse teaches such a theory.[2]

By which arose in both Sāriputta and Moggallāna the knowledge that everything which is having the principle of origination is also having the principle of cessation according to the law of cause and effect. Especially from the fact that Sāriputta, after having become a monk, took an active part as a true reasoner, we see that the reason why false reasoning arises is ignorance of the causal law or the fourfold truth. This matter can be also realized from the fact that the word '*ariyañāya*' indicates "to understand the theory of the dependent origination."[3]

8.5 Let us return to the subject. Since the same word may be used in countless situations by millions of people, contexts can go some way towards solving the vagueness of word-meanings. Another *Sutta* text states as follows:[4]

1. There are, Bhāradvāja, some recluses and brahmans who value tradition. Having attained to the accomplishment of super-knowledge in this world through tradition, they

---

1. D. I, 16, 21, 23, 29, etc. In the Chinese version of the *Brahmajāla-sutta* (T. 1, 88 b-94 a), the word corresponding to *takka* cannot be seen.
2. Vin. I, 40, T. 22, 110 b, 798 c. etc.
3. See S. V, 388 and SA. II, 73.
4. M. II, 211.

acknowledge the beginning of pure life—such as brahmans of the Three Vedas.

2. There are, Bhāradvāja, some recluses and brahmans. Having attained to the accomplishment of super-knowledge in this world by means of mere confidence, they acknowledge the beginning of pure life—such as reasoners and investigators.

3. There are, Bhāradvāja, some recluses and brahmans who understand fully *dhamma* (truth), by themselves only, which had not been heard before. Having attained to the accomplishment of super-knowledge in this world by means of understanding the truth, they acknowledge the beginning of pure life. Now, I (the Buddha) am one of those recluses and brahmans.

The above remark fits naturally the case we are arguing. That is to say, there is a definite distinction between reasoning that is based on the truth and reasoning that is based on mere confidence. The former is the standpoint of Buddhism and the latter is false reasoning. In this case, what the reasoner states he is unable to generalize. Nevertheless, he concludes by saying that the world is eternal, the soul is eternal, and so on. This is said to be merely false reasoning. As we have already mentioned in chapter **8.4**, words have a number of different facets depending on the situation of the speaker (in the above case, the Buddha and his disciples), so that the word '*takka*' was used in the sense of false reasoning, in spite of the fact that the word '*takka*' itself did not contain the concept of 'false'. In other words, one who does not understand the causal law or the dependent origination is addicted to reasoning for the sake of reasoning, and is called a false reasoner or sophist. On the other hand, the Buddha and some of his disciples are true reasoners, because they understand the causal law in Buddhism. In this sense, we would say that the word '*takka*' had the neutral sense of 'reasoning', which could be favourable or unfavourable according to the standpoint of the speaker. As the Buddha and his disciples used it as "false reasoning", the original sense fell into disuse particularly in the early Buddhist canon.

8.6 What kind of word, then, did Buddhists use in expressing "true reasoning" ? Prior to answering this question, let us turn our eyes to the words '*duṭṭakkita*' and '*sutakkita*'.

In Pāli, the prefix *su* added to nouns, adjectives, etc. means 'well', 'good', and the prefix *du*(*r*), 'ill', 'bad' (and they cover a wide range of similar conceptions : easy difficult, pleasant unpleasant, etc.[1]). Therefore, *duttakkita* is used with the meaning of 'badly reasoned', and *sutakkita*, with the meaning of 'well reasoned'. For example, we see : "He is a sophist (*takkin*) and his view is badly reasoned (*duṭṭakkita*)." On the other hand, since it seems that 'well reasoned' means "skilfully reasoned" rather than "reasoned correctly" from sound assumptions, we could say that 'well reasoned' does not always indicate "true reasoning." In the *Sandakasutta*, the following explanation can be seen :[2]

> (Ānanda says :) Sandaka, there is some teacher who is a reasoner and investigator; he teaches *dhamma* on the basis of his own understanding, beaten out by his argumentations (*takkapariyāhata*), followed by his investigation (*vimaṁsānucarita*). To the teacher who is a reasoner and investigator, his view is well reasoned (*sutakkitam pi hoti*) and badly reasoned (*duttakkitam pi hoti*) ; his view is well and badly reasoned (*tathā pi hoti aññathā pi hoti*).

In reference to this, the commentator throws no light, so that we cannot grasp the meaning (e.g. what the words '*sutakkitam pi hoti*', '*tathā pi hoti aññathā pi hoti*', etc. signify) in full. It is, however, understood from the above that there was a neutral reasoner as distinguished from a so-called reasoner (who is possessed of false reasoning). The neutral reasoner can be regarded as one who is possessed of neutral reasoning. Properly speaking, such a case is unthinkable. But, judging from the explanation in the *Sandakasutta*, the neutral case seems to be partly true and partly false reasoning. On the whole, the *Sandakasutta* must have tried to give a description of this point.

1. The prefix *su* meaning 'very' may be prefixed to adjectives in poetry. See A. K. Warder, *Introduction to Pāli*, p. 414.
2. M. I, 520.

Regrettably, we cannot see many materials dealing with the neutral case. Thus,

"A neutral reasoner's view is well and badly reasoned."

8.7 Once again, let us consider the word '*takka*' and its associative field together with the meaning of the words '***sutakkita***' and '***duttakkita***':

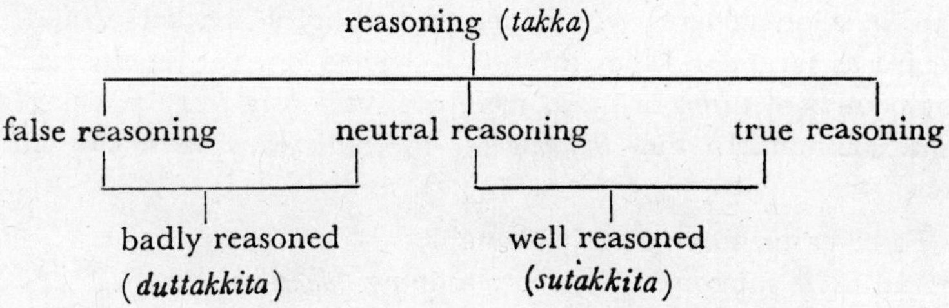

From the preceding explanations, we have also learned the two words '*takka-pariyāhata*' (beaten out by argumentations) and '*vīmaṁsānucarita*' (followed by investigation). According to S. C. Vidyabhusana,[1] the two words would suggest a Buddhist disbelief in logical reasoning and its validity as a means of knowledge. As we have already mentioned in chapter **8.4** and also as pointed out by G. S. P. Misra,[2] what is rejected by the Buddha and his disciples is certainly not the logical method or its validity but a vicious and unnecessary dialectic. It is, therefore, said that non-Buddhists are false reasoners (*takkins*) or that sophists (*takkins*) formulate false reasoning (*takka*).

From the standpoint of Buddhism, true reasoning is called *dhammatakka* or *ariyañāya*, which indicates the position of *vimuttiñāṇadassana* : the realm of newly discovered verbal expressions and thinking. *Dhammatakka* is a compound word made up of two independent words : *dhamma* and *takka*. Compounds, which are occasionally formed to show which of two or more homonyms is meant, may be regarded as borderline cases between words

1. *History of the Mediaeval School of Indian Logic*, p. 59.
2. "Logical and Scientific Method in Early Buddhist Texts," JRAS, Part 1 and 2, p. 55.

and phrases.[1] The meaning of the compound word '*dhamma-takka*' can be understood without losing the respective sense of both *dhamma* and *takka*. The word '*dhamma*' means 'true' (of course, *dhamma* includes various meanings, such as doctrine, merit, principle, etc., see chapter **2.7**), and the word '*takka*' means 'reasoning'. Therefore, *dhammatakka* can be considered to be 'reasoning based on the truth'. Compounds are very freely formed in Pāli (much more freely than in English, except perhaps in some modern styles which many English speakers would regard as jargon[2]). They are not restricted to two members, compounds of three or more members, variously related, being quite common. In the *Suttanipāta*, the following verse can be seen:

> To be calm, to be pure in thought,
> And to be supported by true reasoning (*dhammatakka*),[3]
> These are the result of the highest insight,
> And the breaking up of ignorance. Thus, I teach. (1107)

According to the commentary, *Cūḷaniddesa*,[4] *dhammatakka* is right intention (*sammāsaṅkappa*), right theory (*sammādiṭṭhi*), the insight (*vipassanā*) of the fourfold way (for recluse), and the starting-point of release through the highest insight. The right intention (also, the right theory) is reckoned as one of the eight factors of the noble way. But whether the right intention or the right theory, it will be accompanied by the other seven factors. Also, the eight factors of the noble way are inseparable from the fourfold truth. Therefore, the reasoning based on the truth (*dhammatakka*) is no other than the reasoning that occurs from the knowledge of the fourfold truth or dependent origination (which signifies intrinsically *ariyañāya*). In the *Majjhimanikāya*, the explanation of right intention can be seen as follows:

> What, monks, is the right intention that is noble, passionless, super-mundane, a factor of the way ? In one who, by culti-

1. L. Bloomfield, *Language*, p. 180.
2. See A. K. Warder, *Introduction to Pāli*, p. 78.
3. In the Chinese version, the words "to see the truth" are used (T.2, 256 a).
4. Nd2. p. 176.

> vating the noble way, is of noble thought, of passionless thought and is conversant with the noble way, whatever is reasoning (*takka*), reflective thought (*vitakka*), intention (*saṁkappa*), the complete focussing (*appanāvyappanā*), the application of the mind (*cetaso abhiniropanā*), and an activity of speech (*vācāsaṁkhāra*)—this, monks, is the right thought that is noble, passionless, super-mundane, a factor of the way.[1]

There is no denying the fact that the Buddha's line of argument was logical. According to Sunakkhata,[2] the son of a Licchavi, the Buddha teaches *dhamma* (doctrine) skilfully. To be skilful is not always to be logical. But we see that in any discourses given by the Buddha, there is a certain element characterized by force and persuasiveness. On this point, the Sthaviravāda text states as Sunakkhata's words : The recluse Gotama teaches *dhamma* on the basis of his own devising, beaten out by his argumentations, followed by his investigation; and the *dhamma* taught for the sake of something specific only leads the doer of it to the cessation of unhappiness.[3]

The Buddha points out that it is important to attain to the state of *atakkāvacara* 'beyond logic', i.e. 'the realm of a well-established conclusion which cannot be controverted' or to the position of *vimutti* 'the realm of no verbal expression and no thinking'. However, after his enlightenment the Buddha did not make light of argument, but regarded it as the first principle. In other words, his teachings are for a certainty expressed logically and reasonably. If we think of the distinction between true and false reasoners (or between those with understanding and those with weak understanding), the true reasoner would be, contrary to the false reasoner who was addicted to mere reasoning, the person who not only attained to the state of profound profitable *dhamma* which is beyond logic, but also realized *dhammatakka*. In this context, the following explanation,

1. M. III, 73. But, in the Chinese version, there is no term corresponding to *takka* (see T. 1, 735 c).
2. T. 17, 591 c.
3. M. I, 68, 71, 77.

as indicated in chapter **6.2**, shows how rigorous methods of argument were established:

> A person by discussing with another knows thus : judging from this reverend's approach to a question, judging from his intention, judging from his behaviour towards a question, he has understanding, ...As to the *dhamma* (teaching) the reverend talks, he is competent both in brief and in detail, is competent to explain its meaning, to expound it, to make it clear, to lay it down, to open it up, to analyze it and to make it plain. This reverend has understanding, he is not weak in understanding.

From the latter part of the above, we can see in particular some of the thinking actions (which are attended by the functions of comparison, discrimination, analysis, synthesis, etc.) of the person called one with understanding.

8.8 In spite of the fact that the Buddha was a man of profound thought, much was said in criticism of him. He was said abusively to be unenlightened (e.g. there are no states of enlightenment, excellent knowledge and insight suitable to the noble in the recluse Gotama).[1] He was also called "a juggler (*māyāvin*) who knows a trick of enticement (*āvaṭṭani māyā*) by which he entices away the followers of those holding other views."[2] But this does not express the truth. The reason why some recluses and brahmins said such words to the Buddha is that they did not understand completely what the *dhamma* (truth) taught by the Buddha is, and that they were not possessed of great understanding (*mahā paññā*), nor wide understanding (*puthu paññā*), nor profound understanding (*gambhira paññā*), nor incomparable understanding (*asamatta paññā*), nor penetrating understanding (*nibbedhika paññā*). To those who spoke ill of the Buddha, he explained his meaning to their satisfaction.[3] Yet, what the

---

1. M. I, 68.
2. A. II, 190, M. I, 375, T. 1, 629 a, etc.
3. As one of the most representative *suttas*, we see the *Kasibhāradvājasutta* of the *Suttanipāta* (pp. 12-6).

Buddha was deeply concerned about must have been that, among his disciples (especially novices), there were some who listened to the views of certain recluses and brahmins (perhaps known as reasoners) and yet could not discriminate truth from falsity. Accordingly, the Buddha probably protected such novices from making an error in judgement. At this point, the following explanation is worth noticing:[1]

> Do not accept these things (which certain reasoners spoke to you) by tradition (*anussava*), nor by a succession (*parampară*, of teachers handing something down on their authority), nor by history (*itikirā*), nor by texts (*piṭakasampadāna*), nor by (mere) logic (*takka*), nor by schemes (*naya*: a predetermined or a priori system of ideas, according to A. K. Warder[2]), nor by reflection on peculiarities (*ākāraparivitakka* as merely superficial aspects of things which do not show their real nature), nor by approving after considering (mere) opinion (*diṭṭhinijjhānakkhanti*), because (the person speaking) appears to be capable (*bhavyarūpatā*), and because the philosopher is our teacher (*samaṇo no gurū*, which may also be translated : our teacher is a philosopher). If you know for yourselves : these things (these non-reasons) are unprofitable, blameworthy, censured by those with understanding : these things, when performed and undertaken, conduce to loss and suffering, ...then, you indeed reject them.

The Buddha urges his disciples to find things out by themselves, to have personal knowledge of the conditions through which things happen, that is, to pursue a deep knowledge based on the truth.

From the above discussion, we have learned that only the person called one with understanding is a true reasoner, who attained to the state of *atakkāvacara* which means "profound profitable *dhamma* (truth) being beyond logic" and at the same

---

1. A. I, 189, 193, II, 191, 193. Cf. S. II, 115-7 and T. 2, 98 c.

2. *Outline of Indian Philosophy*, p. 49. Later on, *naya* was used in a good sense as an instrument of logical analysis—a tetralemma, for example, would be a *naya*, likewise a *duka* or a *tika* and so on.

time, who had a right understanding of *dhammatakka* which means "reasoning based on the fourfold truth or dependent origination." The fourfold truth and dependent origination are two teachings closely connected. In other words, the one is the corollary of the other. And it is universally acknowledged that all the Buddha's teachings are summarized in the formula of the fourfold truth. However, in clarifying more thoroughly the ways of thinking of the early Buddhists, we need to examine the conclusions arrived at in the *Nikāyas* by means of true reasoning.

8.9 As we have already mentioned at the very beginning of this chapter, it is clear that certain words occupy a significant position in the evolution of thought, and that as time goes by, changes in the meaning of the words come to produce changes in meaning in the text. We have learned that the word '*takka*' is no exception to the rule. This can be also said about the word '*anumāna*' (inference). For instance, we see the *Anumānasutta* in the *Majjhimanikāya*[1] and see "*anumānapañha*" in the *Milinda-pañha*.[2] But the significance of *anumāna* used in both texts is very different. In this sense, it is extremely important to examine and to clarify the meaning of words which occupy a special position in any field of philosophy. It is, therefore, said that contemporary semantics is characterized by an absorbing interest in relations between language and thinking; language is no longer regarded as a mere instrument for expressing our thoughts, but as an influence in its own right, which shapes and predetermines them and directs them into specific channels,[3] though these ideas were already prominent in the theory of 'semantic field'.[4]

---

1. M. I, 95-100, T. 1, 571 b-572 c, 842 b-843 b.
2. Miln. pp. 329-47.
3. On this, see S. Ullmann, *Semantics*, p. 9. Also, refer to ed. L. Linsky, *Semantics and the Philosophy of language*.
4. See S. Ullmann, *The Principles of Semantics*, pp. 152-70. Also refer to N. Chomsky, *Syntactic Structures*, p. 15, pp. 92-105, and B. K. Matilal, *The Navya-nyāya Doctrine of Negation*, pp. 19-20.

9

FORMS OF REASONING AND ARGUMENT

9.1 The Buddha states in a discussion with the wanderer Dīghanakha that a discerning person (*viññū purisa*) does not adhere to any of the three opinions: (1) I do approve of everything (that annihilationists, eternalists and other heretics assert), (2) I never approve of anything they assert, and (3) I approve of some things they assert and not others. The Buddha also states that he does not affirm : This alone is the truth, any other view is false (*idam eva saccaṃ mogha aññaṃ*), for by giving a categorical reply, there is a quarrel (*viggaha*) between them; if there is a quarrel, there is a dispute (*vivāda*); if there is a dispute, there is remorse (*vighāta*); if there is remorse, there is trouble (*vihesā*).[1] His explanation similar in essence to the above can also be found in the *Mahāviyūha-sutta* of the *Suttanipāta* (Nos. 895-914). Although the above indicates the Buddha's way of thinking to some extent, it does not mean that the Buddha maintained a dubious or uncertain attitude towards their assertions.

As mentioned in chapter **6.11**, the Buddha regarded all the metaphysical problems as meaningless because he thought that the objects mentioned are neither real nor existent. Nevertheless, he had to express his views and to exchange them with his disciples and non-Buddhists; consequently, he used the four *pañhabyākaraṇas* properly and encouraged his disciples to learn

1. M. I, 498-99, T. 2, 249 b-c, 449 a-b.

them. This point must be clarified further by examining the ways of thinking of the Buddha and his disciples. In this chapter, we would like to make clear forms of reasoning and argument appearing in the *Nikāyas*.

9.2 The *Saṁyuttanikāya* deals with varieties of synonym denoting the conception of *nibbāna*, which is also called *asaṁkhata* 'unactivated' or 'unsynthesized'.[1] When we classify those synonyms, we find that there are negative expressions and positive expressions, as already mentioned in chapter **5.3**. In other places, *nibbāna* means the absence of *kilesas* represented by three poisons, namely : 1. passion (*rāga*), 2. aversion (*dosa*) and 3. delusion (*moha*);[2] and also means the extinction of desire for all the pleasant matter seen, heard, felt and known:

All that you do think, Mettagu,
Thus the Master said,
Above, below, transversely, midst—in such;
Eliminate pleasure (*nandi*) and attachment (*nivesana*),
And consciousness (*viññāṇa*) will never stay in transmigration (*bhava*). (Sn. 1055)

And also, we see:

In this world, to get rid of desire and passion
For all the pleasant matter (*piyarūpa*) seen
And heard and felt and known, Hemaka,
Is the way to the stable enlightenment. (Sn. 1086)

Yet, from the very beginning, *nibbāna* as the ultimate truth seems to have been expressed by using negative prefixes or by using *nipātas* in the sense of negation. For example, we see the following explanations of *nibbāna*:[3]

(1) Monks, there exists that condition wherein is neither earth, nor water, nor fire, nor air; wherein is neither the sphere of infinite space, nor of infinite consciousness, nor of

1. S. IV, 368-73, T. 2, 224 a.
2. S. IV, 251, 261, etc.
3. Ud. pp. 80-1, Itv. p. 37.

nothingness nor of neither-consciousness-nor-unconsciousness; wherein is neither this world, nor a world beyond, nor both the moon and the sun. Monks, I declare it to be no coming; no going; no standing; no vanishing; and no arising. It is without help; without continuance; and without sense-object. This indeed is the end of unhappiness.

(2) It is hard to see non-ego; it is not easy to see truth; one who penetrates knows craving; and there is nothing for one who sees.

(3) Monks, there is a not-born; a not-become; a not-made; and an unactivated. Monks, if that not-born; not-become; not-made; and unactivated are not, there will not be apparent the departure from being born; becoming; being made; and being activated. Monks, because there is a not-born; a not-become; a not-made; and an unactivated, there is the departure from being born; becoming; being made; and being activated.

(4) For one who clings, there is wavering; for one who does not cling, there is no wavering; wavering not being, there is calm; calm being, there is no attachment; attachment not being, there is no coming and going; coming and going not being, there is no death and birth; death and birth not being, there is neither 'here', nor 'yonder', nor anything between the two. This indeed is the end of unhappiness.

The explanations mean that the ultimate truth cannot be directly expressed in affirmative words. That is : the ultimate truth is beyond all descriptions. Therefore, at the stage of trying to explain what the ultimate truth is, there is no method of doing so other than using a negative phrase such as "this is not *A*", "not *B*", "not *C*", and so on.

9.3 However, a noteworthy matter at this point is that the early Buddhists accepted such a dichotomising tendency not only in the explanations of the ultimate truth, but also in those of Buddhist doctrine; moreover, by means of a double negative in statements, the early Buddhists must have attempted advancing the theory of Buddhism. In other words, it was probably not difficult for the early Buddhists to apply the principle of contradiction in statements, because they had a good supply of both *upasaggas* and *nipātas* expressing the negative. The following affords a striking illustration of the fact:

1. Example of *na ahaṃ na jānāmi* coming out in a dialogue between Ānanda and Kokanuda. That is, while the venerable Ānanda was staying at Rājagaha in the Tapoda park, the wanderer Kokanuda approached him, saying:[1]

K. : I would like to ask you a question on a certain point, if you could give the opportunity for answering my question.

A. : Ask on, friend. When we hear, we shall know.

K. : What about this, friend ? Do you hold the view: The world is eternal; this is the truth; any other view is useless (*mogha*) ?

A. : No indeed, friend, I do not hold such a view.

K. : Then, do you not know, not see ?

A. : No indeed, friend, I am not one who knows not, sees not, I know. I see (*na kho ahaṃ āvuso na jānāmi na passāmi, jānām' ahaṃ āvuso passāmi' ti*).[2]

. . . .

A. : As regards groundless view (*diṭṭhigatā*), friend, as regards a tenet of speculative philosophy (*diṭṭhiṭṭhāna*), as regards self-determining view (*adhiṭṭhāna*), as regards prejudiced view (*pariyuṭṭhāna*), as regards rising up from view (*samuṭṭhāna*), as regards rooting up view (*samugghāta*), I am one who knows, who sees.

2. Example of *no a-manasikāra*.[3]

Monks, these four conditions are to be understood by four other conditions. What are the four ? It is by association

---

1. A. V, 196-8, T. 2, 248 b-c, 448 a.
2. We see in the Chinese version : "非不知非不見。悉知悉見", corresponding exactly to the statement in Pāli (see T. 2, 248 b).
3. A. II, 187, S. I, 78, T. 2, 305 c-306 a.

that (one's) virtue is to be understood, and that for a long time, not shortly, by attention, not by inattention (*no amanasikāra*),[1] by one who has understanding, not by one who is weak in understanding. It is by living with (one) that (one's) integrity is to be understood, and that for a long time, . . . not by inattention, . . . It is in time of distress that (one's) courage is to be understood and that for a long time, . . . not by inattention, . . . It is by discussion that (one's) understanding is to be understood, and that for a long time, . . . not by inattention, . . .

3. Example of *na an-attamana.*[2]

Monks, a teacher teaches *dhamma* (doctrine) to disciples, compassionate, seeking their welfare, out of compassion, saying: "This is for your welfare, this is for your happiness." Some of his disciples do not listen, do not lend ear, do not prepare their minds for profound knowledge and, turning aside, move away from the teacher's instruction. But some disciples listen, lend ear, prepare their minds for profound knowledge and, not turning aside, do not move away from the teacher's instruction. Herein, monks, the thus-gone is neither delighted nor does he experience delight and neither is he not delighted (*na anattamano hoti*), nor does he not experience delight (*na anattamanataṁ paṭisaṁvedeti*[3]). Having got rid of both delight and non-delight, he dwells with equanimity, mindful (*sata*), clearly conscious (*sampajāna*). This, monks, is the second base of self-possession (*satipaṭṭhāna*) that a noble man practises and, practising it, is the noble man who is a teacher competent to instruct a group.

The statements represented by the double negative in the

1. The Chinese version states: "不以不智" (literally, meaning 'not by not understanding'). See T. 2, 306 a. In general, "智" means 'understanding', but in this place it should be regarded as meaning 'pondering' or 'attention'.

2. M. III, 221, T. 1, 693 c-694 a (esp. see 693 c).

3. In the Chinese version, the second expression cannot be seen.

Nikāyas are too numerous to mention. The statement "*x* is not non-*A*" expressed by the double negative is logically equivalent to the affirmative proposition "*x* is *A*." Double negation in statements can be a strong expression in some cases. And it can also become a weak expression in the sense of the suggestion of uncertainty of expression in some cases. Except for these two facts, we must realize that for those who form the basis of negative thinking, the use of double negative is very important, because they do not want to give apparently an expression of dogmatic affirmative, though internally positive. As a characteristic of the dialogue on *dhammas*, we can see that there are four methods of answering questions, in which the first method is to give a categorical reply or to answer directly in the affirmative (see chapter **6.10**). This method is generally based on the principle of identity expressed by the formula of "(All) *S* is *S*." Most of the discernible logical forms which we find in the *Nikāyas* seem to be statements founded on this principle. However, at the same time we cannot fail to see the fact that in the *Nikāyas* there are statements which are expressed according to the principle of contradiction. This principle is that which forms the foundation of negative thinking, whilst the principle of identity is what forms the basis of affirmative thinking. However, in statements the former reaches substantially the same result as the latter.

9.4 Throughout early Buddhism, "nothing is permanent in this world" persists as a universal proposition. Furthermore, we can find the following statement based on the principle of contradiction:[1]

> He has not this view (*na pi hevaṃ diṭṭhi hoti*): That self, after death, becomes permanent, lasting, eternal, and does not have the principle of change (*aviparināmadhammo*)

In the *Nikāyas* and *Āgamas*, the three words '*anicca*', '*dukkha*', and '*viparināmadhamma*' (having the principle of change) are dealt with together as a stereotyped expression[2], and the

1. S. III, 98-9. T. 2, 13 c, in which the same explanation as in Pāli cannot be seen.
2. See M. III, 20, 272, 278, T. 2, 14 c, 73 a, etc.

subject of these words is the five *khandhas* or the six *āyatanas*, which are also represented by the word '*sabba*' (all, everything in the world).[1] Therefore, on this basis the statement should be expressed as follows :

> Everything in the world is impermanent, unhappy and having the principle of change.

However, when we look at the paragraph *na pi hevaṃ diṭṭhi hoti* and the words '*a-viparināmadhammo*' (of which the subject is of course "*sabbo*") mentioned previously, the whole statement becomes: "he has not indeed such a view: everything is not having the principle of change." In other words, "Everything is not *a-viparināmadhammo* (not having the principle of change)," which is expressed by the formula of "*S* is not non-*P*". According to the rules of the symbolism of modern logic, the above statement might be changed into the following expression :

> It is not the case that everything is not having the principle of change.

We would say that the *Nikāyas* (especially, the "*Khandha*-chapter"[2] in the *Saṁyuttanikāya*) teach us both the statements "Everything is having the principle of change" and "It is not the case that everything is not having the principle of change." If we use the letter p to symbolize the statements, the former is p, and the latter, $--p$. The latter is equivalent to the former :

$$--p \equiv p$$

And also we can learn from the statements : "It is not the case that everything is having the principle of change and that everything is not having the principle of change." Symbolically :

$$-(p . -p)$$

The principle of contradiction is used in general to defeat an opponent rather than to assert emphatically one's own opinion. "Having the principle of change," this is the standpoint of Buddhism and "not having the principle of change," this is the viewpoint of eternalists. But the Buddha does not give a flat

1. S. IV, 15.
2. S. III, 1-188.

denial to them. As he points out, if a Buddhist (or Buddhists) affirms or adheres to the opinion : "I never approve of yours," there is a quarrel,...a trouble. In this sense, it might be considered that the Buddha gave an expression of passivity by the use of the principle of double negation and tried to use the principle of contradiction, though the latter is not expressed yet in concrete form in the *Nikāyas*.

The practical use of a double negation such as "I am not one who knows not, sees not. I know. I see" can certainly be considered an expression of emphatic affirmation. But, in view of the fact that the four types of ambiguous answers and the four kinds of possible answer are applied widely in the *Nikāyas* (see Chapter **7.1**, **2** and **3**), and the fact that the Buddha himself mentions clearly to Dīghanakha that a discerning person does not adhere to any one of the three opinions (chapter **9.1**), the practical use of a double negation seems to be an expression lacking positive affirmation. This is also a very important point when we come to consider the characteristics of the forms of argument in the *Nikāyas*. From the above, we can see to a certain extent the principles of thinking appearing in the *Nikāyas*. In order to clarify this point further, let us give another example.

The example is from the *Mahāparinibbānasutta*, in which the Buddha said the following words to a great disciple, Ānanda, who was in deep grief, having heard the news that the Buddha was going to pass away:[1]

> Enough, Ānanda. Do not mourn; do not lament. Have I not already told you that it is in the very nature of all things most near and dear to us that we must separate from them, leave them, sever ourselves from them ? How, then, Ānanda, can this be possible, that whatever is born, existing, activated and having the principle of breakage should not be dissolved (*yan taṃ jātaṃ bhūtaṃ saṅkhataṃ paloka-dhammaṃ, taṃ vata mā palujjiti*) ? No such case can exist (*n'etaṃ ṭhānaṃ vijjati*).

The form of expression is entirely the same as in the first example. Therefore, "Whatever is born, existing, activated and

1. D. II, 144, T. 1, 16c.

having the principle of breakage should not be dissolved" is a case which cannot exist. Although his expression might seem an involved construction, it becomes :

It is not the case that whatever is born, existing, activated and having the principle of breakage is not dissolved.

As pointed out before, it is understood that, with the help of both *upasaggas* and *nipātas* to express negation, the early Buddhists probably tried to develop further a theory of Buddhism. In this sense, if we disregard the negative way of thinking appearing in the *Nikāyas*, we cannot understand the theory of dependent origination and the process of its development. So we would like to enlarge further upon this point with the statements expressed in other logical forms.

9.5. As mentioned in chapter **8.8**, the whole doctrine of the Buddha is summarized in the formula of the fourfold truth (*sacca*), and from the standpoint of Buddhism, the true reasoning is that which was based on the knowledge of the fourfold truth or dependent origination (*paṭiccasamuppāda*)—which could be displayed by the words '*dhammatakka*' or '*ariyañāya*'. As is well known, the formula of the fourfold truth is:[1]

1. This is the noble truth of unhappiness: birth (*jāti*) is unhappy, so is old age (*jarā*), sickness (*vyādhi*), death (*maraṇa*), (and grief, lamentation, pain, depression, and misery are unhappy: *sokaparidevadukkhadomanassupāyāsā pi dukkhā*[2]). Contact with unpleasant things (*appiya-sampayoga*) is unhappy, separation from pleasant things (*piya-vippayoga*) is unhappy, not getting what one wishes (*yam iccham na labhati*) is unhappy. In short, the five attachment groups (*pañcupādānakkhandhā*) are unhappy.
2. This is the noble truth of origination of unhappiness : desire which leads to rebirth, desire which is connected with pleasure and passion, desire which finds pleasure here and there, namely: the desire for passion, the desire for existence, and the desire for non-existence.

---

1. S. V, 420-24, T. 2, 103 c-104 a, T. 2, 503 b-c, etc.
2. These l ist omitted by the *Vinaya* text (see Vin. I, 10). Cf. T. 2, 103 c-104 a, T. 2, 503 b.

3. This is the noble truth of the cessation of unhappiness: the absolute cessation in dispassion of, the abandonment of, rejection of, freeing from, not clinging to, that same desire.

4. This is the noble truth of the way leading to the cessation of unhappiness: this is the noble eightfold way, namely: 1. right theory (*sammādiṭṭhi*), 2. right intention (*sammāsaṃkappa*), 3. right speech (*sammāvācā*), 4. right action (*sammākammanta*), 5. right livelihood (*sammā-ājiva*), 6. right effort (*sammāvāyāma*), 7. right self-possession (*sammāsati*) and 8. right concentration (*sammāsamādhi*).

And as the extension of the fourfold truth, we see the theory of the twelve-linked chain of causation in direct and reverse orders, which is formulated in a scientific manner and contains strictly logical deductions, as we shall see below. Also, from the *Nikāyas* and *Āgamas*, we can learn the fact that the early Buddhists made an effort to examine what unhappiness and its origination are. For example, the first *dhamma*, *kāyānupassànā*, in the four *satipaṭṭhānas*, Nos. 274, 276, 448-450, 453, 1093 in the *Theragāthā*, Nos. 205, 206 in the *Suttanipāta*, etc. are the most representative doctrines which teach the impurity and decrepitude of the body, and also which lead to a comprehension of *anicca*, *dukkha* and *anattan* in the world. Therefore, it may be that the following universal propositions can be formulated:[1]

> The five *khandhas* (or six *āyatanas*) are impermanent. What is impermanent, that is unhappy (*yad aniccaṃ taṃ dukkhaṃ*). What is unhappy, that is egoless (*yaṃ dukkhaṃ tad anattā*). What is egoless, that is not mine (*yad anattā taṃ netam mama*): I am not it (*neso ham asmi*); it is not my self (*na meso attā*).

In dealing with the above, we must use discretion. That is, according to western logic (strictly speaking, since Aristotle's time), such a statement is regarded as a sorites, which is like a categorical syllogism in that all premisses are categorical propositions; but the above statement is a sorites which is composed of hypothetical judgments. On this point, we stand in need of more detailed explanation.

1. S. III, 22, 23, 112, IV, 1, T. 2, 2 a, 30 c, etc.

9.6. In connection with the fourfold truth, we see further the generalization : "Whatever is having the principle of origination is having the principle of cessation" (*yaṃ kiñci samudayadhammaṃ sabbaṃ taṃ nirodha-dhammaṃ*).[1] This proposition can be expressed by:

1. "If anything is having the principle of origination, then it is also having the principle of cessation."

This must be viewed as affirming a bundle of individual conditionals : If *a* is having the principle of origination, *a* is having the principle of cessation; if *b* is having the principle of origination, *b* is having the principle of cessation; and so on. In short :

2. "For all *x*, if *x* is having the principle of origination, then *x* is having the principle of cessation."

This can also be rewritten as :

3. For all *x*, it is not the case that *x* is both having the principle of origination and not having the principle of cessation.

Item 1 is called a "*generalized conditional.*"[2] At this point, we must keep items 1, 2 and 3 in mind.

Now, the statement "Whatever is having the principle of origination is having the principle of cessation" teaches the close relationship of *anicca, dukkha* and *anattan*. In contrast to the penetration of *attan* as a basic idea through Brahmanism, "everything is impermanent (unhappy and egoless) in the world" penetrated as a universal proposition through early

---

1. Vin. I, 40. Besides, we see the same expression in D. I, 110, M. III, 280, S. IV, 47, 107, V, 423, etc. On the other hand, in Chinese texts we see the words "遠塵離垢得法眼浄", which correspond to Pāli : *virajaṃ vītamalaṃ dhamma-cakkhuṃ udapādi* (seeT. 22, 110 b, 798 c, 1.88 a, 2, 104 a, 503 c, 504 b, 26, 479 c, etc.), but we cannot see the words corresponding exactly to the words *yaṃ kiñci . . . nirodhadhammaṃ*'. Also, we see another expression "*yaṃ bhūtam taṃ nirodhadhammaṃ*" (what has come to be is having the principle of cessation). On this, see "*nidāna-saṁyutta*" (S.II,48), the Chinese version of "*nidāna-saṃyukta*" (T. 2, 95 b), and E. Waldschmidt, "Skt. fragments of *Nidānasaṃyukta*," (ed. Tripāṭhī, Berlin, DAWB, VIII, 1962), p. 201. From this, it is supposed that the words '*kiñci*' and '*sabbaṃ*' in *yaṃ . . . nirodhadhammaṃ* were added in the later period.

2. On this, see W. V. Quine, *Methods of Logic*, p. 14.

Buddhism. In this case, not only the Buddha, but also his disciples must have been required to prove why everything is impermanent, unhappy, and egoless. The Buddha postulates that the five *khandhas* (or six *āyatanas*, which can be expressed by *sabba*) are non-ego, because they cannot be controlled, and then he gives an apt illustration of 'matter', one of the five *khandhas*, as we have already seen in chapter **5.7**:[1]

> If matter (as physical principles) were ego, it would not be involved in sickness, and one could say of matter: "Thus let it be. Thus let it not be." But, inasmuch as matter is non-ego, that is why matter is involved in sickness, one cannot say of matter: "Thus let it be. Thus let it not be."

As can be realized from the above, the statement "matter is non-ego" is actually conditional. In other words, the starting-point in the *Nikāya*-Buddhism is in the observation that everything is *anicca*. In spite of the fact that everything in the world is impermanent, one is possessed by the belief that everything is permanent. From such an illusion, *dukkha* arises. And as one of the four *dukkhas*, the above *sutta* text deals with "sickness" and tries to treat of the fact that nothing is substantial (*anattan*) from the standpoint of sickness. Therefore, it is understood that the relationship of (A) *anicca*, (B) *dukkha*, and (C) *anattan* is that if there is *A*, then there is *B*; if there is *B*, then there is *C* (or if there is not *A*, then there is not *B*; if there is not *B*, then there is not *C*). Such a case is a sorites which is composed of hypothetical judgements. Concerning this, we see a more detailed explanation:[2]

> Whenever such subjects as matter, sensation, perception, forces, or consciousness occur, one understands them wholly as impermanent principles, as an ill, as a disease (*roga*), a boil (*gaṇḍa*), a sting (*salla*), a hurt (*agha*), an affliction (*ābādha*), as something alien (*para*), breakable (*paloka*), void, egoless.

This explanation is what teaches fully a series of facts in the world that begins from *anicca* and ends in *anattan*. The later work

1. S. III, 66, Vin. I, 13. T. 2, 7 c, etc.
2. A. IV, 422-3, M. I. 435, 436, 500, etc.

Paṭisambhidāmagga (which seems to be a supplement of the *Vibhaṅga*) treats of these points as follows:[1]

> What is impermanent, that is unhappy (*yaṃ aniccaṃ, taṃ dukkhaṃ*); what is impermanent and unhappy, that is egoless (*yaṃ aniccañ ca dukkhañ ca, taṃ anattā*); what is impermanent... and egoless, that is real (*yaṃ aniccañ ca...anattā ca, taṃ tathaṃ*); what is impermanent ... and real, that is the truth (*yaṃ aniccañ ca . . . tathañ ca, taṃ saccaṃ*); what is impermanent . . .and the truth, that is included in one[2] (*yaṃ aniccañ ca . . . saccañ ca, taṃ ekasaṅgahitaṃ*).

The form of expression mentioned above is entirely the same as in the explanation of *anicca*, *dukkha* and *anattan* mentioned in chapter **9.5**. The statement "what is *A*, *B*, *C* . . .and *S*, that is *P*" is considered to be a kind of compound judgement (Das Mehrheitsurteil), because it has many subjects such as "that which is *A*, that which is *B*, that which is *C* . . .and that which is *S*, these are *P*." But this statement can also be understood from the standpoint of a variety of sorites indicating that if there is (not) *A*, then there is (not) *B*; if there is (not) *B*, then there is (not) *C* and so on. Apart from the examination of the *Paṭisambhidāmagga*, what can be considered as the most basic sorites expressing hypothetical judgement in the *Nikāyas* is the formula: "This being, this is (*imasmiṃ sati idaṃ hoti*); from the arising of this, this arises (*imassuppādā idam uppajjati*). This not being, this is not (*imasmiṃ asati idaṃ na hoti*); from the cessation of this, this ceases (*imassa nirodhā idaṃ nirujjhati*)."[3] And such a sorites of the most developed form is, we could say, the twelve *paṭiccasamuppādas*.[4]

The twelve *paṭiccasamuppādas* in direct order are:

---

1. Pṭm. II, 106.
2. This means that it is penetrated (or comprehended) by one knowledge (or one cognition). See Pṭm. II, 105-6. Also, see the Commentary, p. 594 : the 4 truths (or many truths) may be understood as one truth.
3. S. II, 28, M. II, 32, III. 63, T. 1, 723 c, 2, 98 b, 100 a, etc.
4. S. II, 1-2, 42-3, V, 338, M. III, 63-4, A. I, 177, Vin. I, 1, T. 2, 85 a-b, 216 a, 723 c, etc.

Conditioned by ignorance are the forces (*avijjāpaccayā saṃkhārā*) ; conditioned by the forces is consciousness (*saṃkhārapaccayā viññānaṃ*); conditioned by consciousness is a sentient body (*viññāṇapaccayā nāmarūpaṃ*) ; conditioned by a sentient body are the six spheres of the senses (*nāmarūpapaccayā saḷāyatanaṃ*) ; conditioned by the six spheres of the senses is contact (*saḷāyatanapaccayā phasso*) ; conditioned by contact is sensation (*phassapaccayā vedanā*) ; conditioned by sensation is desire (*vedanāpaccayā taṇhā*) ; conditioned by desire is attachment (*taṇhapaccayā upādānaṃ*); conditioned by attachment is existence (*upādānapaccayā bhavo*); conditioned by existence is birth (*bhavapaccayā jāti*) ; conditioned by birth there come into being old age and death, grief, lamentation, pain, depression and misery (*jātipaccayā jarāmaraṇaṃ sokaparidevadukkhadomanassupāyāsā sambhavanti*).

Those in reverse order are:

From the absolute dispassion and cessation of ignorance is the cessation of the forces (*avijjāya asesavirāganirodhā saṃkhāranirodho*) ; from the cessation of the forces is the cessation of consciousness; from the cessation of consciousness is the cessation of a sentient body; from the cessation of a sentient body is the cessation of the six spheres of the senses; from the cessation of the six spheres of the senses is the cessation of contact; from the cessation of contact is the cessation of sensation; from the cessation of sensation is the cessation of desire; from the cessation of desire is the cessation of attachment; from the cessation of attachment is the cessation of existence; from the cessation of existence is the cessation of birth; from the cessation of birth, old age and death, grief, lamentation, pain, depression and misery cease.

Such are the twelve *paccayākāras* (aspects of condition) in direct and reverse orders, in which it is impossible in fact to indicate which one is the first cause, because the twelve make a continuous circle which is called the wheel of life. The wheel of life is a circle with no beginning, but it is customary to begin its exposition at "ignorance" (*avijjā*).

Among the twelve, the former is always the cause of the latter, so that the relationship between the former and the latter is expressed by the term "if . . .then. . . .", i.e. "ignorance is the cause of the (blind) forces," "the (blind) forces are the cause of consciousness,". . .and "birth is the cause of old age and death"; in other words, "if there is *A* (ignorance), then there is *B* (the forces)," "if there is *B*, then there is *C* (consciousness). . . ." We have stated the above from the standpoint of direct order, but it can be viewed as "if there is not *A*, then there is not *B*," "if there is not *B*, then there is not *C*" and so forth. This is no doubt a sorites, not in the form of a categorical judgement, but in the form of a hypothetical judgement.

In fact, a sorites itself can be viewed as a sort of shorthand presentation of a chain of categorical syllogisms. For instance, from two premisses: "All *A*'s are *B*" and "All *B*'s are *C*," we can get as the conclusion of a perfect syllogism: "All *A*'s are *C*." The latter, with the following premiss: "All *C*'s are *D*," will yield the perfect conclusion: All *A*'s are *D*." This in turn, with the following premiss: "All *D*'s are *E*," yields the conclusion of the sorites: "All *A*'s are *E*." However, in the sorites, the intermediate conclusions—"All *A*'s are *C*." and "All *A*'s are *D*"—are left out.[1] The twelve *paṭiccasamuppādas* are apt to be regarded as a kind of argument called a sorites above. But as mentioned already, the twelve as well as the fourfold truth can be viewed as being based on a sorites which can be cast into the form of a sequence of hypothetical statements.

9.7. It is likely that in the *Nikāyas* and *Āgamas* the twelve *paṭiccasamuppādas* in direct and reverse orders are the most elaborate doctrine which teaches why the world is filled with hardships, and at the same time, which teaches the way leading to the cessation of them.[2] The central point of the twelve is

---

1. On this, see R. B. Angell, *Reasoning and Logic*, pp. 111-3.

2. Besides the twelve *paṭiccasamuppādas*, we can find in the Sn. (Nos. 862-877) the different type of dependent origination, in which the actual phases of human life are dealt with analytically on the basis of hypothetical judgement.

that everything in the world consists of "existence depending upon a series of causes," that is, only when there are causes, is there existence; without causes there can be no existence; no existence is permanent nor conclusive. To obtain such a knowledge, this is *dhammatakka* or *ariyañāya* from the standpoint of Buddhism (see chapter **8.7**). In order to help a listener obtain the knowledge, the Buddha and his disciples made an effort to give a simile (which is represented by the word '*upamā*' or '*opamma*', see chapter **6.7** and **8**).

We would say that the forms of argument in the *Nikāyas* are characterized by a sorites which is composed of hypothetical statements, and afterwards, such a tendency did find acceptance in one ***Abhidhamma*** text, the *Kathāvatthu*, in which we see a strictly formalized system of debate—especially, hypothetical syllogisms, which will be discussed in another chapter.

9.8 Another style of argument appearing in the *Nikāyas* and *Āgamas* is that which is based on alternative judgement. Alternative propositions are compound propositions in which the components are connected by "or" or "either ... or ..." The components are called *alternants* and there may be two or more of them. As mentioned in chapter **5.4**, the interpretation of "either p or q" is treated as implying that one alternant or the other must be true. In other words, the most important thing is that either p is true or q is true, but not both of them together. The "or" has an exclusive sense. In the *Nikāyas*, the following argument can be widely seen:[1]

Ques. : Now, what do you think, monks? Is everything permanent or impermanent?
Ans. : Everything is impermanent, Sir.
Ques. : What is impermanent, is that happy or unhappy?
Ans. : That is unhappy, Sir.
Ques. : What is impermanent, unhappy, having the principle of change, ... is it proper concerning that to think "This is mine. I am this. That is my self?"
Ans. : No, indeed, Sir.

1. S. III, 181, 182, IV, 45, 47, 54, 106, T. 2, 41 c, 42 a, etc.

The starting-point in the above is "Everything is either permanent or impermanent" (schematized by (x) $(Fx \vee -Fx)$—Whatever x may be, x is permanent or x is not permanent). From the standpoint of Buddhism, the answer is "Everything is impermanent." Therefore, the next point is "Everything is either happy or unhappy" (i.e. (x) $[(x \text{ is happy}) \vee -(x \text{ is happy})]$). In this case, the answer is of course "Everything is unhappy." And the last point is "Everything is either substantial or not substantial" (i.e. (x) $[(x \text{ is substantial}) \vee -(x \text{ is substantial})]$). The answer is "Everything is not substantial." Such a style of argument is one of the characteristics of the *Nikāyas* and *Āgamas*. In this case, if we replace "permanent" with P, "happy" with H, "substantial" with S, the above argument could be schematized as follows:

(x) Px or $(x) - Px$?
(x) $-Px$*
(x) $(-Px \supset Hx)$ or (x) $(-Px \supset -Hx)$?
(x) $(-Px \supset -Hx)$*
(x) $(-Px.-Hx \supset Sx)$ or (x) $(-Px.-Hx \supset -Sx)$?
(x) $(-Px.-Hx \supset -Sx)$*

Hence, $(x) - Sx$

According to the history of western logic, the Stoics, chiefly Chrysippus (280-209 B.C.), developed a logic of hypothetical and alternative arguments. And the logic called "traditional logic" includes Aristotle's analysis of propositions, his treatment of immediate inference, and especially, his theory of the categorical syllogism, as well as the Stoics' analysis of hypothetical and alternative syllogisms with related types of arguments. On the other hand, in early Buddhism we cannot see such definite classifications as in the history of western logic mentioned above. However, it must be noted that the forms of argument of the early Buddhist are characterized by hypothetical and alternative statements rather than categorical statements. Let us introduce from the *Nikāyas* another example which is composed of alternative judgements:[1]

1. M. I, 500, D. II, 66, T. 1, 61 c, 2, 249 c, etc.

There are three feelings, Aggivessana: (1) happy feeling, (2) unhappy feeling, and (3) feeling that is neither unhappy nor happy. Aggivessana, whenever one feels item 1, one feels neither item 2 nor item 3. Whenever one feels item 2, one feels neither item 1 nor item 3. Whenever one feels item 3, one feels neither item 1 nor item 2. The three feelings, Aggivessana, are impermanent, synthesized (*sankhata*), generated by the law of causation (*paṭiccasamuppanna*), having the principle of destruction (*khayadhamma*), having the principle of decay (*vayadhamma*), having the principle of dispassion (*virāgadhamma*), having the principle of cessation (*nirodhadhamma*).

From the standpoint of Buddhism, there are two classes of people, namely: one whose members are ignorant, and whose members do not understand the fourfold truth (and therefore, feel either happiness or unhappiness), and one whose members have understood the fourfold truth (*arahant*: perfected one), or whose members have attained to the ideal state of emotional habits (and therefore, feel neither-happiness-nor-unhappiness). But, unless we discriminate between the two, the above expression would be "All men feel either happiness or unhappiness or neither-happiness-nor-unhappiness." (On this schematization, see chapter **5.5**.)

9.9 We cannot deny the fact that the forms of argument expressed by alternative judgement exerted a great influence on the development of *Abhidhamma* philosophy. For instance, all *dhammas* (principles) in the early *Abhidhamma*, especially the *Dhammasaṅgaṇi*, were systematized according to the criteria of *kusala* (good) *akusala* (bad) and *avyākata* (neither-good-nor-bad). Such criteria cannot be seen in the *Nikāyas* and *Āgamas*. The noteworthy point here is that what the word '*akusala*' means is not always equivalent to that which is expressed by the negative of *kusala*, namely: *a-kusala*, not good, although the word '*a-kusala*' is philologically contradictory to *kusala*. In other words, because *a-kusala* is not a member of the *Mātikas* consisting of couplets (*dukas*), but of the *Mātikas* consisting of triplets (*tikas*), it should be regarded as having the meaning of 'bad' which is contrary to 'good' (*kusala*). We must also realize that the usage of *avyākata* in the *Nikāyas* and *Āgamas* is not the same as that of *avyākata*, one of the *tika-mātikā*, in the *Dhammasaṅgaṇī*. As we have already pointed out (see chapter **6.11** and chapter **7.2**), the Buddha did not give any answer on metaphysical questions in some cases, because these were regarded as that which should be waived or undetermined (*avyākata*). Therefore, in the *Nikāyas* the chapter dealing with metaphysical subjects is named *avyākata-saṁyutta*[1] or *avyākata-vagga*.[2] On the other hand, the word '*avyākata*' in the *Dhammasaṅgaṇī* is used in the meaning of "neither-good-nor-bad." To illustrate this, we can take the expression "The root of one's mind is either good or bad or neither-good-nor-bad." (On this schematization, see chapter **5.5**.)

Also, in one of the *Abhidhamma* texts, the *Yamaka*, we see an enormous number of pairs of questions formalized by alternative statements and see the answers to these questions which are given throughout. The main purpose of these exercises is, as pointed out by A. K. Warder,[3] to prepare Buddhists against the logical traps inherent in conversion. In fact, we are inclined to say that such exercises had been already conducted in early Buddhism, and afterwards were transmitted to *Abhidhamma* Buddhism by setting them in array systematically.

9.10 In considering the explanations above, we might make the following points as the conclusions which we have reached:

1. The methods of Sañjaya's answer must have influenced more or less the early Buddhists. The reason for this is that in a sense the four kinds of possible answer coming out in the *Nikāyas* are similar to Sañjaya's answers.

2. This can be also demonstrated from the fact that the way of thinking of the early Buddhists was mainly based on the principle of contradiction. From a logical point of view the principle of identity is equivalent to that of contradiction; however, it seems that the early Buddhists avoided the expression

---

1. S. IV, 374-403. In the Chinese text, there is no chapter corresponding to "*avyākata-saṁyutta*."

2. A. IV, 67-98. In the Chinese text, there is no chapter corresponding to "*avyākata-vagga*."

3. *Outline of Indian Philosophy*, p. 93.

of emphatic affirmatives; rather, they tried to give the expression lacking positive affirmatives by the practical use of double negative (see chapter **9.4**).

3. From the above, we are inclined to think that the forms of argument in the *Nikāyas* were built up, i.e. the forms of argument characterized by a sorites, being cast into the form of a sequence of hypothetical statements. This point can also be understood from the fact that the Buddha admonished his disciples not to say "This alone is the truth, any other view is false" (*idam eva saccaṃ mogham aññaṃ*)—e.g. M.II, 171, A.V, 193, T.2, 245 c, etc.

4. In addition, as one of the styles of argument in the *Nikāyas* and *Āgamas*, we see a form of argument expressed by alternative judgements. Such a style of argument must have been important in discussing with non-Buddhists to decide which doctrine is proper to Buddhism, and also must have been useful in arranging many doctrinal topics (*mātikās*) in Buddhism.

5. The tendency of item 3 was especially accepted in the *Kathāvatthu*, in which a strictly formalized system of debate, in particular hypothetical syllogisms, came to be developed.

6. The tendency of item 4 was in course of time accepted in the *Dhammasaṅgaṇi* and the *Yamaka*. Above all, in the latter an enormous number of pairs of questions came to be formalized by alternative propositions.

10

LOGICAL ARGUMENTS IN THE DIALOGUES (*SUTTAS*)

10.1. On the basis of what we have learned in chapter 9, we would like to examine a few *suttas* (dialogues) and to derive argument forms from them as clearly as possible.

10.2. Let us start with the *Kalahavivādasutta* of the *Suttanipāta*, which deals with the origin of contentions, disputes, etc.[1] In the *sutta* the following subjects are treated:

1. Contentions (*kalahas*).
2. Disputes (*vivādas*).
3. Lamentation (*parideva*).
4. Griefs (*sokas*).
5. Stinginess (*macchara*).
6. Pride (*māna*).
7. Conceit (*atimāna*).
8. Slander (*pesuṇa*).
9. Dear things (*piyas*).
10. Greed (*lobha*).
11. Hope (*āsā*)
12. Fulfilment (*niṭṭhā*).
13. Will (*chanda*).
14. Decision (*vinicchaya*).
15. Anger (*kodha*).

---

1. See T. 4, 181 b-c.

16. Falsity (*mosavajja*).
17. Uncertainty (*kathaṃkathā*).
18. Principles declared by the recluse (*dhammā samaṇena vuttā*).
19. The pleasant (*sāta*).
20. The unpleasant (*asāta*).
21. Existence (*bhava* of items 19 and 20).
22. Non-existence (*vibhava* of both items 19 and 20).
23. Contact (*phassa*).
24. Possessing (*pariggaha*).
25. Selfishness (*mamatta*).
26. A sentient body (*nāma-rūpa*).
27. Wish (*icchā*).

The *sutta* states as follows:

From whence arise contentions, disputes, lamentation, griefs,
stinginess, pride, conceit and slander?
Whence arise these? Please tell me that. (862)
From dear things arise the above eight,
Contentions and disputes are connected with stinginess;
And slander is born amid disputes. (863)
From whence arises dear things in the world,
And arises greed in the world?
From whence arise hope and fulfilment
Which bring man to the next world? (864)
Dear things and greed are caused by will.
From that arise hope and fulfilment. (865)
From whence arise will and a decision in the world?
From whence arise anger, falsity, uncertainty and principles declared by the recluse? (866)
The pleasant and the unpleasant, says the world;
From such conditions arises will.
Man sees existence and non-existence in matter;
And shapes a decision about the world. (867)
Anger, falsity and uncertainty,
Principles arise when the state of the pleasant and the unpleasant exist.
Let a man who depends on uncertainty train in the path of knowledge.
Principles by the recluse are taught—he knows. (868)

From whence arise the pleasant and the unpleasant ?
What being absent, causes these not to be ?
Tell me the meaning of existence and non-existence
And from what reason the pleasant and the unpleasant arise. (869)

The pleasant and the unpleasant are caused by contact;
Contact being absent, causes these not to be.
I tell you the meaning and the reason of existence and non-existence. (870)

From whence arises contact in the world ?
And from whence arises possessing ?
What being absent, causes selfishness not to be ?
What being absent, do contacts no longer exist ? (871)
Contact exists because of a sentient body;
Possessing is caused by wish,
When wish is absent, selfishness is not;
When a sentient body decays, contacts no longer exist. (872)
What state is his so matter decays for him ?
How indeed do happiness and unhappiness decay ?
Please tell me as to the decay.
I would like to know—this ever is my thought. (873)
When there is no perceiving of perceptions.
Nor not perceiving of perceptions,
And there is still no not-perceiving then,
Nor has perceiving ceased.
When thus his state, then matter decays for him.
From perceptions arise signs of obsession. (874)
You have declared to us all that we asked;
But one thing more we ask; please tell us this:
Say not some wise men that the highest thing
Is e'en the cleansing of (human) beings there ?
Or say they there is something after that ? (875)
Some wise men declare the highest thing
To be the cleansing of (human) beings here;
Again, some experts on 'the unattached
Where naught remains' say it's to pass away. (876)
The silent sage knows such as trusting still,
He studies and knows where they put their trust;

Knowing, released, the wise seeks no dispute,
Seeks not about becoming this or that. (877)

The above is based on analytical questions and answers (*vibhajja-pañhabyākaraṇa*). What we must note first concerning this *sutta* is the explanations of Nos. 869 and 870, in which we see the expression : "What being absent, causes these not to be ?" (i.e. items 19 and 20, *kismiṃ asante na bhavanti hi ete*), "Contact being absent, causes these not to be" (*phasse asante na bhavanti hi ete*) and the like. This is indicative of the close relationship between the antecedent (i.e. "What being absent ?" or "Contact being absent") and the consequent (i.e. "causes these not to be"). In other words, the statement has something in common with the negative formula expressing hypothetical judgement : "This not being, this is not; from the cessation of this, this ceases" (from the standpoint of *bhava*, this becomes the formula affirmative : "This being, this is; from the arising of this, this arises"). So, if by convention we use the letters p and q, the statement above and the formula negative can be viewed as the form (or schema) $-p \supset -q$, which is called the reverse of $p \supset q$. In this connection, $q \supset p$ is called converse and $-q \supset -p$ is called contraposition. The form $p \supset q$ is equivalent to $-q \supset -p$, but not equivalent to $-p \supset -q$ and $q \supset p$.

As we have learned already, a sorites which is composed of hypothetical judgements is one of the characteristics in the *Nikāyas* and *Āgamas*. To the same effect, the *sutta* mentioned above must be also viewed as such a sorites.

10.3. In order to understand the whole of the *sutta* with ease, let us make the following table:[1]

A. Items 26, 27
↓ ↓
B. Items 23, 24, (25)
↓
C. Items 19, 20 21, 22
↓ ↓
D. Items 13, 15, 16, 17, 18, 14

1. For the sake of brevity, numbers are used instead of words. For meaning see the beginning of chapter **10.2**.

↓
E. Items 9, 10, 11, 12

↓
F. Items 1, 2, 3, 4, 5, 6, 7, 8 (1, 2 R 5. 2 R 8)

From the table, we can see without fail section *A* is related to section *B*, *B* is related to *C*, . . .and *E* is related to section *F*. We could call such a relation "a direct relation." At the same time, we cannot overlook that which is called an indirect relation. That is : section *A* is related indirectly to *C*, *D*, *E* and *F*, whilst *A* is related directly to *B*. In other words, each section is related to every other section both directly and indirectly. Concerning this, we can make up the following diagram:

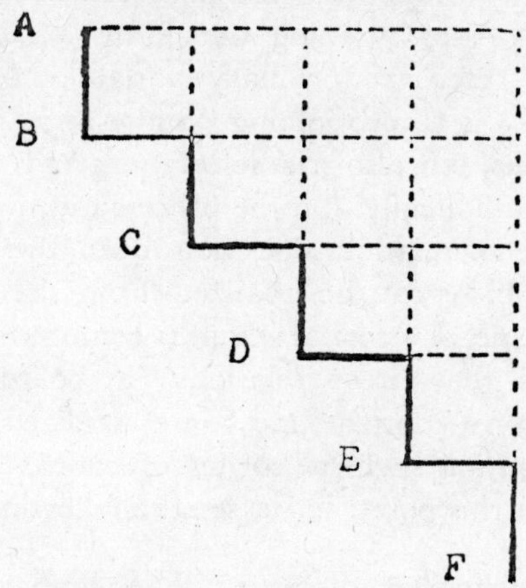

A bold-faced line indicates a direct relation, and dotted lines vertical and horizontal indicate indirect relations. The teachings which the Buddha preached in regard to a sorites being composed of hypothetical judgements can be, we would say, clarified only by understanding clearly the direct and indirect relations. This can be realized from the fact that the Buddha made use of the words *dhammacakkhu* and *yathābhūtaṃ* in the explanation of his doctrine. The former means 'the eye of truth', and the latter, 'as it really is' or 'in its true nature'. If one understands only the direct relation indicated by a bold-faced line, one has just the divine eye (*dibba-cakkhu*, e.g. see D. I, 82). On the other hand, if one understands the direct relation and at the same time understands indirect relations, one has the eye of truth and can see everything as it really is. In the same way, we would say that to realize truly the dependent origination which is a central concept in Buddhism is in fact to realize systematically the fact that all principles (or phenomena) are composed of involved relations. In this respect, the twelve (or nine) *paṭiccasamuppādas* are the most representative of the real logic of relations, because they make clear the relationships between the origination and the cessation of unhappiness.

The logic of relations in modern logic is complicated. For example, in dyadic relations, to say that x bears the relation R to y, or in other words that the pair of x and y belongs to R, we write 'xRy'. Also, by using the forms '$x \in \alpha$' and '$y \in \beta$' and the like (x, y, etc. are ordinary variables, α, β, etc. are class variables and $\in$ is a verb joining x and α or y and β), not only dyadic relations, but also triadic relations and tetradic relations are treated symbolically. On the other hand, what we call here the real logic of relations does not mean the logic of relations in modern logic. As can be realized from the diagram above, the characteristic of a sorites which is composed of hypothetical judgements is that direct relations (a bold-faced line) and indirect relations (dotted lines) are realized simultaneously. The realization of such a sorites of course depends on the individual. On this point, let us see the following illustration:[1]

> To him who has discerned the elimination of the five obstacles (*nīvaraṇas*), a great delight (*pāmujja*) arises; to him who is greatly delighted, joy (*pīti*) arises; to him who is joyous, the body becomes tranquil; to him who has a tranquil-body, happiness arises; to him who feels happy, his thought (*citta*) comes to one-pointedness (*samādhiyati*).

This can be expressed by the "if. . .then. . ." form, i.e. "if one eliminates the five obstacles, then a great delight arises," and "if one feels happy, then one's thought comes to one-pointed-

---

1. D. I, 182, T. 1, 110 a.

ness." If using the letters p, q, r, s, etc. to symbolize the statements, and replacing section A of the diagram with p, section B of it with q, section C of it with r, etc., we can see that p is related directly to q, and at the same time p is related indirectly to r and so forth. From such relations, it is possible to derive at least a mixed hypothetical syllogism and a pure hypothetical syllogism. In this case, the direct relation between p and q, or the direct relation of p, q and r always becomes a premiss (or premisses), and the indirect relations of them can be regarded as the conclusion.

10.4. Now, by using diagrams, let us demonstrate the above fact. A mixed hypothetical syllogism is a syllogism in which one premiss is hypothetical and the other asserts or denies one of the components of the first. So a mixed hypothetical syllogism affirmative (traditionally, called *modus ponens*) is one of the most pervasive of all valid argument forms: $p \supset q$, p, hence, q. A mixed hypothetical syllogism negative (traditionally, called *modus tollens*) means that if the consequent of a true hypothetical is found false, then the antecedent must be false also : $p \cup q$, $-q$, hence, $-p$. In a mixed hypothetical syllogism affirmative, the following diagram could be drawn :

Diagram A :

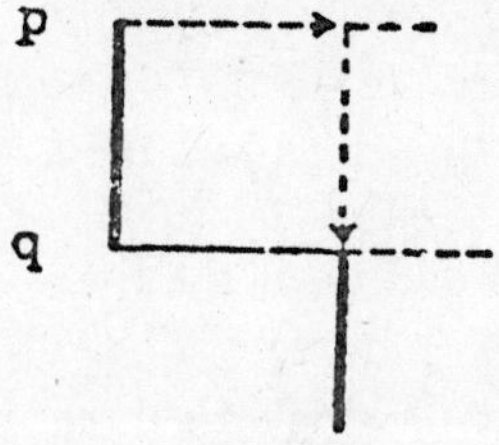

$p \supset q$ (shown by a bold-faced line, because it can be regarded as the "if ... then. . ." form on the basis of a sorites being indicative hypothetical judgement.)

p (a point of intersection between dotted lines horizontal and vertical.)[1]

Hence, q (a point of intersection between a dotted line vertical and a bold-faced horizontal.)

A noteworthy point here is that the direction of the arrow is always as shown if the conclusion is affirmative and true, because

1. The direction of the arrow means that r can be obtained from p without specifying q, s can be obtained from p without specifying q and r, and so forth.

the following form is invalid logically: $p \supset q$, q, hence, p. In this connection, we must know that the form $p \supset q$, $-p$, hence, $-q$ is also invalid. We have, however, learned that the form $p \supset q$, $-q$, hence, $-p$ is valid. In such a case we could view it by making a diagram as follows:

The left side means that any conclusion is always negative and true.

The right side means that any conclusion is always affirmative and true.

Diagram B :

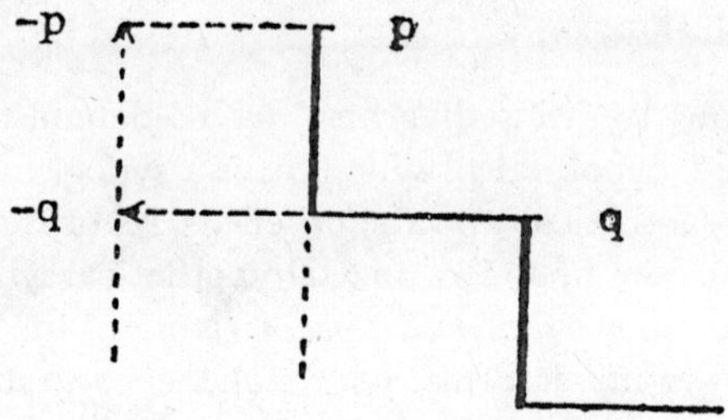

In case the conclusion is negative and true, the direction of the arrow always comes up.

According to the logic of propositions, the form $p \supset q$ becomes:

$$(p \supset q) \overset{1}{\equiv} (-q \supset -p) \overset{2}{\equiv} (-p \vee q) \overset{3}{\equiv} -(p . -q)$$

And from the above, we see the following syllogisms:

1. $-q \supset -p$, p, hence, q
2. $-p \vee q$, p, hence, q
3. $-(p . -q)$, p, hence, q

But it is unlikely that such syllogisms are found until the time of *Abhidhamma* Buddhism.

Pure hypothetical syllogisms are arguments in which all three propositions are hypotheticals. On this we could draw the following diagram :

Diagram C:

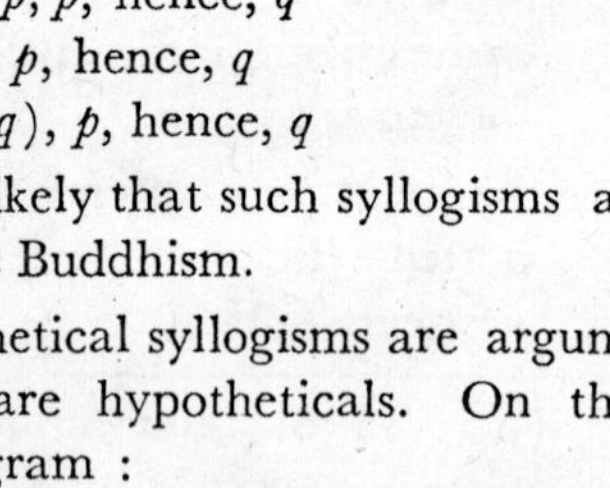

$p \supset q$

$q \supset r$

Hence, $p \supset r$

In the same way as diagram *A*, the direction of the arrow must always come down; if it does not, the conclusion will be, even though affirmative, false. For instance, the following forms are invalid :

1. $p \supset q$, $r \supset q$, hence, $p \supset r$
2. $\underline{q \supset p}$, $q \supset r$, hence, $p \supset r$
3. $\underline{q \supset p}$, $\underline{r \supset q}$, hence, $p \supset r$

In such syllogisms, underlined forms do not serve as obtaining a valid syllogism with the conclusion $p \supset r$, so that each conclusion could become false without inconsistency. From a logical point of view, the pure hypothetical syllogism $p \supset q$, $q \supset r$, hence, $p \supset r$ can be proved valid, because the following is regarded as a truth-functionally valid proposition:[1]

$$[(p \supset q) \cdot (q \supset r)] \supset (p \supset r)$$

This is called the principle of transitivity of implication.

In connection with the most basic valid form of pure hypothetical syllogism mentioned above, it would be possible to enumerate additional forms of pure hypotheticals if we allow each proposition to appear either affirmed or denied, and of these some, like the following, will be valid :

1. $p \supset q$, $r \supset -q$, hence, $p \supset -r$
2. $q \supset r$, $-q \supset p$, hence, $-p \supset r$
3. $q \supset p$, $r \supset q$, hence, $-p \supset -r$

But we must note that most additional forms of pure hypothetical syllogisms, in any exhaustive enumeration, will be invalid. It is therefore said that, in any case, traditional logic dealt chiefly with the first valid form (which is indicated by diagram *C*) ; it remained for mathematical logicians to provide a theory which would systematically account for all possibilities.[2] This can be also applied without modification in examining statements of the *Nikāyas* as well as of *Abhidhamma* texts.

---

1. Truth-functionally valid proposition is called tautology, and truth-functional equivalence and implication is called tautologous equivalence and implication. On this, see W. V. Quine, *Elementary Logic*, p. 35.

2. R. B. Angell, *Reasoning and Logic*, p. 148.

Moreover, from a sorites which consists of direct and indirect relations, the forms such as $p.q \supset r$, $p.q.r \supset s$ and the like can be obtained. These forms are composed of a compound proposition (refer to chapter **9.6**). But it must be noted that the form $p.q \supset r$ is equivalent to the form $p \supset (q \supset r)$, namely:

$$(p.q \supset r) \equiv [p \supset (q \supset r)]$$

This is the tautology called the principle of exportation. Similarly we can make the following form:

$$(p.q.r \supset s) \equiv [p \supset (q \supset (r \supset s))]$$

On the whole, we would say that in a sorites composed of hypothetical judgements various forms of argument are involved, insofar as such a sorites is called the real logic of relations.

10.5 We have already learned that the *Kalahavivādasutta* of the *Suttanipāta* has many subjects of some interest. In the *Mahānidānasutta*, subjects in common with those in the *Kalahavivādasutta* are treated, such as 'decision' (*vinicchaya*), 'will' (*chanda*), 'possessing' (*pariggaha*), 'contention' (*kalaha*), 'dispute' (*vivāda*), 'slander' (*pesuñña*), etc.[1] The arrangement of these subjects on the whole is dealt with at random, as compared with that in the *Kalahavivādasutta*. Here let us pay attention once more to No. 872 of the *Kalahavivādasutta*:

> Item 23 (contact) exists because of item 26 (a sentient body),
> Item 24 (possessing) is caused by item 27 (wish),
> When item 27 is absent, item 25 (selfishness) is not;
> When item 26 decays, contacts no longer exist.

Exclusive of items 26 and 23, the relationship of items 27, 25 and 24 is worth noticing. The statement "Item 24 is caused by item 27" can be expressed in the form $p \supset q$, and the statement "When item 27 is absent, item 25 it not" can be expressed in the form $-p \supset -r$ which is equivalent to the form $r \supset p$. From

1. D. II, 58-9. We see four Chinese recensions of the *Mahānidānasutta*, in which parallel subjects are treated. These may be compared with a great interest : "大縁方便経" (T. 1, 60 c), "人本欲生経" (T. 1, 242 b), "佛説大生義経" (T. 1, 884 c) and "大因経" (T. 2, 579 a).

the above we see the form $r \supset q$. Therefore, the arrangement of the three items neither becomes:

Wish⟶ Possessing ⟶ Selfishness,

nor becomes:

Wish⟶ Selfishness⟶ Possessing,

but becomes:

Selfishness (25) ⟶ Wish (27) ⟶ Possessing (24)

This arrangement is, however, not always invariable. In another context of the *Suttanipāta*, we see the following expression:

Metagū: From whence arise these various kinds of unhappiness which are so varied in the world? (1049)
Buddha: They are caused by attachments (*upādhis*)
Which are so varied in the world. (1050)

From this we see the arrangement:

Attachment ⟶ Unhappiness

According to the *Mahāniddesa*, wish is called thirst (*icchā vuccati taṇhā*), and thirst (*taṇhā*, which could be used as meaning 'desire', 'craving', 'thirst') is almost regarded as the synonym for attachment.[1] Therefore, the following arrangement would be possible:

Selfishness ⟶ Attachment ⟶ Unhappiness

And in another context of the *Suttanipāta*, the following expression can be seen:

Ajita: Covered by what is the world? (1032)
Buddha: Covered by ignorance (*avijjā*) is the world. (1033)

Furthermore, the Buddha explains:

One who is ignorant forms attachment,
And meets unhappiness again. (1051)

Therefore, we see here another arrangement:

Ignorance ⟶ Attachment ⟶ Unhappiness.

1. Nd1. p. 276.

The examination of such arrangements is of importance not only from a logical point of view, but also in the sense of bringing light on the development of the sequence of dependent origination.

When we turn our eyes to Nos. 873 and 874 of the *Suttanipāta* with item 26 (a sentient body) and item 23 (contact), we can learn that there is the indication that item 26 is caused by perception (*saññā*). Accordingly, the following arrangement can be seen:

Perception ⟶ Sentient body ⟶ Contact.

But in another place, the Buddha explains to Ajita about the cessation of a sentient body:

A. : Understanding (*paññā*), self-possession (*sati*) and a sentient body (*nāma-rūpa*), in what case do these things cease (*uparujjhati*)? (1036)

B. : When there is the cessation (*nirodha*) of consciousness (*viññāṇa*), these things cease. (1037)

From this we see that a sentient body is caused by consciousness:

Consciousness ⟶ Sentient body ⟶ Contact.

The arrangement is that which can be seen in the twelve (or nine) *paṭiccasamuppādas*. In this connection, there is a certain problem to be discussed in detail. That is, in spite of the fact that the Buddha claimed non-ego (or non-soul, *anattan*), not only non-Buddhists, but also some of the Buddha's disciples maintained that "sensation is my self" (*vedanā me attā*),[1] "perception is the soul of a man" (*saññā purisassa attā*),[2] "this consciousness passes on, transmigrates, not another" (*idam viññāṇaṃ sandhāvati saṁsarate, anaññaṁ*)[3] and so on.[4] It goes without saying that the doctrinal topic *anattan* occupies an important position throughout the whole of Buddhism. In the period of *Abhidhamma* Buddhism, the *Kathāvatthu* and the *Vijñānakāya* set

1. D. II, 66, T. 1, 61 c.
2. D. I, 180, T. 1, 110 c.
3. M. I, 256, T. 1, 766 c.
4. As to the collection of *suttas* in the *Nikāyas* which deal with "ego," see H. Saddhatissa, *Upāsakajanālaṅkāra*, pp. 19, 20, 25, 26, etc.

down the chapter of *puggalakathā* (discussion of the 'person') as one of the controversial topics, in which heated discussions on *attan* and *anattan* are recorded. We have referred briefly to *anattan* in connection with *anicca* and *dukkha* in early Buddhism (see chapter **9.6**). But it is necessary here to examine a certain *sutta* and to clarify the forms of argument in early Buddhism. So let us scrutinize the *Mahātaṇhāsaṅkhayasutta* (Greater Discourse on the Ending of Desire).[1]

10.6. In a word this *sutta* states that the Buddha refuted the heresy of a monk, Sāti by name, who thought that one and the same consciousness transmigrated, not another. But the most important thing is examining the *sutta* in how the Buddha refuted the heresy of Sāti. As we shall see later, the method of the Buddha's refutation is quite logical. We would say that "to be logical" means that what was firmly established by the Buddha is critical, reasonable and scientific.

Sāti's view is :

> Insofar as I understand *dhamma* taught by the Buddha, it is that this consciousness passes on, transmigrates, not another. The reason for this is that the person who speaks (*vado*),[2] the person who knows and feels (*vedeyyo*), experiences the result of good and bad *karmans* (actions).[3]

On the other hand, the Buddha's view is :

> I indeed stated in various ways that consciousness arises from a cause : There is no arising (*sambhava*) of consciousness without a cause (*aññatra paccayā n'atthi viññāṇassa sambhavo ti*).

And the proof of the above is established, then is followed by taking an example.

The proof is :

> Whatever consciousness arises due to a cause, it is identified (*saṅkhaṁ gacchati*) by that name :

1. M. I, 256-71, T. 1, 766 b-770 a.
2. On this, see MA. I, 71, II, 305.
3. We see the same expression in M. I, 8, T. 1, 432 a, 813 b, 2, 740 c, etc.

1. Conditioned by eye and sights (or visible objects), arises consciousness. It is identified by 'eye-consciousness' (*cakkhuviññāṇa*);

2. Conditioned by ear and sounds, arises consciousness. It is identified by 'ear-consciousness' (*sotaviññāṇa*);

3. Conditioned by nose and odours, arises consciousness. It is identified by 'nose-consciousness' (*ghānaviññāṇa*);

4. Conditioned by tongue and tastes, arises consciousness. It is identified by 'tongue-consciousness' (*jivhāviññāṇa*);

5. Conditioned by body and tangible objects (*phoṭṭhabba*), arises consciousness. It is identified by 'body-consciousness' (*kāyaviññāṇa*);

6. Conditioned by mind and principles (*dhammas*), arises consciousness. It is identified by 'mind-consciousness' (*manoviññāṇa*).

And the example given is in the form of an analogy:

Just as (*seyyathā*) whenever fire burns due to a cause, it is identified by that name:

1. Conditioned by sticks, burns fire. It is identified by 'stick-fire' (*kaṭṭhaggi*);

2. Conditioned by chips, burns fire. It is identified by 'chip-fire' (*sakalikaggi*);

3. Conditioned by grass, burns fire. It is identified by 'grass-fire' (*tiṇaggi*);

4. Conditioned by cow-dung, burns fire. It is identified by 'cow-dung-fire' (*gomayaggi*);

5. Conditioned by chaff, burns fire. It is identified by 'chaff-fire' (*thusaggi*);

6. Conditioned by rubbish, burns fire. It is identified by 'rubbish-fire' (*saṅkāraggi*).

In the Chinese text we see only three kinds of statements, namely: items 2, 3 and 4 mentioned above (see T. 1,767 a).

From a logical point of view, analogy is a form of reasoning in which one thing is inferred to be similar to another thing in a certain respect, on the basis of the known similarity between the things in other respects. When one is trying to solve a problem for which no answer is deducible from logical considerations or available knowledge, it is sometimes helpful to look for suggestions in analogous situations in which similar problems of analysis are found. Especially in modern logic, analogies are used in inductive arguments, and although the consideration of analogies often leads investigators down wrong tracks, as well as successful ones, the investigation of appropriate analogies has an important role in the organon of good reasoning.[1]

On the other hand, an example called analogy which is found in the *Nikāyas* and *Āgamas* is, as mentioned in chapter **6.7** and **8**, always that which can be judged by general knowledge. In other words, a statement by analogy is only one way to help a listener (or listeners) understand an argument. Let us here compare item 1 in the proof mentioned before and item 1 in the statement by analogy. Both of them may be rephrased as follows to bring out their form :

	Statement of proof		*Analogy*
(A)	Conditioned by eye and sights, arises consciousness.	(a)	Conditioned by sticks, burns fire.
(B)	It is identified by eye-consciousness.	(b)	It is identified by stick-fire.

We see from the above that the small letter (*a*) analogously suggests the situation of the capital letter (*A*), the small letter (*b*) analogously suggests the situation of the capital letter (*B*) ; consequently, the small letters (*a*) and (*b*) analogously suggest the situation of the capital letters (*A*) and (*B*), as mentioned in chapter **6.8**. Thus the form of the statements would be :

A — a
B — b

Hence, B/A — b/a

The form B/A — b/a means that the capital letter (*B*) based on the letter (*A*) is similar to the small letter (*b*) based on the letter (*a*). In other words, the small letters (*a*) and (*b*) are

---

1. On this, see R. B. Angell, *Reasoning and Logic*, p. 296.

important ways to help a listener understand that the capital letters (A) and (B) are reasonable. We would say that an analogy which agrees with the statement of proof (or argumentation) is in a sense an analogy based on the method of agreement.

After the argument by analogy, the Buddha continues by explaining to Sāti four kinds of nutriment (*āhāra*), which either maintain living beings or help those seeking birth, and refutes the objection raised against him by Sāti.

10.7. Prior to introducing the Buddha's further refutation, we would like here to clarify to a certain extent how the Buddha and his disciples argued and concluded by giving the following verse:[1]

Māra: Who made this (human) being (*bimbaṃ*) ?[2]
Where is the maker of the human being ?
From whence has it come to be (*samuppanna*) ?
Where will it cease (*nirujjhati*) ?

Selā : Neither self-made (*attakata*) the (human) being is,
Nor other-made (*parakata*) it is.
Because of a cause (*hetu*), it has arisen (*sambhūta*),
By the dissolution (*bhaṅga*) of the cause, it will cease.
Just as a certain seed sown in the field
Grows by depending on both the taste of earth and moisture (*sineha*).
Thus the (five) groups, elements (*dhātus*)
And these six spheres of the senses (*āyatanas*)
Have arisen because of a cause,
And will cease by the dissolution of the cause.

The word *māra* imports 'Death' that is regarded as a temptation or *kilesas* (defilements) disturbing one's mind, so that Māra's questions above can be considered to be the suspicion which occurred to a nun, Selā by name. Now, we can see that Selā's argumentation is composed of four steps. The first two paragraphs are propositions which deny Māra's questions. This may

1. S. I, 134, T. 1, 327 c.
2. The word *bimbaṃ* is applied to the individual being (*attabhāva*). Refer to *The Kindred Sayings*, vol. 1, p. 168.

be called the first argument. The third and fourth paragraphs are propositions that Selā supports to reach a conclusion. This may be called the second argument (or premiss). The fifth and sixth paragraphs are statements by example (or simile). The last four paragraphs are regarded as a conclusion. Selā's argumentation seems to be inductive, because, by stating that one of the five *khandhas* (which are represented by *sabba*) exists because of a cause, it is stated in the conclusion that the five *khandhas* exist because of a cause. Thus we see:

Matter, *rūpa*, exists because of a cause.	*M/c*
(Sensation, *vedanā*, exists because of a cause).	(*S/c*)
(Perception, *saññā*, exists because of a cause).	(*P/c*)
(Forces, *saṅkhāra*, exists because of a cause).	(*F/c*)
(Consciousness, *viññāṇa*, exists because of a cause).	(*C/c*)

Hence, everything exists because of a cause. Hence, (*x*) (*x/c*)

This is, however, not always a consistent argumentation in the *Nikāyas*. We also see the fact that the five *khandhas* or the six *āyatanas* are explained by deductive reasoning, for example :[1]

> The Buddha said to his monks : Everything, monks, is on fire (*sabbaṃ bhikkhave ādittaṃ*). What everything is on fire ? The eye is on fire, visible object (*rūpa*) is on fire, eye-consciousness is on fire, eye-contact (*cakkhusamphassa*) is on fire, that which arises due to eye-contact, namely : feeling, either happiness or unhappiness or neither-happiness-nor-unhappiness, is also on fire.

What is metaphorically called fire is said to be the fire of greed, of aversion, of delusion, of old age and death, of grief, lamentation, pain, depression and misery. In the above, "everything" means not only eye, but also the other five spheres of the senses. It is, therefore, possible to explain deductively as follows:

Everything is on fire.	(x) (x is on fire)
Eye is on fire.	E is on fire.
Ear is on fire.	Ea is on fire.

1. S. VI, 19.

Nose is on fire.	N is on fire.
Tongue is on fire.	T is on fire.
Body is on fire.	B is on fire.
Hence, mind is on fire.	Hence, M is on fire.

But what we want to emphasize here is that in any argumentation appearing in the *Nikāyas* an example is always indicated. Especially, an example in the form of analogy does not appear to be felt as a weak form of argument. It is also, as pointed out by A. K. Warder,[1] undoubtedly effective for propaganda purposes. But we see no distinction actually recognized between analogy and strict inference, although in some dialogues analogy is apparently advanced as actual proof, as we have seen in chapter **6.8**. But we would say that the Buddha's and his disciples' line of argument is in a sense loose and informal.

We have already discussed the Buddha's first argument and example in the *Mahātaṇhāsaṅkhayasutta*. But we see his more logical refutation in this *sutta*. So we would like to examine it and to derive argument forms from it.

10.8 The Buddha points out that there are four kinds of nutriment as follows:[2]

1. *Kabaḷiṅkārāhāra*: bodily nutriment, either *oḷārika* 'gross', 'solid' or *sukhuma* 'fine', 'minute'.
2. *Phassāhāra* : nutriment of contact.
3. *Manosañcetanāhāra*: nutriment of volition of the mind.
4. *Viññāṇāhāra* : nutriment of consciousness.

Then he asks the following points of his disciples including Sāti:

(I)

1. Do you see, monks, that this has come to be? (*Bhūtam idan ti bhikhave passathāti.*) (Ans. : Yes, Sir.)
2. Do you see that this is arising from nutriment? (*Tadāhārasambhavam ti bhikkhave passathāti.*) (Ans. : Yes, Sir.)
3. From the fact that this is the cessation of nutriment, do you see that what has come to be is having the principle of

1. "The Earliest Indian Logic," p. 57.
2. Also, see S. II, 11-2, T. 2, 101 c-102 a

cessation? (*Tadāhāranirodha yaṁ bhūtaṁ taṁ nirodhadhamman ti bhikkhave passathāti.*) (Ans. : Yes, Sir.)

(II)

1. From doubt (*kaṅkhā*), monks, does the uncertainty (*vicikicchā*) arise : This has come to be, might it not have? (Ans.: Yes, Sir.)
2. From doubt, does the uncertainty arise : This is arising from nutriment, might it not be? (Ans.: Yes, Sir.)
3. From doubt, does the uncertainty arise : What has come to be, from the cessation of nutriment, is having the principle of cessation, might it not be? (Ans.: Yes, Sir.)

(III)

1. By seeing as it really is by means of right understanding (*sammappaññā*), monks, that this has come to be, is an uncertainty renounced (*pahīyāti*)? (Ans. : Yes, Sir.)
2. By seeing as it really is by means of right understanding that this is arising from nutriment, is an uncertainty renounced? (Ans. : Yes, Sir.)
3. By seeing as it really is by means of right understanding that what has come to be, from the cessation of nutriment, is having the principle of cessation, is an uncertainty renounced? (Ans. : Yes, Sir.)

(IV)

1. For you, is there the absence of uncertainty : This has come to be? (Ans. : Yes, Sir.)
2. For you, is there the absence of uncertainty : This is arising from nutriment? (Ans. : Yes, Sir.)
3. For you, is there the absence of uncertainty : What has come to be, from the cessation of nutriment, is having the principle of cessation? (Ans. : Yes, Sir.)

(V)

1. This has come to be. Was this well seen by means of right understanding as it really is? (Ans. : Yes, Sir.)
2. This is arising from nutriment. Was this well seen by means of right understanding as it really is? (Ans.: Yes, Sir.)

3. What has come to be, from the cessation of nutriment, is having the principle of cessation. Was this well seen by means of right understanding as it really is? (Ans. : Yes, Sir.)

It seems that the five sections above elucidate how to realize accurately the relationship of "nutriment," "existence" and "cessation." The fifth section is as a matter of course the final stage to which all Buddhists must reach. In the Chinese text we cannot see the word corresponding to *āhāra*. Instead, we see the words '如来真說' (*tāthāgata*'s true words). A translator of this text must have regarded *āhāra* as *araha*. The word *araha* means 'to be worthy of'. In this sense, the translator presumably imagined the relationship between "worthy" and *tathāgata* (see T. 1,767 b-c).

Now, the relationship of nutriment, existence and cessation can be viewed as (1) "nutriment is the cause of existence" and (2) "existence is the cause of cessation." By using the initial letters N, E and C, the statements of nutriment, existence and cessation could be expressed by the universal quantificational schemata :

$$(x)\ (Nx \supset Ex) \text{ —— } (1)$$
$$(x)\ (Ex \supset Cx) \text{ —— } (2)$$

$$(x)\ (Nx \supset Cx) \text{ —— } (3)$$

The statement of item (3) is "nutriment is the cause of cessation."

It is clear that the Buddha tried logically to inform his disciples that as far as any one depends on nutriment and is having the principle of cessation, no one has soul (or ego). Rather than refer to the discussion on non-soul, let us give attention to the Buddha's further argument. He says:

The four kinds of nutriment have desire as source (*taṇhānidāna*), desire as origination (*taṇhāsamudaya*), desire as birth (*taṇhājātika*) and desire as provenance (*taṇhāpabhava*). The desire has sensation as source, ...sensation as provenance. The sensation has contact as source, ... contact as provenance. The contact has the six spheres of the senses as source, ... the six spheres of the senses as provenance.

> The six spheres of the senses have a sentient body as source, ... a sentient body as provenance. The sentient body has consciousness as source, . . . consciousness as provenance. The consciousness has forces as source . . . forces as provenance. The forces have ignorance as source,. . .ignorance as provenance.

And the twelve *paṭiccasamuppādas* in direct order (beginning its exposition at "ignorance") are mentioned. So we could make the above clearer as follows :

1. Ignorance	1. Ignorance
2. Forces	2. Forces
3. Consciousness	3. Consciousness
4. A sentient body	4. A sentient body
5. The six spheres of the senses	5. The six spheres of the senses
6. Contact	6. Contact
7. Sensation	7. Sensation
8. Desire	8. Desire
9. Nutriment. . . .	9. Attachment
. . . . .	10. Existence
	11. Birth
. . . . .	12. Old age and death

We can realize from the above that item 9 in the first column is related to items 10 and 12 (regarded as cessation) in the second column. In other words, it is pointed out that in the first column "nutriment" itself does not exist independently and that it is the direct cause of "existence" and the indirect cause of "cessation." Furthermore, we see the analytical explanations of the twelve *paṭiccasamuppādas*. For instance, concerning the relationship between birth and old age (also, death), the following explanation can be seen :

> It has been said: Conditioned by birth is old age and death. Conditioned by birth, monks, is there old age and death or is there not old age and death (*jātipaccayā nu kho bhikkhave jarāmaraṇaṁ no vā*), how is it as to this (*kathaṁ vā ettha hoti*)? Conditioned by birth, Sir, is old age and death.

Thus it is for us as to this: Conditioned by birth is old age and death.

In the same way, each *paccayākāra* (the aspect of condition) is analytically elucidated. The above explanation tempts us to try rephrasing into a mixed hypothetical syllogism (affirmative). If we use the letters p, q to symbolize the statements between the Buddha and monks.

B. : It is true that if there is birth, then there is old age and death. $p \supset q$

B. : Is it true that if there is birth, then there is old age and death or is it true that if there is birth, then there is not old age death? $(p \supset q)$? or $(p \supset -q)$?

M. : It is, Sir, true that if there is birth, then there is old age and death. $p \supset q$

M. : Thus it is for us as to this: It is true that if there is birth, then there is old age and death. $p \supset q$

The last words of monks are regarded as the repetition of the Buddha's first words. But we may be allowed to rephrase the last words into two separate statements:

It is true that there is birth. p
It is true that there is old age and death. q

Consequently, the Buddha's question and monks' answers become:

B. : $(p \supset q)$? or $(p \supset -q)$?
M. : $p \supset q$

At this point, it might be possible to think that from the above answer of monks to the Buddha's question and the two separate statements mentioned previously, the mixed hypothetical syllogism (affirmative): $p \supset q$, p, hence, q can be formed. In other words, the repetition of the Buddha's words by his disciples is in a fair way to develop as mixed hypothetical syllogisms and as pure hypothetical syllogisms. These arguments of the

Buddha and his disciples are characterized by the use of double negative, and by hypothetical and alternative judgements.

10.9 In connection with the above, we would like to introduce the following expression which is recorded as the Buddha's saying:[1]

1. Monks, renounce bad (*akusala*). It can be done. If it were impossible to renounce bad (*no ce taṃ sakkā abhavissa akusalaṃ pajahituṃ*), I would not say so (*nāham evaṃ vadeyyaṃ*). But since (*yasmā*) it can be done, therefore I say so (*tasmāhaṃ evaṃ vadāmi*).
2. If (*ca*) this renouncing of bad conduced to disadvantage (*ahita*) and unhappiness, I would not say "renounce bad." But since it conduces to advantage (*hita*) and happiness, therefore I say so.
3. Monks, cultivate good (*kusalaṃ bhikkhave bhāvetha*). It can be done. If it were impossible to cultivate good, I would not say so. But it can be done, therefore I say so.
4. If this cultivating of good conduced to disadvantage and unhappiness, I would not say "cultivate good." But since it conduces to advantage and happiness, therefore I say so.

This is expressed by the conditional (*kālātipatti*) tense, which appears regularly when a false or impossible hypothesis (in the view of a speaker, and usually of a hearer also) is stated. The above could be rephrased as follows:

It is good to renounce bad if it can be done (obvious).
If it could not be done it would be unreasonable to command it, but if it can be done it is reasonable.
It can be done.
Therefore, I command it.

We must note here that sections 1 and 2 above are not independent of each other, neither are sections 3 and 4. For section 2 (also section 4) gives a second consideration that would restrain the Buddha from his commandment. Therefore,

1. A. I, 58.

he is not arguing simply "It can be done, therefore I say so," but rather "It can be done, and it conduces to advantage and happiness, therefore I say so." In other words, each saying presupposes the assumption, "If nothing else interferes." While there is something like a mixed hypothetical syllogism in each of these, the reasoning is a good deal more elaborate than that.

In this context, we must note that every statement in the *Anumānasutta* is expressed by the term "*sace* (if) . . *tena* (then) . . ." It is recorded that this *sutta* was preached by Moggallāna, one of the chief disciples of the Buddha, and that there is no reference to the Buddha throughout the whole of the *sutta*. But since it deals with the admonishing of monks and with self-examination, sentence verbs of the consequent in hypothetical statements mostly have the suffix *tabba*, which is usually called the future passive participle. The sense of the future passive participle is generally not simply future but rather imperative or optative: "this must be done," "this should be done," "this ought to be done," also "this can be done."[1] Let us see one example in the *Anumānasutta*:[2]

> If, while a monk is reflecting (*paccavekkhamāna*), he knows thus: "I am one who is attached to this (mundane) life (*sandiṭṭhiparāmāsī*), who grasps it tightly (*ādhānagāhī*) and who cannot abstain from it (*duppaṭinissaggi*)," then the monks should strive (*vāyamitabba*: should be strived in the strict sense of the word) to get rid of (these) evil bad principles (*pāpakākusala-dhammas*).

By contrast, we see the simile of the above in which a sentence verb in the consequent has no suffix *tabba*:

> Just as a young woman or a young man who is desirous of ornaments reflects them in a mirror or in a bowl of water which is so clear, so pure that his appearance is reflected; if he sees dust of blemish there, he (will) strive (*vāyamati*) to get rid of it.

---

1. See A. K. Warder, *Introduction to Pāli*, p. 104.
2. M. I, 99-100.

It is clear that, among many disciples of the Buddha, some really understood a logical explanation of his teachings and some did not understand it. Therefore, as pointed out in the latter half of chapter **10.7**, "the Buddha's and his disciples' line of argument is in a sense loose and informal" involves the fact that the Buddha and his chief disciples avoided explaining Buddhist teachings logically under certain circumstances. A main point here is that the style of argument of the Buddha and his disciples is characterized specifically by using double negatives, and by hypothetical and alternative judgements. In other words, for the Buddha's disciples who clearly understood the real logic of relations in early Buddhism, it must have been not difficult to develop mixed hypothetical syllogisms, pure hypothetical syllogisms and the like.

10.10 Now, let us return to the *Mahāṭaṅhāsaṅkhayasutta*. After the explanation of the twelve *paṭiccasamuppādas* in reverse order, the Buddha states dialogically that if one really understands dependent origination, one does not have any suspicion of eternal existence, namely:

1. Now, monks, would you, knowing thus, seeing thus, run back to (*paṭidhāvati*) the past (*pubbanta*), thinking: Were we in the past (*atītam addhānaṁ*), were we not in the past, what were we in the past, how were we in the past; having been what, what did we become in the past ? (Ans. : No, Sir.)
2. Now, monks, would you, knowing thus, seeing thus, run forward to (*ādhāvati*) the future (*aparanta*), thinking : Will we come to be in the future (*anāgatam addhānaṁ*), will we not come to be in the future, what will we come to be in the future, how will we come to be in the future; having been what, what will we come to be in the future ? (Ans. : No, Sir.)
3. Now, monks, would you, knowing thus, seeing thus, come to be internally doubtful now about the present (*paccuppannam addhānaṁ*), thinking : Am I, am I not, what am I, how am I; from whence has this being come, where is it going ? (Ans. : No, Sir.)

Moreover, the Buddha asks several questions, then brings interrogations to a close with the following question :

> Do you not speak of that which of yourselves you have known (*ñāta*), seen (*diṭṭha*) and discerned (*vidita*) ? (Ans. : Yes, Sir.)

In the Chinese text, before the final question above, the Buddha asks many questions which do not correspond to the Pāli text, e.g. on the five *ānantarikakammas* 'actions (that find retribution) immediately' (namely, 1. killing one's father, 2. killing one's mother, 3. killing an *arahant*, 4. causing disunity in the Buddhist community and 5. injuring the body of a *buddha*), on breaking the Buddhistic precepts, and so on.[1] At any rate, "that which of yourselves you have known, seen and discerned" is as a matter of course indicative of the dependent origination which the Buddha has explained before in this *sutta*.

To the Buddha's questions, answering by saying "Yes" or "No" is characteristic of dialogues in the *Nikāyas* and *Āgamas*. This is very important in the sense of preparing his disciples against the logical traps inherent in conversion (see chapter **5.10** and chapter **9.9**). For example.

1. Is all eye eye-sphere ('eye-sphere' is the sense of sight) ?
2. Is all eye-sphere eye ?

From the standpoint of Buddhism, the answer to the first question is "No," and the answer to the second question is "Yes". Such questions and answers can be seen especially one of the *Abhidhamma* texts, the *Yamaka*. But it can be readily said that these exercises were transmitted from early Buddhism to *Abhidhamma* Buddhism.

The *Mahātaṇhāsaṅkhayasutta* is concluded with the explanation of there being two classes of people in this world, namely : one whose members are ignorant, and whose members do not realize the origination of groups of unhappiness (*dukkhakkhandhasamudaya*) and the cessation of groups of unhappiness (*dukkhakkhandhanirodha*), and one whose members are learned, and whose members

1. T. 1, 769 a-b.

do realize both of them. In other words, what the Buddha means in any case is that for each condition something is the cause (*hetu*), the source (*nidāna*), the origination (*samudaya*) and the condition (*paccaya*) for each thing; if the condition did not occur, this thing would not happen. This is emphasized not only in the *Mahātaṇhāsaṅkhayasutta*, but also in any *sutta* in the *Nikāyas* and *Āgamas*.

10.11 Laying stress on the *Kalahavivādasutta* and the *Mahātaṇhāsaṅkhayasutta*, we have tried to make clear the style of argument used by the early Buddhists and to find out its characteristics. As a result, in the forms of the dialogue on *dhammas* based on the four *pañhabyākaraṇas* we find certain embryonic anticipations of formal logical procedures. It can be understood from the *Kathāvatthu* and the *Vijñānakāya* that such anticipations have greatly contributed to the growth of *Abhidhamma* philosophy.

In clarifying further the development of *Nikāya*-Buddhism, it may be necessary to look at not only the *Kalahavivādasutta* and the *Mahātaṇhāsaṅkhayasutta*, but also the following *suttas* :

1. *Poṭṭhapādasutta* (D. I, 178-203, T. 1,109 c-112 c).
2. *Pāyāsisutta* (D. II, 316-358, T. 1, 42 b-47 a, 525 a-532 b, 831 a-835 c).
3. *Pāṭikasutta* (D. III, 1-35. T. 1, 66 a-70 a).
4. *Sammādiṭṭhisutta* (M. I, 46-56, T. 2, 797 b-798 a).
5. *Rathavinītasutta* (M. I, 145-151, T. 1, 429 c-431 c, 2, 733 c-735 b).
6. *Cūḷasaccakasutta* (M. I, 227-236, T. 2, 35 a-37 b, 715 a-717 b).
7. *Mahāvedallasutta* (M. I, 292-298, T. 1, 790 b-792 c, 2, 60 b-c)
8. *Cūḷavedallasutta* (M. I, 299-305, T. 1, 788 a-790 b).
9. *Aggivacchagottasutta* (M. I, 483-489, T. 2, 245 b-246 a, 444 c)
10. *Subhasutta* (M. II, 196-209, T. 1, 666 c-670 a).

11

ADVANCED FORMS OF QUESTIONS AND ANSWERS IN THE *KATHĀVATTHU* AND THE *VIJÑĀNAKĀYA*

11.1 The forms of questions and answers in the *Abhidhamma* texts are, as compared with those in the *Nikāyas* and *Āgamas*, quite improved. In this chapter, we would like to take up the *puggala* (Skt. *pudgala* : person) chapter in both the *Kathāvatthu* and the *Vijñānakāya* and to see how questions and answers are treated in it.

11.2 Compared with the *Vijñānakāya* which contains six chapters, the *Kathāvatthu* is divided into twenty-three chapters. We see in it a collection of more than 200 debates, which are refutations in strict logical form of propositions maintained by many schools of Buddhism.[1] Above all, in controversial topics of the *Kathāvatthu*, such as "*puggalakathā*" (discussion of the 'person'), "*brahmacariyakathā*" (discussion of the best life), "*jahatikathā*" (discussion of renouncing), "*sabbamatthītikathā*" (discussion of 'everything exists') and so forth, the Sthaviravādin refutes the views of other schools of Buddhism by using a variety of logical methods.

In clarifying below the forms of questions and answers in "*puggalakathā*" (or "*pudgalaskandha*") and finding *Abhidhammic*

---

1. As to the names of different schools of Buddhism, see tr. Shwe Zan Aung and Mrs. Rhys Davids, *Points of Controversy*, pp. xviii-xxvii, and Nyanatiloka Mahathera, *Guide Through the Abhidhamma-Piṭaka*, pp. 60-2.

differences in argument forms, first of all, we must know the reason why the topic "*puggala*" was set down in the *Kathāvatthu* and the *Vijñānakāya*. The concept of *puggala* appeared in the third century B. C.[1] The followers of an elder named Vajjiputta, who came to be known as Vajjiputtakas (Skt. Vātsīputrīya) probably maintained that the 'person' is in some sense real, even though it is not an eternal soul such as non-Buddhists believed in. All other Buddhists, however, maintained that the word '*puggala*', sometimes used by the Buddha himself, contained no more meaning than a mere pronoun. Although the doctrinal topic *anattan* (non-ego) occupies an important position throughout the whole of Buddhism, even in the *Nikāyas* and *Āgamas*, it is recorded that for lack of a full understanding of *anattan*, some disciples of the Buddha regard "sensation" as the soul or "perception" as the soul (see chapter **10.5**). It seems that from the very beginning, some disciples were interested in meaningless problems such as "Who desires ?" or "Who is conscious ?" etc. rather than the proper formulations "Through what condition is there desire ?" or "Through what condition is there consciousness ?" etc. In this sense, it is natural that a heated discussion was conducted between the Sthaviravādin and the opponent, called the Pudgalavādin here (or between the Sarvāstivādin and the Pudgala school) and that such an event was later recorded as "*puggalakathā*" (or "*pudgala-skandha*") in both the *Kathāvatthu* and the *Vijñānakāya*.

The Pudgala school is subdivided into the Sammitiyas (Saṃmitīya), the Dhammuttarīyas (Dharmottarīya), the Bhadrayānikas (Bhadrayānīya), the Channāgarikas (Ṣaṇnagarika), all seceded from the Vajjiputtakas. In connection with the word '*puggala*', we see the *Puggalapaññatti* (the Concept of the 'Person') as one of the Pāli *Abhidhamma* texts, and see "*pudgala*" chapter in the *Śāriputrābhidharmaśāstra* (T. 28, 584 c-589c). But neither of them treat of a positive entity as a person, but deal with the brief definitions of various types of human and a great number of important specifically doctrinal terms

1. On this, see E. Lamotte, *Histoire de Bouddhisme Indien*, pp. 575-606, pp. 673-4 and A. K. Warder, *Indian Buddhism*, pp. 240-42.

concerning human types. Since the matter in hand is to see the forms of questions and answers in the *puggala* chapter in the *Kathāvatthu* and the *Vijñānakāya*, let us proceed to the main subject.

11.3 In the sections below, we follow the lead of A. K. Warder's study named "The Earliest Indian Logic."[1]

The *puggalakathā* is composed of nineteen sections in which eight possible sections, called *niggaha* (refutation) are given. Again, each of these refutations, consists of five sub-sections, called *pañcaka* (pentad), or *catukka* (tetrad). They are as follows:

1. The first refutation. (Nos. 1-5 : pp. 1-4)
   - i. Affirmative pentad (*anuloma-pañcakaṃ*).
   - ii. Rejoinder tetrad (*paṭikamma-catukkaṃ*).
   - iii. Refutation tetrad (*niggaha-catukkaṃ*).
   - iv. Application tetrad (*upanayana-catukkaṃ*).
   - v. Conclusion tetrad (*niggamana-catukkaṃ*).
2. The second refutation. (Nos. 6-10 : pp. 4-7)
   - i. Adverse controversy pentad (*paccanika-pañcakaṃ*).
   - ii. Rejoinder tetrad.
   - iii. Refutation tetrad.
   - iv. Application tetrad.
   - v. Conclusion tetrad.
3. The third refutation. (No. 11 : p. 8)
4. The fourth refutation. (No. 12 : pp. 8-9)
5. The fifth refutation. (No. 13 : p. 9)
6. The sixth refutation. (No. 14 : pp. 9-10)
7. The seventh refutation. (No. 15 : p. 10)
8. The eighth refutation. (No. 16 : pp. 10-11)
9. Simple collation (*suddhika-saṃsandanā*). (Nos. 17-129 : pp. 11-4)
10. Comparison (*opamma-saṃsandanaṃ*). (Nos. 130-37 : pp. 14-20)

1. *Proceedings of the 25th International Congress of Orientalists* (1963), vol. 4, pp. 56-68. The statements of the *puggalakathā* in the *Kathāvatthu* are paraphrased and sometimes expanded from A. K. Warder's study, since his article is not easily accessible and also contains numerous printing errors, as the author could not proofread it.

11. Collating by the tetrad scheme (*catukkanaya-saṃsandanaṃ*). (Nos. 138-45 : pp. 20-4)
12. Definition-judgement-discussion (*lakkhaṇāyuttikathā*). (Nos. 146-7 : p. 24)
13. Clarification of terms (*vacanasodhanaṃ*, here actually indicating the distribution of terms). (Nos. 148-53 : pp. 24-5)
14. Examination of concepts (*paññattānuyogo*). (Nos. 154-57 : pp. 25-8)
15. Examination of future courses (*gatianuyogo*). (Nos. 158-70 : pp. 28-34)
16. Examination of derivative concepts (*upādāpaññattānuyogo*). (Nos. 171-99 : pp. 34-45)
17. The first section of ethical goodness (*kalyāṇavaggo paṭhamo*). (Nos. 200-16 : pp. 45-55)
18. Examination of supernormal power (*abhiññānuyogo*). (Nos. 217-8 : pp. 55-6)
19. Adducing *suttas* (*suttāhāra*). (Nos. 219-45 : pp. 56-69)

According to A. K. Warder, the pentad and tetrad in the first refutation mentioned above are analyzed as follows on the basis of statements in the *puggalakathā*:[1]

Pentad : normal (*anuloma*) consequent (*pāpanā*).
normal disproof (*āropaṇā*).
reverse (*paṭiloma*) antecedent (*ṭhapanā*).
reverse consequent.
reverse disproof.

Tetrad : normal consequent.
normal disproof.
reverse consequent.
reverse disproof.

It may be expedient to examine the actual debates between the Sthaviravādin and the Pudgala school.

11.4. We would like to start with the debate comprising the affirmative pentad in the first refutation :

1. "The Earliest Indian Logic," p. 61.

St. : Does the person exist (*upalabbhati*) in the real, ultimate sense (*saccikaṭṭhaparamaṭṭha*)?[1]

Pu. : Yes.

St. : Does the person exist in the real, ultimate sense in the same way (*tato*) as the real and ultimate things?[2]

Pu. : No, that cannot indeed be said thus.

St. : Acknowledge the refutation:

i. If (*hañci*) the person exists in the real, ultimate sense, then (*tena*) indeed you should also say, the person exists in the real, ultimate sense in the same way as the real and ultimate things.
ii. What you say here is wrong (*micchā*), namely : You say "Yes" in the former, and "No" in the latter.
iii. If the latter cannot be admitted,
iv. then the former should not be admitted.
v. What you say here is wrong, because the former is affirmed and the latter is negated.

As pointed out in chapter 9, hypothetical (or conditional) statements are most frequently identifiable by "if. . .then. . ." Those are two component propositions: the "antecedent" which comes between the "if" and the "then," and the "consequent" which comes after the "then". Unlike a conjunction, the assertion of the "if. . .then. . ." statement as a whole does not imply that any one of its component propositions is true. What is asserted is not the truth of either components, separately or together, but the relation of conditionality between them.[3] Therefore, in the above debate the Sthaviravādin subdivides his refutation of the opponent into the five steps and explains that

1. According to the *Kv.-Commentary* (p. 8), the word '*saccikaṭṭha*' is that which is real (*bhūtattho*) and is that which cannot be grasped in a false way (*abhūtākārena agahetabbo*) like a deceptive appearance (*māyā*), a mirage (*marīci*), etc.; and *paramaṭṭha* means 'highest' (*uttamaṭṭha*) and is that which cannot be grasped under the influence of report, etc. (*anussavādivasena agahetabbo*).

2. This means to ask whether or no the person exists in the same way as the 57 principles (i.e. the 5 *khandhas*, the 12 *āyatanas*, the 18 *dhātus* and the 22 *indriyas*) exist. On this, see the *Kv-Commentary*, p. 8.

3. See R. B. Angell, *Reasoning and Logic*, p. 144.

if the antecedent should be true, then the consequent should be also true, and if the consequent is false, then the antecedent will be also false, namely :

(i) $p \supset q$
(ii) $-(p. -q)$
(iii) & (iv) $-q \supset -p$
(v) $-(p. -q)$[1]

We must note here that the form $p \supset q$ becomes :

$$(p \supset q) \equiv -(p. -q) \equiv (-q \supset -p) \equiv (-p \vee q)$$

Thus, in the affirmative pentad we see that the Pudgala school is defeated by the Sthaviravādin. In other words, the Sthaviravādin points out that the forms $-p \supset -q$, $p \supset -q$, $-p \supset q$ taken together are inconsistent with the forms $p \supset q$.

Now, let us see the rejoinder tetrad in which the opponent takes the initiative:

Pu.: Does the person not exist in the real, ultimate sense ?
St. : No.[2]
Pu.: Does the person not exist in the real, ultimate sense in the same way as the real and ultimate things ?

---

1. As for the affirmative pentad mentioned above, a further attempt would be made by paraphrasing the statements of items i, ii, iii, iv and v as follows :

i. If the person exists in the real, ultimate sense, then indeed you should also say, the person exists in the real, ultimate sense in the same way as the real and ultimate things.
ii. What you say here is wrong, namely: You say "Yes" in the former, and "No" in the latter.
iii. But the latter cannot be admitted.
iv. Therefore, the former should not be admitted.
v. The former is affirmed and therefore it is wrong to negate the latter. Symbolically:

i. $p \supset q$
ii. $-(p. -q)$
iii. $-q$
iv. Therefore, $-p$
v. p, therefore, $- -q$

2. The word '*āmantā*' meaning "Yes" is used according to Pāli idiom. But the answer in this case actually means "Yes : it *does* not exist," so that *āmantā* here should be rendered negatively in English.

St. : No, that cannot indeed be said thus (it does not exist).

Pu. : Acknowledge the rejoinder :

i. If the person does not exist in the real, ultimate sense, then indeed you should also say, the person does not exist in the real, ultimate sense in the same way as the real and ultimate things.

ii. What you say here is wrong, namely : You say "No" in the former, and "It is not the case that the person does not exist" in the latter. (That is, "Yes.")

iii. If it is not the case that the latter cannot be admitted, then it is not the case that the former should not be admitted.

iv. What you say here is wrong, because the former is negated and the latter is negated twice.

Thus, to sum up:

(i) $-p \supset -q$

(ii) $-(-p. --q)$

(iii) $--q \supset --p$

(iv) $-(-p. --q)$[1]

It seems that by showing the form $-p \supset -q$ which is equivalent to the form $q \supset p$, in the above the Pudgala school tries to demonstrate sophistically p and $-q$, which are both the standpoint of the Pudgala school. This can be understood from the fact that the Pudgala school shows the form $-p \supset -q$ (item i above) and the form $--q \supset --p$ (item iii above). The form $--q \supset --p$ becomes the form $q \supset p$ from a logical point of view. The form $q \supset p$ is called the converse of the form $p \supset q$, and the latter is equivalent to the form $-q \supset -p$ which is called contraposition, but not equivalent to the form $--q \supset --p$ (or $q \supset p$).

Let us turn our eyes to the refutation tetrad, which is stated by the Pudgala school :

---

1. As for the rejoinder tetrad, we could see symbolically as follows :
   i. $-p \supset -q$
   ii. $-(-p. --q)$
   iii. $--q$, therefore, $--p$
   iv. $-p$, therefore, $-q$

i. But if you think "We say 'No' in the former and 'It is not the case that the person does not exist' in the latter," then, you who have assented to the propositions, should indeed be refuted; let us then refute you, for you are well refuted. If you say "No" in the former, then you should say "No" in the latter.
ii. What you say here is wrong, namely : You say "No" in the former and "It is not the case that the person does not exist" in the latter.
iii. If it is not the case that the latter cannot be admitted, then it is not the case that the former should not be admitted.
iv. What you say here is wrong, because the former is negated and the latter is negated twice.[1]

At this point, we see that the Pudgala school sophistically tries to point out that the form $-p \supset -q$ is valid, but the form $-p \supset --q$ is invalid.

Furthermore, the Pudgala school mentions in the application tetrad as follows :

i. If this (refutation tetrad) is a faulty refutation (*dunniggaha*), see the affirmative pentad. We said there "Yes" in the former, and "No" in the latter. We, who assented there to these propositions, should not indeed be refuted. Then, (You perhaps say) you have refuted us, but we are not well refuted. (Your argument) is "If the person exists in the real, ultimate sense, then indeed you should also say, the person exists in the real, ultimate sense in the same way as the real and ultimate things."
ii. What you say here is wrong, namely : You say, the person exists in the real, ultimate sense, and the person does not exist in the real, ultimate sense in the same way as the real and ultimate things.

---

1. As for the refutation tetrad, we could see symbolically as follows :
   i. $-(-p . --q)$
   ii. $--q$
   iii. $--p$
   iv. $--p$, therefore, $--q$

iii. If it is not the case that the person exists in the real, ultimate sense in the same way as the real and ultimate things, then it is not the case that the person exists in the real, ultimate sense.

iv. The same as item ii. Thus you are wrong.[1]

And at the conclusion of the first refutation, the Pudgala school mentions as follows :

i. We are not to be refuted thus. What you refute us is "If the person exists in the real, ultimate sense, then indeed you should also say, the person exists in the real, ultimate sense in the same way as the real and ultimate things."

ii. What you say here is wrong, namely : You say, it is the case that the person exists in the former and it is not the case that the person exists in the latter.

iii. If the latter cannot be admitted, then the former should not be admitted.

iv. What you say here is wrong, because the former is affirmed and the latter is negated. Therefore, what was refuted (by you) was badly done. (Our) rejoinder was well done. Our sequel to the argument (*paṭipādanā*) was well done.

If we sum up items i, ii, iii and iv above on the basis of what the Pudgala school states, they become :

i. $p \supset q$

ii. $-(p.-q)$

iii. $-q \supset -p$

iv. $-(p.-q)$[2]

---

1. As for the application tetrad, we could see symbolically as follows :
 i. $p \supset q$
 ii. $—(p.—q)$
 iii. $—q$, therefore, $—p$
 iv. $—p$, therefore, $—q$

2. As for the conclusion tetrad, we could see symbolically as follows :
 i. $p \supset q$
 ii. p, therefore, $--q$
 iii. $—q$, therefore, $—p$
 iv. $—(p.—q)$

These forms are apparently correct. According to the Pudgala school, the refutation of the Sthaviravādin was badly done, whilst the sequel to the argument by the Pudgala school was well done. Nevertheless, we cannot see any true reasoning from what the Pudgala school stated in the application tetrad and the conclusion tetrad. Rather we see only the sophistical (or equivocal) refutation by the Pudgala school. From the debate in the first refutation between the two schools, therefore, we can learn the following forms:

St. : $p \supset q$

$-(p.-q)$

$-q \supset -p$

Pu. : $-p \supset -q$

$$\left.\begin{array}{l} p \supset -q \\ -p \supset q \\ -p \supset --q \end{array}\right] \equiv p.-q$$

$-(-p.---q)$

$--q \supset --p$

11.5. The following is the adverse controversy pentad in the second refutation, where the Pudgala school takes the initiative :

Pu. : Does the person not exist in the real, ultimate sense ?

St. : No.[1]

Pu. : Does the person not exist in the real, ultimate sense in the same way as the real and ultimate things ?

St. : No, that cannot indeed be said thus.

Pu. : Acknowledge the refutation:

i. If the person does not exist in the real, ultimate sense, then indeed you should also say, the person does not exist in the real, ultimate sense in the same way as the real and ultimate things.

ii. What you say here is wrong, namely : You say "No" in the former and "It is not the case that the person does not exist" in the latter.

1. This also means "Yes : it *does* not exist." So this should be rendered negatively in English.

iii. If it is not the case that the latter cannot be admitted,
iv. then it is not the case that the former cannot be admitted.
v. What you say here is wrong, because the former is negated and the latter is negated twice.

This is similar to the rejoinder tetrad in the first refutation. Whilst the first refutation is in a word viewed as an affirmative refutation, the second one is viewed as a negative refutation. In order to simplify further the arguments between the two schools, let us express them symbolically by using only the letters p, q, etc.

In the rejoinder tetrad, which is similar to the affirmative pentad in the first refutation, we see:

St. : p ?
Pu. : Yes.
St. : q ?
Pu. : No.
St. : i. $p \supset q$
ii. $-(p.-q)$
iii. $-q \supset -p$
iv. $-(p.-q)$

In the refutation tetrad we see :

St. : i. $-(p.-q) \equiv (p \supset q)$
ii. $-(p.-q)$
iii. $-q \supset -p$
iv. $-(p.-q)$

The following is the application tetrad :

St. : i. $-(-p.--q) \equiv (-p \supset -q)$
ii. $-(-p.--q)$
iii. $--q \supset --p$
iv. $-(-p.--q)$

As the conclusion tetrad, the following can be seen :

St. : i. $-p \supset -q$
ii. $-(-p.--q)$
iii. $--q \supset --p$
iv. $-(-p.--q)$

As we have seen already, the first and second refutations form a complete debate in themselves, consisting of five subsections or four subsections, called simply pentads (*pañcaka*) or tetrads (*catukka*). Such a way of refutations is covered throughout the *Kathāvatthu*. Therefore, we would like here to introduce only the topics of questions and answers in the other six refutations.

In the third refutation affirmative, the Pudgala school is defeated. The noteworthy point here is that the term 'everywhere' is used :

St. : Does the person exist in the real, ultimate sense ?
Pu. : Yes.
St. : Does the person exist everywhere (*sabbattha*) in the real, ultimate sense ?
Pu. : No, that cannot indeed be said thus.

In the fourth refutation affirmative, the Pudgala school is defeated:

St. : Does the person exist in the real, ultimate sense ?
Pu. : Yes.
St. : Does the person exist always (*sabbadā*) in the real, ultimate sense ?
Pu. : No, that cannot indeed be said thus.

In the fifth refutation affirmative, the Pudgala school is defeated:

St. : Does the person exist in the real, ultimate sense ?
Pu. : Yes.
St. : Does the person exist in everything (*sabbesu*) in the real, ultimate sense ?
Pu. : No, that cannot indeed be said thus.

In the sixth refutation negative, the Sthaviravādin is defeated:

Pu. : Does the person not exist in the real, ultimate sense ?
St. : No.
Pu. : Does the person not exist everywhere in the real, ultimate sense ?
St. : No, that cannot indeed be said thus.

In the seventh refutation negative, the Sthaviravādin is defeated:

Pu. : Does the person not exist in the real, ultimate sense ?
St. : No.
Pu. : Does the person not exist always in the real, ultimate sense ?
St. : No, that cannot indeed be said thus.

In the eighth refutation negative, the Sthaviravādin is defeated :

Pu. : Does the person not exist in the real, ultimate sense ?
St. : No.
Pu. : Does the person not exist in everything in the real, ultimate sense ?
St. : No, that cannot indeed be said thus.

The terms 'everywhere,' 'always,' 'in everything' in the above are important in examining the essential qualities of the word '*puggala*' itself.[1] But what is more important here is the relationship between two different propositions, which are always analyzed from a logical point of view by the respective schools. As already stated, in the first refutation the Sthaviravādin begins by refuting the Pudgala school in the pentad which contains the essential argument, but is defeated by sophistry or equivocation when the Pudgala school has the initiative in the four tetrads (esp. refer to chapter **11.4**); in the second refutation the Pudgala school begins by repeating its rejoinder argument as the pentad, but the Sthaviravādin then has the rejoinder and in the four tetrads he develops his argument strictly, eliminating the sophistry, and establishes his refutation of the Pudgala school.

Thus we can see from the above eight refutations that both the Sthaviravādin and the Pudgala school conduct quite logical investigations into the existence or non-existence of *puggala* in the real sense. In other words, the first two refutations deal with

1. On this, see the *Kv.-Commentary*, p. 15 and the *Abhidhammattha-saṅgaha*, Part VII.

what is called *existential quantification* and what is called *universal quantification*. If we substitute "*F*" for "*puggala* in the real, ultimate sense," the Pudgala school maintains "There are *F*" or "*F* exist," symbolized by $(\exists x)Fx$. On the other hand, the Sthaviravādin maintains "There are no *F*" or "*F* do not exist," symbolized by $-(\exists x)Fx$. But to say that "there are no *F*" is the same as saying that "everything is non-*F*," symbolized by $(x)-Fx$. Therefore, we come to know from the first two refutations :

1. $(\exists x)Fx$ (existential quantification).
2. $-(\exists x)Fx$ (universal quantification).

And the last six refutations also indicate some kind of universal quantification: 'everywhere', 'always', 'in everything', though these are qualified in space, in time, and in particulars.

11.6 In the simple collation (*suddhika-saṃsandanā*), the Sthaviravādin takes the initiative in the following manner:

St. : Does the person exist in the real, ultimate sense, and does matter (*rūpa* as physical principles) exist in the real, ultimate sense ?

Pu. : Yes.

St. : Is matter different from the person (*aññaṃ rūpam añño puggalo*) ?

Pu. : No, that cannot indeed be said thus.

St. : Acknowledge the refutation:

i. If the person exists in the real, ultimate sense, and matter exists in the real, ultimate sense, then you should also say, matter is different from the person.
ii. What you say here is wrong, namely: You say "Yes" in the first two propositions, and "No" in the third proposition.
iii. If the third one cannot be admitted, then the first two should not be admitted.
iv. What you say here is wrong, because the first two are affirmed and the third is negated.

The same form of refutation is then pursued concerning whether or not the other four *khandhas*, the twelve *āyatanas*, the eighteen *dhātus* and the twenty-two *indriyas* (faculties) exist in the real, ultimate sense. Hereon, we see that the above is an example of a compound propositional form, and that the argument form is composed of the form $p.q \supset r$ which is equivalent to the form $[p \supset (q \supset r)]$, called the principle of exportation. Thus the Sthaviravādin's statements above could be expressed symbolically as follows :

i. $p.q \supset r$
ii. $-(p.q.-r)$
iii. $-r \supset -(p.q)$
iv. $-(p.q.-r)$

The form $p.q \supset r$ is also equivalent to the form $[q \supset (p \supset r)]$. An important thing in such a compound proposition is to see relation between terms in the sentences rather than to see relations between the sentences and the way they are connected together. In this respect, we must note that the word '*saṃsandanā*' (or *–aṃ* neuter) is used in debate (see chapter **11.3**).

According to A. K. Warder (see "The Earliest Indian Logic," p. 60), the word *saṃsandanā* means 'checking', 'collating', 'putting together', 'substitution', and the object of this is to see whether a given term, concept, or entity is distinct from the other terms, etc., used in Buddhist philosophy. So, *suddhika-saṃsandanā* (simple checking) means setting the given term beside all the terms of the *Mātikā* system in rotation and asking whether it is different. If *a* is not different from *b*, then it cannot be said that *a* exists in the real, ultimate sense; only *b* so exists and *a* is just a name. In this sense, it is logically significant that in the ninth section, called *suddhika-saṃsandanā*, each term (of the five *khandhas*, the twelve *āyatanas* and so on) is examined by asking whether or no it is different from the person. Moreover, as other forms of *saṃsandanā* we see *opamma* (section 10) and *catukkanaya* (section 11). The former means 'comparison', in which related but contrasted terms are substituted for some terms of the disputed proposition. The latter means 'collating by the tetrad scheme, in which the following questions are given:

Is the term under discussion :

(1) identical with another term in the system,

(2) part of that other term,
(3) different from that other, or
(4) is that other part of it ?

In the *opamma-saṃsandanaṃ*, on the other hand, we can see the following dialogue:

St. : Matter exists in the real, ultimate sense, and so does feeling. Is matter different from feeling ?
Pu. : Yes.
St. : Does the person exist in the real, ultimate sense, and does matter exist in the real, ultimate sense ?
Pu. : Yes.
St. : Is matter different from the person ?
Pu. : No, that cannot indeed be said thus.
St. : Acknowledge the refutation :

i. If matter and feeling exist in the real, ultimate sense, matter is different from feeling, and the person and matter exist in the real, ultimate sense, then you should also say, matter is different from the person.
ii. What you say here is wrong, namely : You say "Yes" in the first three propositions, and "No" in the fourth proposition.
iii. If the fourth one cannot be admitted, then the first three should not be admitted.
iv. What you say here is wrong, because the first three are affirmed and the fourth is negated.

This is also an example of a compound propositional form. The above refutation could be schematized as follows:

i. $p.q.r \supset s$
ii. $-(p.q.r.-s)$
iii. $-s \supset -(p.q.r)$
iv. $-(p.q.r.-s)$

In this section, the same argument as the above is then applied to the case of each of the other three *khandhas*, substituted for feeling, and the permutations of the five *khandhas*, the twelve *āyatanas*, the eighteen *dhātus* and the twenty-two *indriyas* are proceeded with as the above. As pointed out in chapters 9 and 10, the argument forms of early Buddhists are characterized by a sorites, being composed of hypothetical statements and from such a sorites various forms of argument can be derived. Therefore, we are almost certain that the same tendency would have been followed by Buddhists in the time of *Abhidhamma* Buddhism.

11.7 Besides the word '*saṃsandanā*', we see other important words such as *lakkhaṇāyuttikathā* (definition-judgement-discussion), *vacanasodhanaṃ* (clarification of terms), *paññattānuyogo* (examination of concepts) and so forth. Especially, in the *vacanasodhanaṃ* (section 13) we see some arguments which are known as simple conversion. These arguments can also be expressed by "Some *F* are *G*," symbolized by $(\exists x)(Fx . Gx)$ and "Some *F* are not *G*," symbolized by $(\exists x)(Fx . -Gx)$. For example,

St. : Does the person exist, (and) is that which exists the person ?

Pu. : The person exists, some (*kehici*) of what exists is the person, and some is not the person.

St. : Does some of what is the person exist, and some not exist ?

Pu. : No, that cannot indeed be said thus.

But the most remarkable thing throughout the *puggalakathā* is that it can be divided into two kinds of debates. One belongs to a primary debate, called *vādayutti* (sections 1-8), and the other, to a varying number of secondary discussions (sections 9-19).[1] The word '*vādayutti*' is regarded as meaning 'judgement of (the opponent's) statement', so that in the primary debate (or theorem) eight refutations are, as mentioned already, set out according to a logical analysis. On the other hand, in the various secondary discussions the terms and propositions used, or entities referred to, in the primary debate are examined and are fully elaborated for the first debate. Accordingly, in the secondary discussions we can see more logical arguments than

1. On this, see A. K. Warder, "The Earliest Indian Logic," p. 64.

in the first debate. Therefore, let us examine some of the logical arguments in the secondary discussions. In the *upādāpaññattānuyogo* (section 16), we see the following dialogue:

Pu. : Is it not the case that the person passes on (*sandhāvati*) from this world to the other world (*para loka*), and from the other world to this world ?

St. : No.

Pu. : Was the following not said by the Buddha ? Transmigration (*saṃsāra*) is, monks, without a known beginning (*anamatagga*) ; unthinkable (*na paññāyati*) is the beginning and the end of beings (*sattas*), who pass on (*sandhāvati*) and who transmigrate (*saṃsarati*). Is the *sutta* thus ?[1]

St. : Yes.

Pu. : Then the person indeed passes on from this world to the other world, and from the other world to this world.

It is clear that the quotation from the early canon mentioned above is misused by the Pudgala school.[2] But if we view only the argument form of the Pudgala school, it is composed of a mixed hypothetical syllogism (affirmative), namely:

If it is true that the Buddha preached: "Transmigration is without a known beginning; unthinkable...," then it is true that the person passes on from this world to the other world, and from the other world to this world.	$p \supset q$
It is true that the Buddha preached.	p
Hence, it is true that the person passes on.	Hence, q

As we have learned in chapter **10.4**, this is named *affirming the antecedent* because the second premiss affirms the *antecedent* of the

1. S. III, 149, T. 2, 69 b.

2. Besides this *sutta*, we see on the same page the following quotation from the early canon : Seven times at the most reborn, the person yet passing on, through the destruction of all fetters, is relieved of unhappiness. On this, see S. II, 185, T. 2, 242 b, Itv. p. 18, T. 17, 662 c-663 a, etc.

hypothetical premiss to be true by itself; this, taken with the hypothetical as a whole, necessitates the affirmation of the consequent. From the standpoint of the Sthaviravādin, however, the antecedent must be false, for the consequent of a true hypothetical is found false, namely:

$p \supset q$, $-q$, hence, $-p$

This is called *denying the consequent* because in the second premiss we hold the *consequent* of the hypothetical to be false when taken alone; this, assuming that the hypothetical itself is true, necessitates the denial of the antecedent.

Contrasted with these two valid forms, we must notice the following two forms which are invalid:[1]

1. $p \supset q$, q, hence, p (named *affirming the consequent*).
2. $p \supset q$, $-p$, hence, $-q$ (named *denying the antecedent*).

11.8 After all, the Sthaviravādin defeats the Pudgala school by using the mixed hypothetical syllogism denying the consequent. It seems that in it the Sthaviravādin gives the most conclusive proof that no person exists. To put it briefly (p. 65):

If the person exists in the real, ultimate sense, then everything is [inferred to be] of soul (*attan*).	$p \supset q$
It is not the case that all principles are of soul (*sabbe dhammā anattā*).	$-q$
Hence, it is not the case that the person exists.	Hence, $-p$

In spite of the fact that such an argument form cannot be found in the *Nikāyas*, it is used widely in the *puggalakathā* of the *Kathāvatthu* (e.g. p.43, p.61, etc.) in order to defeat the opponent. We would say that this marks the development of the Buddhists' thinking of the time, as compared with that at the time of the

---

1. Moreover, we see the following four forms which are obviously invalid :

1. $p \supset q$, p, hence, $-q$
2. $p \supset q$, $-q$, hence, p
3. $p \supset q$, q, hence, $-p$
4. $p \supset q$, $-p$, hence, q

On this, see R. B. Angell, *Reasoning and Logic*, p. 149.

Buddha. From a logical point of view, the proposition "(All) *S* is *P*" has the status as "(All) *S* is not *P*." The former as well as the latter can be true or false. Nevertheless, negative judgement can be construed as 'nonbeing' as opposed to 'being', though the problem of negation has perplexed thinkers of different ages. In other words, in order to furnish an irrefragable proof that no person exists, the Sthaviravādin seems to have used the mixed hypothetical syllogism denying the consequent in particular. But it must be noticed that the problem of negation is nowadays receiving minute study, and that there is a scholar who suggests that every significant negation "A is not B" can be analyzed as "A is X, which excludes B" where X is an unknown property which excludes the property B,[1] and also that there is another who criticizes adversely such an analysis.[2] Apart from the relationship between negation and ontology, it is certain that by using negative statements the Sthaviravādin made an effort to give full proof of the fact that the person does not exist in the real, ultimate sense.

11.9 We have found various forms of argument in the *puggalakathā*. These are all refutations of propositions maintained by the school. Finally, let us introduce one more example in which an analogy is used (p.41):

St. : Is the concept (*paññatti*) of the person based on (*upādāya*) matter (*rūpa*), just as the concept of villager (*gāmika*) is based on village (*gāma*)? And if that is so, is matter different from the person, just as village is different from villager?

Pu. : No, that cannot indeed be said thus.

St. : Acknowledge the refutation. . . .

It is clear that the above analogy is based on the method of agreement, which was brought over from the *Nikāyas* and *Āgamas* to the *Abhidhamma* texts, in the sense that the investigation of

1. B. Bosanquet, *The Essentials of Logic*, p. 135.
2. On this, see Bimal K. Matilal, *The Navya-nyāya Doctrine of Negation*, pp. 87-95.

appropriate analogies has an important role in the organon of good reasoning. Thus the Sthaviravādin points out:

It is not the case that the concept of villager is based on village and that village is not different from villager.	$-(p.-q)$
The concept of villager is based on village.	p
Hence, village is different from villager.	Hence, q

In quite the same way, we can see the relationship between 'person' and 'matter', stated by the Sthaviravādin. As mentioned in chapter **11.4**, the form $-(p.-q)$ becomes :

$$(p \supset q) \equiv (-q \supset -p) \equiv (-p \vee q)$$

Therefore, the following forms of argument are equivalent to one another :

1. $-(p.-q)$, p, hence, q
2. $p \supset q$, p hence, q
3. $-q \supset -p$, p, hence, q
4. $-p \vee q$, p, hence, q

On the whole, the *Kathāvatthu* is a polemical text, consisting of refutations in strict logical form, so that we have tried to elucidate this point in the first chapter, *puggalakathā*. According to A. K. Warder, the *Kathāvatthu* is the earliest known Indian philosophical work which proceeds on the basis of a set of established logical techniques : definition, distribution of terms, classification, relations between propositions as biconditionals or ponentials, quantification, the use of logical words to give a standard formal presentation of all the arguments, and so on.[1]

11.10 On the other hand, the *pudgalaskandha* in the *Vijñānakāya* seems to be composed of nine sections. As we shall see later, under the name of the Śūnyatāvādin, the Sarvāstivāda school which does not accept the existence of the person (*pudgala*) refutes the Pudgala school, which asserts the existence of the person. Let us begin by introducing the chapters of the *Vijñānakāya*. It was translated into Chinese by Hiuen-Tsang in 649 A.D. and contains six chapters (*skandhas*) :

1. *Indian Buddhism*, pp. 299-300.

1. Maudgalyāyana (T.26,531 a-537 a).
2. *Pudgala* (person) (T.26, 537 a-547 a).
3. *Hetupratyaya* (cause as condition) (T.26, 547 a-559 a).
4. *Ālambanapratyaya* (mental object as condition) (T.26,559 a-582 b).
5. *Saṃyukta* (conjoined) (T.26, 582 b-593 a).
6. *Samanvāgama* (accomplishment) (T.26, 593 b-614 b).

As we have stated briefly in chapter **5.13,** the first chapter deals with the knowing of three roots of bad (*akusalamūlas*) : greed (*lobha*), aversion (*doṣa*) and delusion (*moha*) in the past, present and future principles (*dharmas*) (see T.26, 513 a):

Maudgalyāyana states thus : The past and future do not exist, but the present and the unactivated (or the unsynthesized : *asaṃskṛta*) do exist.

Śūnyatāvādin : Do you recognize what was well taught, well said and well stated by the Buddha, namely, there are three roots of bad, which are greed, aversion and delusion?

Mau. : Yes.

Śūn. : Do you recognize in the bad root of greed as follows: It has been known that this is bad, it is known that this is bad, and it will be known that this is bad?

Mau. : Yes.

Śūn. : In which time are they known? In the past or in the present or in the future?

If there is the bad root of greed known in the past, you should say that there is the past. You should not say that there is not the past.

If you say that there is not the past, this is unreasonable.

If there is the bad root of greed known in the future, you should say that there is future. You should not say that there is not the future.

If you say that there is not the future, this is unreasonable.

If there is the bad root of greed known in the present, you should say that there is the simultaneity of two kinds of thought (*citta*) at the same moment in the person (*pudgala*).

> If there is the bad root of greed known in the present, you should say that there is the simultaneity of two kinds of thought at the same moment in the person; one is the thought of the bad root of greed; the other is the thought of seeing the bad root of greed.
>
> This is unreasonable.
>
> If you do not say that there is the simultaneity of two kinds of thought at the same moment in the person; one is the thought of the bad root of greed and the other is the thought of seeing the bad root of greed, you should not say that there is the bad root of greed known in the present. It is unreasonable that there is the bad root of greed known in the present.
>
> If you say that there is not the bad root of greed known in the past, present and future, then you do not have to recognize concerning the bad root of greed as follows : It has been known that this is bad, it is known that this is bad, and it will be known that this is bad. . . .

Thus Maudgalyāyana's view concerning the non-existence of past and future principles is refuted.

The third chapter deals with the relations of many types of thought (*citta*), which might be called mental (active) phenomena, (as can be seen in the *Dhammasaṅgaṇi* in which 89 *cittas* are distinguished). Also this chapter treats of four kinds of *pratyaya* (condition), namely : 1. *hetu* (cause), 2. *samanantara* (quite immediate), 3. *ālambana* (mental object), and 4. *adhipati* (dominant), whilst the *Paṭṭhāna* operates with twenty-four kinds of *paccaya* (*pratyaya*) and the *Śāriputrābhidharmaśāstra* explains thirty-three *hetus* including ten *pratyayas* and *sarvatraga* (universal).

The fourth chapter deals with the problem of cognition and explains the six kinds of consciousness (*vijñāna*) which are in the past, present and future, and which are good, bad, and neither-good-nor-bad, the interrelation of them, etc.

The fifth chapter is devoted to epistemological explanations of the six *vijñānas*, twelve *āyatanas*, eighteen *dhātus*, etc.

The sixth chapter deals with the mental functions of a person under training and explains the mental phenomena of the *arhant*.

11.11 Now what we are concerned with here is the second chapter named *pudgalaskandha*, so that we would like to see each of the nine sections.

1. Discussion of the transmigration of the 'person' in the five *gatis* (T.26,537 a-538 b), which may be compared partly with section 15 of the *puggalakathā* (see chapter **11.3**).
2. Discussion of eight types of person (T.26,538 b-540 c), which may be compared in part with No. 164 of section 15.
3. Discussion of the three *rāśis* (heaps or classes) and the person (T.26,540 c-542 a).
4. Discussion of the three trainings (*śaikṣas*) and the person (T.26,542 a-b).
5. Discussion of the three sensations, *karmans* and the person (T.26,542 b-543 b), which may be compared partly with No. 210 of section 17 and No. 229 of section 19.
6. Discussion of principles seen, heard, sensed and cognized and the person (T.26, 543 b-c).
7. Discussion of the cause of benevolence (*maitrā*) and the person (T.26,543 c-545 b).
8. Discussion of *saṃskṛta, asaṃskṛta* and the person (T. 26, 545 b), which may be compared partly with No. 225 of section 19.
9. Discussion of the six kinds of consciousness (*vijñāna*) and the person (T.26,545 b-547 a).

Only in section 7, the Sarvāstivādin's (strictly speaking, Śūnyatāvādin's, as stated in chapter **11.10**) view is given at the beginning, whilst the view of the Pudgala school is given in the opening sentences of the other sections.

The following (Nos. 1 to 5)[1] is the argument of whether or not the person transmigrates from *niraya* to *tiryagyoni.*

—Translation of section 1 (T. 26,537 b-c)—

1. The Pudgala school states thus : The person is known, recognized, and exists actually and exists in the real, ultimate sense. Therefore, the person certainly exists.

1. The numbers are mine. The same thing follows below.

The Śūnyatāvādin[1] asks thus : Did the Buddha teach well, say well and state well in the *sūtra* : There are certainly five kinds of future courses (*gatis*) and they are established as different, namely : 1. *niraya* 'purgatory', 2. *tiryagyoni* 'animals', 3. *pitryaviṣaya* 'the dead', 4. *devā* 'gods', and 5. *manuṣyā* 'human beings'; then *niraya*, . . .and *manuṣyā* are certainly different ?

Pud. : Yes.

Śūn. : Does the (same) person decease and is the (same) person born from *niraya* into *tiryagyoni* ?

Pud : Yes.

Śūn. : Acknowledge the refutation.

If you say that there are certainly five *gatis* and they are established as different, namely, 1. *niraya*, . . .and 5. *manuṣyā*; then *niraya*, . . .and *manuṣyā* are certainly different, then you should not say that the person deceases and is born from *niraya* into *tiryagyoni*.

What you say here is unreasonable.

If you say that the person deceases and is born from *niraya* into *tiryagyoni*, then you should not say that there are certainly five *gatis* and they are established as different, namely, 1. *niraya*, . . .and 5. *manuṣyā*; then *niraya*, . . .and *manuṣyā* are certainly different.

It is unreasonable that you say : There are certainly five *gatis* and they are established as different, . . .then *niraya*, . . .and *manuṣyā* are certainly different.

2. The Pudgala school states thus : The person certainly deceases and is born from *niraya* into *tiryagyoni*.

The Śūnyatāvādin questions, saying ; Is this (the same as) that ? (This means "Whether or not the person in *niraya* is the same as the person in *tiryagyoni*.")

Pud. : No.

Śūn. : Acknowledge the refutation.

If the person certainly deceases and is born from *niraya* into *tiryagyoni*, then you should say that this (person) is (the same as) that (person).

---

1. The Śūnyatāvādin in this chapter indicates the Sarvāstivādin.

What you say here is unreasonable.

If you do not say that this (person) is (the same as) that (person), then you should not say that the person certainly deceases and is born from *niraya* into *tiryagyoni*.

It is unreasonable that you say : The person certainly deceases and is born from *niraya* into *tiryagyoni*.

3. In the case that the Pudgala school says thus : This (person) is (the same as) that (person), the Śūnyatāvādin will question, saying : Is the *niraya* (the same as) the *tiryagyoni* ?

Pud. : No.

Śūn. : Acknowledge the refutation.

If this (person) is (the same as) that (person), then you should say that the *niraya* is (the same as) the *tiryagyoni*.

What you say here is unreasonable.

If you do not say that the *niraya* is (the same as) the *tiryagyoni*, then you should not say that this (person) is (the same as) that (person).

It is unreasonable that you say : This (person) is (the same as) that (person).

4. In the case that the Pudgala school says thus : This (person in *niraya*) is different from that (person in *tiryagyoni*), the Śūnyatāvādin will question, saying : Is this (person in *niraya*) annihilated and is that (person) born in *tiryagyoni* different ?

Pud. : No.

Śūn. : Acknowledge the refutation.

If this (person in *niraya*) is different from that (person in *tiryagyoni*), then you should say that this (person in *niraya*) is annihilated and that (person) born in *tiryagyoni* is different.

What you say here is unreasonable.

If you do not say that this (person in *niraya*) is annihilated and that (person) born in *tiryagyoni* is different, then you should not say that this (person in *niraya*) is different from that (person in *tiryagyoni*).

It is unreasonable that you say : This (person in *niraya*) is different from that (person in *tiryagyoni*).

5. In the case that the Pudgala school says thus : It cannot be said that this (person) is either (the same as) that (person) or different from that (person), the Śūnyatāvādin will question, saying : Is it impossible to say that this (person) is either (the same as) that (person) or different from that (person) in the case that the person deceases and is born from *niraya* into *tiryagyoni* ?

Pud. : No. It is impossible to say so.

Śūn. : Acknowledge the refutation.

If it cannot be said that this (person) is either (the same as) that (person) or different from that (person), then you should say that it is impossible to say that this (person) is either (the same as) that (person) or different from that (person) in the case that the person deceases and is born from *niraya* into *tiryagyoni*.

What you say here is unreasonable.

If you do not say that it is impossible to say that this (person) is either (the same as) that (person) or different from that (person) in the case that the person deceases and is born from *niraya* into *tiryagyoni*, then you should not say that it cannot be said that this (person) is either (the same as) that (person) or different from that (person).

It is unreasonable that you say : It cannot be said that this (person) is either (the same as) that (person) or different from that (person).

In the same way as the person deceases and is born from *niraya* into *tiryagyoni*, the person deceases and is born from *niraya* into *pitryaviṣaya*.

The following (Nos. 1 to 6) is the argument of whether or not the person transmigrates from *niraya* to *manuṣyā*.

—Translation of Section 1, continued (T. 26, 537c-538 b)—

1. The Pudgala school states thus : The person is known, recognized, and exists actually and exists in the real, ultimate sense. Therefore, the person certainly exists.

The Śūnyatāvādin asks thus : Did the Buddha teach well, . . . ? (This is the same as in No. 1 of the above.)

Pud. : Yes.

Śūn. : Does the (same) person decease and is the (same) person born from *niraya* into *tiryagyoni* ?

Pud. : Yes.

Śūn. : Acknowledge the refutation.

. . .the same as in No. 1 of the above.

2. The Pudgala school states thus : The person certainly deceases and is born from *niraya* into *manuṣyā*.

Śūn. : Is this (person) (the same as) that (person) ?

Pud. : No.

Śūn. : Acknowledge the refutation.

If the person certainly deceases and is born from *niraya* into *manuṣyā*, then you should say that this (person) is (the same as) that (person).

What you say here is unreasonable.

If you do not say that this (person) is (the same as) that (person), then you should not say that the person certainly deceases and is born from *niraya* into *manuṣyā*.

It is unreasonable that you say : The person certainly deceases and is born from *niraya* into *manuṣyā*.

3. In the case that the Pudgala school says thus : This (person) is (the same as) that (person), the Śūnyatāvādin will question, saying : Is the *niraya* (the same as) the *manuṣyā* ?

Pud. : No.

Śūn. : Acknowledge the refutation.

If this (person) is (the same as) that (person), then you should say that the *niraya* is (the same as) the *manuṣyā*.

What you say here is unreasonable.

If you do not say that the *niraya* is (the same as) the *manuṣyā*, then you should not say that this (person) is (the same as) that (person).

It is unreasonable that you say : This (person) is (the same as) that (person).

4. In the case that the Pudgala school says thus : This (person) is (the same as) that (person), the Śūnyatāvādin will question, saying : Is there no capacity of producing the five faculties, the five strengths and the seven factors of enlightenment of 'without influence' (*anāsrava*) in *niraya*, and is there a capacity in *manuṣyā* ?[1]

Pud. : Yes.

Śūn. : Is that there is no capacity (the same as) that there is a capacity ?

Pud. : No.

Śūn. : Acknowledge the refutation.

If this (person) is (the same as) that (person), then you should say that that there is no capacity is (the same as) that there is a capacity.

What you say here is unreasonable.

If you do not say that that there is no capacity is (the same as) that there is a capacity, then you should not say that this (person) is (the same as) that (person).

It is unreasonable that you say: This (person) is (the same as) that (person).

5. In the case that the Pudgala school says thus : This (person) is different from that (person), the Śūnyatāvādin will question, saying : Is this (person in *niraya*) annihilated and is that (person) born in *manuṣyā* different ?

Pud. : No.

Śūn. : Acknowledge the refutation.

If this (person) is different from that (person), then you should say that this (person in *niraya*) is annihilated and that (person) born in *manuṣyā* is different.

What you say here is unreasonable.

If you do not say that this (person in *niraya*) is annihilated and that (person) born in *manuṣyā* is different, then you should not say that this (person) is different from that (person).

---

1. At this point, "入趣" (meaning 'enter *gati*') is to be read as "人趣" (meaning '*manuṣyā*'). (See T. 26, 538 a.)

It is unreasonable that you say : This (person) is different from that (person).

6. In the case that the Pudgala school says thus : It cannot be said that this (person) is either (the same as) that (person) or different from that (person), the Śūnyatāvādin will question, saying : Is it impossible to say that this (person) is either (the same as) that (person) or different from that (person) in the case that the person deceases and is born from *niraya* into *manuṣyā* ?

Pud. : No. It is impossible to say so.

Śūn. : Acknowledge the refutation.

If it cannot be said that this (person) is either (the same as) that (person) or different from that (person), then you should say that it is impossible to say that this (person) is either (the same as) that (person) or different from that (person) in the case that the person deceases and is born from *niraya* into *manuṣyā*.

What you say here is unreasonable.

If you do not say that it is impossible to say that this (person) is either (the same as) that (person) or different from that (person) in the case that the person deceases and is born from *niraya* into *manuṣyā*, then you should not say that it cannot be said that this (person) is either (the same as) that (person) or different from that (person).

It is unreasonable that you say : It cannot be said that this (person) is either (the same as) that (person) or different from that (person).

In the same way as the person deceases and is born from *niraya* into *manuṣyā*, the person deceases and is born from *niraya* into *devā*.

Although it should not be said that in *niraya*, *tiryagyoni* and *pitryaviṣaya* there is a capacity, it should be said that in *devā* and *manuṣyā* there is a capacity.

Although it should not be said that in *devā* and *manuṣyā* there is not a capacity, it should be said that in *niraya*, *tiryagyoni* and *pitryaviṣaya* there is not a capacity.

11.12. The second section treats of whether or not the person can be recognized in eight types of person worth honouring.

—Translation of Section 2 (T. 26, 538 b-539 a)—

1. The Pudgala school states thus : The person is known, recognized, and exists actually and exists in the real, ultimate sense. Therefore, the person certainly exists.

The Śūnyatāvādin asks thus : Did the Buddha teach well, say well and state well in the *sūtra* : There are certainly eight types of person and they are established as different, namely : 1. *srota-āpatti-pratipannaka* '(one who is) obtaining the realization of the fruit of stream-attainment', 2. *srota-āpanna* '(one who has) attained stream', . . . 7. *arhatpratipannaka* '(one who is) obtaining the realization of the fruit of Arahantship', and 8. *arhat* '(one who is) Arahant'; then *srota-āpatti-pratipannaka*, *srota-āpanna*,. . . *arhatpratipannaka* and *arhat* are certainly different ?

Pud. : Yes.

Śūn. : Do persons of *srota-āpatti-pratipannaka* become *srota-āpanna* ?

Pud. : Yes.

Śūn. : Acknowledge the refutation.

If there are certainly eight types of person and they are established as different, namely : 1. *srota-āpatti-pratipannaka*, . . and 8. *arhat*; then *srota-āpatti-pratipannaka*, *srota-āpanna*, . . *arhatpratipannaka* and *arhat* are certainly different, then you should not say that persons of *srota-āpatti-pratipannaka* become *srota-āpanna*.

What you say here is unreasonable.

If you say that persons of *srota-āpatti-pratipannaka* become *srota-āpanna*, then you should not say that there are certainly eight types of person and they are established as different, namely: 1. *srota-āpatti-pratipannaka*, ...and 8. *arhat*; then *srota-āpatti-pratipannaka*, *srota-āpanna*, . . .*arhatpratipannaka* and *arhat* are certainly different.

It is unreasonable that you say : There are certainly eight types of person and they are established as different, namely: 1. *srota-āpatti-pratipannaka*, . . .and 8. *arhat*;

then *srota-āpatti-pratipannaka, srota-āpanna . . .arhatpratipannaka* and *arhat* are certainly different.

2. The Pudgala school states thus : Persons of *srota-āpatti-pratipannaka* become *srota-āpanna.*

The Śūnyatāvādin will question, saying : Is this (the same as) that ? (This means "Whether or not persons of *srota-āpatti-pratipannaka* are the same as persons of *srota-āpanna.*")

Pud. : No.

Śūn. : Acknowledge the refutation.

If persons of *srota-āpatti-pratipannaka* become *srota-āpanna,* then you should say that this (person) is (the same as) that (person).

What you say here is unreasonable.

If you do not say that this (person) is (the same as) that (person), then you should not say that persons of *srota-āpatti-pratipannaka* become *srota-āpanna.*

It is unreasonable that you say : Persons of *srota-āpatti-pratipannaka* become *srota-āpanna.*

3. In the case that the Pudgala school states thus : This (person) is (the same as) that (person), the Śūnyatāvādin will question, saying : Is the *pratipannaka* '(one who is) obtaining' (the same as) the *phala-sthita* '(one who is) established in the fruit' ?

Pud. : No.

Śūn. : Acknowledge the refutation.

If this (person) is (the same as) that (person), then you should say that the *pratipannaka* is (the same as) the *phala-sthita.*

What you say here is unreasonable.

If you do not say that the *pratipannaka* is (the same as) the *phala-sthita,* then you should not say that this (person) is (the same as) that (person).

It is unreasonable that you say : This (person) is (the same as) that (person).

4. In the case that the Pudgala school states thus : This (person) is (the same as) that (person), the Śūnyatāvādin will

question, saying : Do persons of *srota-āpatti-pratipannaka* not accomplish the fruit and do persons of *srota-āpanna* accomplish the fruit ?

Pud. : Yes.

Śūn. : Then, the unaccomplishment is (the same as) the accomplishment ?

Pud. : No.

Śūn. : Acknowledge the refutation.

If persons of *srota-āpatti-pratipannaka* do not accomplish the fruit and persons of *srota-āpanna* do accomplish the fruit, then you should say that the unaccomplishment is (the same as) the accomplishment.

What you say here is unreasonable.

If you do not say that the unaccomplishment is (the same as) the accomplishment, then you should not say that this (person) is (the same as) that (person).

It is unreasonable that you say : This (person) is (the same as) that (person).

5. In the case that the Pudgala school states thus : This (person) is different from that (person), the Śūnyatāvādin will question, saying : Are persons of *srota-āpatti-pratipannaka* annihilated and are persons born as *srota-āpanna* different ?

Pud. : No.

Śūn. : Acknowledge the refutation.

If this (person) is different from that (person), then you should say that persons of *srota-āpatti-pratipannaka* are annihilated and persons born as *srota-āpanna* are different.

What you say here is unreasonable.

If you do not say that persons of *srota-āpatti-pratipannaka* are annihilated and persons born as *srota-āpanna* are different, then you should not say that this (person) is different from that (person).

It is unreasonable that you say : This (person) is different from that (person).

6. In the case that the Pudgala school states thus : It cannot be said that this (person) is either (the same as) that (person)

or different from that (person), the Śūnyatāvādin will question, saying : Is it impossible to say that this (person) is either (the same as) that (person) or different from that (person) in the case that persons of *srota-āpatti-pratipannaka* become *srota-āpanna*?

Pud. : No. It is impossible to say so.

Śūn. : Acknowledge the refutation.

If it cannot be said that this (person) is either (the same as) that (person) or different from that (person), then you should say that it is impossible to say that this (person) is either (the same as) that (person) or different from that (person) in the case that persons of *srota-āpatti-pratipannaka* become *srota-āpanna*.

What you say here is unreasonable.

If you do not say that it is impossible to say that this (person) is either (the same as) that (person) or different from that (person) in the case that persons of *srota-āpatti-pratipannaka* become *srota-āpanna*, then you should not say that it cannot be said that this (person) is either (the same as) that (person) or different from that (person).

It is unreasonable that you say : It cannot be said that this (person) is either (the same as) that (person) or different from that (person).

In section 2 below (T.26,539 a-540 c), the discussion of whether or not persons of *anāgāmipratipannaka* '(one who is) obtaining the realization of the fruit of never-returning' become *anāgāmi* '(one who has) never returned' is recorded in the same way as above.

Section 3 (T.26,540 c-542 a) deals with the person in three *rāśis*, namely: 1. *mithyātvaniyatarāśi* 'heap of wrongness', 2. *samyaktvaniyatarāśi* 'heap of rightness' and 3. *aniyatarāśi* 'heap of the undetermined'. This section is explained in the same way as in sections 1 and 2.

11.13 The fourth section treats of whether or not three types of person accomplish three kinds of training (*śaikṣas*).

—Translation of Section 4 (T.26,542 a-b)—

The Pudgala school states thus : The person is known, recognized, and exists actually and exists in the real, ultimate sense. Therefore, the person certainly exists.

The Śūnyatāvādin asks thus : Did the Buddha teach well, say well and state well in the *sūtra* : There are certainly three types of person and they are established as different, namely : 1. the person as a learner (*śaikṣa*), 2. the person as the learned (*aśaikṣa*), and 3. the person who is neither a learner nor the learned (*naivaśaikṣanāśaikṣa*) ?

Pud. : Yes.

Śūn. : Are there also three *dharmas* (principles), namely : 1. *śaikṣa*, 2. *aśaikṣa*, and 3. *naivaśaikṣanāśaikṣa* ?

Pud. : Yes.

Śūn. : Does the person who is neither a learner nor the learned become the person as a learner, and does he become the person as the learned after having become the person as a learner, and then does he become the person as a learner again after having become the person as the learned ?

Pud. : Yes.

Śūn. : Does the principle of *naivaśaikṣanāśaikṣa* become the principle of *śaikṣa*, and does it become the principle of *aśaikṣa* after having become the principle of *śaikṣa*, and then does it become the principle of *śaikṣa* again after having become the principle of *aśaikṣa* ?

Pud. : No.

Śūn. : Acknowledge the refutation.

If the person who is neither a learner nor the learned becomes the person as a learner, and he becomes the person as the learned after having become the person as a learner, and then he becomes the person as a learner again after having become the person as the learned, then you should say : the principle of *naivaśaikṣanāśaikṣa* becomes the principle of *śaikṣa*, and it becomes the principle of *aśaikṣa* after having become the principle of *śaikṣa*, and then it becomes the principle of *śaikṣa* again after having become the principle of *aśaikṣa*.

What you say here is unreasonable.

If you do not say: the principle of *naivaśaikṣanāśaikṣa* becomes the principle of *śaikṣa*, and it becomes the principle of *aśaikṣa* after having become the principle of *śaikṣa*, and then it becomes the principle of *śaikṣa* again after having become the principle of *aśaikṣa*, then you should not say : the person who is neither a learner nor the learned becomes the person as a learner, and he becomes the person as the learned after having become the person as a learner, and then he becomes the person as a learner again after having become the person as the learned.

It is unreasonable that you say : The person who is neither a learner nor the learned becomes the person as a learner, and he becomes the person as the learned after having become the person as a learner, and then he becomes the person as a learner again after having become the person as the learned.

11.14 The fifth section treats of how the person performs *karmans* based on three sensations (*vedanās*).

—Translation of Section 5 (T.26,542 b-c)—

1. The Pudgala school states thus : There is *ātman* (ego), *sattva* (being), *jīva* (the life principle), *jantu* (being), *poṣa* (man), *puruṣa* (man), and *pudgala*. Because the person exists, he performs *karmans* favouring either a happy sensation or an unhappy sensation or the sensation that is neither unhappy nor happy. He feels a happy sensation after having performed a *karman* favouring a happy sensation, he feels an unhappy sensation after having performed a *karman* favouring an unhappy sensation, and he feels the sensation that is neither unhappy nor happy after having performed a *karman* favouring the sensation that is neither unhappy nor happy.

The Śūnyatāvādin asks thus : Are unhappiness and happiness self-made ?

Pud. : No.

Śūn. : Acknowledge the refutation.

If you say : there is *ātman*, *sattva*, *jīva*, *jantu*, *poṣa*, *puruṣa*, and *pudgala*; because the person exists, he performs *karmans* favouring either a happy sensation or an unhappy sensation or the sensation that is neither unhappy nor happy; he feels a happy sensation after having performed a *karman* favouring a happy sensation, he feels an unhappy sensation after having performed a *karman* favouring an unhappy sensation, and he feels the sensation that is neither unhappy nor happy after having performed a *karman* favouring the sensation that is neither unhappy nor happy, then you should say that unhappiness and happiness are self-made.

What you say here is unreasonable.

If you do not say that unhappiness and happiness are self-made, then you should not say : there is *ātman*, *sattva*, . . .and he feels the sensation that is neither unhappy nor happy after having performed a *karman* favouring the sensation that is neither unhappy nor happy.

It is unreasonable that you say : There is *ātman*, *sattva*, . . .and he feels the sensation that is neither unhappy nor happy after having performed a *karman* favouring the sensation that is neither unhappy nor happy.

2. In the case that the Pudgala school states thus: Unhappiness and happiness are self-made, the Śūnyatāvādin will question, saying : Did the Buddha teach well, say well and state well to Timbaruka, a non-Buddhist in the *sūtra* : "I have never said that the sensation is the same as he that feels and from the beginning beings make for themselves unhappiness and happiness" ?

Pud. : Yes.

Śūn. : Acknowledge the refutation.

If unhappiness and happiness are self-made, then you should not say : the Buddha taught Timbaruka : "I have never said that the sensation is the same as he that feels and that from the beginning beings make for themselves unhappiness and happiness."

What you say here is unreasonable.

If you say : the Buddha taught Timbaruka: "I have never said that the sensation is the same as he that feels and that from the beginning beings make for themselves unhappiness and happiness," then you should not say that unhappiness and happiness are self-made.

It is unreasonable that you say : Unhappiness and happiness are self-made.

3. In the case that the Pudgala school states thus: Unhappiness and happiness are made by another, the Śūnyatāvādin will question, saying : Did the Buddha teach well, say well and state well to Timbaruka in the *sūtra* : "I have never said that the sensation is different from he that feels and that unhappiness and happiness are made by another" ?

Pud. : Yes.

Śūn. : Acknowledge the refutation.

If unhappiness and happiness are made by another, then you should not say : the Buddha taught Timbaruka : "I have never said that the sensation is different from he that feels and that unhappiness and happiness are made by another."

What you say here is unreasonable.

If you say : the Buddha taught Timbaruka : "I have never said that the sensation is different from he that feels and that unhappiness and happiness are made by another," then you should not say that unhappiness and happiness are made by another.

It is unreasonable that you say : Unhappiness and happiness are made by another.

—Translation of Section 5, continued (T.26,542 c-543 b)—

1. The Pudgala school states thus : There is *ātmau*, *sattva*, *jiva*, *jantu*, *poṣa*, *puruṣa*, and *pudgala*. Because the person exists, he performs *karmans* favouring either a happy sensation or an unhappy sensation or the sensation that is neither unhappy nor happy. He feels a happy sensation after having performed a

karman favouring a happy sensation, he feels an unhappy sensation after having performed a *karman* favouring an unhappy sensation, and he feels the sensation that is neither unhappy nor happy after having performed a *karman* favouring the sensation that is neither unhappy nor happy.

The Śūnyatāvādin asks thus : Is he that performs *karman*(*s*) the same as he that feels ?

Pud. : No.

Śūn. : Acknowledge the refutation.

If you say : there is *ātman*, *sattva*, . . .and he feels the sensation that is neither unhappy nor happy after having performed a *karman* favouring the sensation that is neither unhappy nor happy, then you should not say that he that performs *karman* (*s*) is the same as he that feels.

What you say here is unreasonable.

If you do not say that he that performs *karman*(*s*) is the same as he that feels, then you should not say : there is *ātman*, *sattva*, . . .and he feels the sensation that is neither unhappy nor happy after having performed a *karman* favouring the sensation that is neither unhappy nor happy.

It is unreasonable that you say : There is *ātman*, *sattva*, ...and he feels the sensation that is neither unhappy nor happy after having performed a *karman* favouring the sensation that is neither unhappy nor happy.

2. In the case that the Pudgala school states thus : He that performs *karman*(*s*) is the same as he that feels, the Śūnyatāvādin will question, saying : Did the Buddha teach well, say well and state well to a brahman in the *sūtra* : "He who performs *karman* (*s*) and feels (their results) falls into the extreme of eternalism (*śāśvata-anta*)" ?

Pud. : Yes.

Śūn. : Acknowledge the refutation.

If you say that he that performs *karman*(*s*) is the same as he that feels, then you should not say : the

Buddha taught a brahman : "He who performs *karman*(*s*) and feels (their results) falls into the extreme of eternalism."

What you say here is unreasonable.

If you say : the Buddha taught a brahman : "He who performs *karman*(*s*) and feels (their results) falls into the extreme of eternalism," then you should not say that he that performs *karman*(*s*) is the same as he that feels.

It is unreasonable that you say : He that performs *karman*(*s*) is the same as he that feels.

11.15. The sixth section treats of whether or not the person exists in *dharmas* (principles) seen (*dṛṣṭa*), heard (*śruta*), sensed (*mata*), and cognized (*vijñāta*).

—Translation of Section 6 (T. 26, 543 b-c)—

The Pudgala school states thus : There is *ātman*, *sattva*, *jīva*, *jantu*, *poṣa*, *puruṣa* and *pudgala*. Because the person exists, among *dharmas* seen, heard, sensed, cognized, what is obtained (*prāpta*) (or) sought for (*paryeṣita*) is pondered on (*anuvicarita*) by the mind.

The Śūnyatāvādin asks thus : Did the Buddha teach well, say well and state well to the monk Ariṭṭha in the *sūtra* : "Whatever is seen, heard, sensed, cognized, obtained, sought for, pondered on by the mind is regarded as : 'this is not mine; I am not it; it is not my self'. This should be seen in its true nature by means of right understanding" ?

Pud. : Yes.

Śūn. : Acknowledge the refutation.

If you say : there is *ātman*, *sattva*, . . .among principles seen, heard, sensed, cognized, what is obtained (or) sought for is pondered on by the mind, then you should not say : the Buddha taught the monk Ariṭṭha : "Whatever is seen, heard, . . . this should be seen in its true nature by means of right understanding".

What you say here is unreasonable.

If you say : the Buddha taught the monk Ariṭṭha : "Whatever is seen, heard, . . . this should be seen in its true nature by means of right understanding," then you should not say : there is *ātman*, *sattva*, . . . among principles seen, heard, sensed, cognized, what is obtained (or) sought for is pondered on by the mind.

It is unreasonable that you say : There is *ātman*, *sattva*, . . .among principles seen, heard, sensed, cognized, what is obtained (or) sought for is pondered on by the mind.

11.16. The seventh section treats of the relation between the occurrence of benevolence (*maitrā*) and the person.

—Translation of Section 7 (T. 26, 543 c-544 c)—

1. The Śūnyatāvādin states thus : The person is not known nor recognized and never exists actually and does not exist in the real, ultimate sense. Therefore, the person does not exist.

The Pudgala school asks thus : Through what mental object (*ālambana*) is there benevolence ?

Śūn. : *Dharmas* (principles) have a nature which exists. The 'being' (*sattva*) is designated according to recognition (*saṃjñā*) and recognizing (*saṃjñānanā*).[1] In this sense, through the continuance of *skandhas* (groups) there is benevolence.

Pud. : Do you say: through the continuance of *skandhas* there is benevolence ?

Śūn. : Yes.

Pud. : Did the Buddha teach well, say well and state well in the *sūtra* : "In order to make beings happy, he enters meditation charged with benevolence (*maitrā-samāprāpti*) " ?

Śūn. : Yes.

Pud. : Acknowledge the refutation.

If there is benevolence through the continuance of *skandhas*, then you should not say : the Buddha taught:

1. It appears that the word '*saṃjñā*' here is used in the sense of 'recognition' rather than 'perception', in considering the following explanation : "recognition (*saññā*) is the noting of objects such as blue-green, yellow" (see *Visuddhimagga*, p. 437, p. 462, etc.).

"In order to make beings happy, he enters meditation charged with benevolence."

What you say here is unreasonable.

If you say : the Buddha taught : "In order to make beings happy, he enters meditation charged with benevolence," then you should not say that there is benevolence through the continuance of *skandhas*.

It is unreasonable that you say : Through the continuance of *skandhas*, there is benevolence.

2. (The Śūnyatāvādin) asks thus : Did the Buddha teach well, say well and state well in the *sūtra* : "There are six kinds of consciousness, namely : 1. eye-consciousness, 2. ear-consciousness, 3. nose-consciousness, 4. tongue-consciousness, 5. body-consciousness, and 6. mind-consciousness" ?

Pud. : Yes.

Śūn. : Venerable one, with what kinds of consciousness is benevolence connected ? With 'eye-consciousness' ? With 'ear-consciousness' ? With 'nose-consciousness' ? With 'tongue-consciousness' ? With 'mind-consciousness' ? If you say that benevolence is connected with 'eye-consciousness', then benevolence does not depend on the being because 'eye-consciousness' depends only on visible objects (*rūpa*). (This refers to "conditioned by eye and visible objects, arises 'eye-consciousness.')

If you say that benevolence is connected with 'ear-consciousness', then benevolence does not depend on the being because 'ear-consciousness' depends only on sound, . . . if you say that benevolence is connected with 'mind-consciousness', then benevolence does not depend on the being because 'mind-consciousness' depends only on mental objects.

If you say that benevolence is not connected with 'eye-consciousness', . . .'mind-consciousness', then there would be a seventh consciousness of the being and benevolence would be connected with it; but the Buddha did not so understand it.

Venerable one, the Buddha explained with perfect self-confidence (*vaiśāradya*) as follows : "I was perfectly enlightened as to *dharmas* (principles). In spite of the fact that I was enlightened with perfect enlightenment, if strivers, brahmans, its Devas, its Māras, its Brahmās in this world said together that he was not enlightened, I did not see any reason for doubt.[1] Because I was enlightened, I was full of peace (*kṣema*), free from fear (*abhaya*) and gained self-confidence; and I myself established the great wheel of truth in the place called the basis of a great man (*ārṣabha-sthāna*) and roared like a lion in the assembly." Venerable one, if so, why do you not blame the Buddha for his ignorance ?

Pud. : Venerable one, I do not blame the Buddha for his ignorance. He well understood it, but did not explain it.

Śūn. : Venerable one, the Buddha taught venerable Ānanda : "I always explain the four *smṛtyupasthānas*, the four *samyakpradhānas*, the four *ṛddhipādas*, the five *indriyas*, the five *balas*, the seven *saṃbodhyaṅgas*, and the eight *āryamārgāṅgas*. Ānanda, the *tathāgata* never keeps his hand closed (*ācārya-muṣṭi* : teacher's fist) in teaching. If I maintain reserve, another *ātman* (may) be conscious of it. I am afraid of this." Venerable one, if so, why do you not blame the Buddha for keeping his hand closed ?

Pud. : Venerable one, I do not blame the Buddha for his ignorance. I do not blame the Buddha for keeping his hand closed. He well understood it, but did not explain it.

The Buddha explained in *Śiṃśapāvanasūtra* : Monks, although I realized completely and well understood principles as innumerable as the sands on the earth and leaves of a *Śiṃśapā* tree, I did not preach them to others. Thus the Buddha did not explain such a consciousness, though he well understood it.

Śūn. : Is there not a further statement left out in the *sūtra* : Monks, however, such principles are not concerned

1. At this point, we follow a free translation, because the Chinese version seems to make no sense.

with the meaning, with good, with truth (*dharma*), do not lead to the best life (*brahmacariya*), do not conduce to insight (*abhijñā*), to enlightenment, to *nirvāṇa* ?

If there is such a person (*pudgala*), it is not concerned with the meaning, with good, with truth, does not lead to the best life, do not conduce to insight, to enlightenment, to *nirvāṇa*.

That is to say, it is useless. Therefore, the person does not exist.

In section 7 below (T. 26, 544 c-545 b), the relation between the occurrence of benevolence in the four *smṛtyupasthānas* and the seven *saṃbodhyaṅgas* and the person is discussed in the same way as above.

11.17 The eighth section treats of the relation of the person to the unsynthesized and the synthesized.

—Translation of Section 8 (T. 26,545 b)—

The Pudgala school states thus : The synthesized (*saṃskṛta*) is known, the unsynthesized (*asaṃskṛta*) is known, and the person is also known.

The Śūnyatāvādin asks thus : Venerable one, is the person the synthesized or the unsynthesized ?

If you say that the person is the synthesized, then the person is established in the same way as the synthesized, and there is *jāti* (birth), *anityatā* (impermanence), *sthiti* (persistence), and *anyathātva* (difference).

If you say that the person is the unsynthesized, then the person is established in the same way as the unsynthesized, and there is no birth, nor impermanence, nor persistence, nor difference.

Venerable one, the Buddha taught the monks : "There are two classes, that is, 1. the synthesized and 2. the unsynthesized. There is no other class than the synthesized and the unsynthesized."

Therefore, it is not the case that the person exists.

11.18 The ninth section deals with the relation of the six kinds of consciousness and the person.

—Translation of Section 9 (T. 26,545 b-547 a)—

1. There are six kinds of consciousness, namely : 1. eye-consciousness, 2. ear-consciousness, 3. nose-consciousness, 4. tongue-consciousness, 5. body-consciousness, and 6. mind-consciousness. Conditioned by eye and visible objects, 'eye-consciousness' arises. Such an 'eye-consciousness' presents (lit. cognizes) only visible objects, and is not the person. The person is not what is presented by 'eye-consciousness'. There are only visible objects, which are presented by 'eye-consciousness'. Therefore, the 'eye-consciousness' is not the consciousness of the person.

And conditioned by eye and visible objects, 'eye-consciousness' arises, and because of the connection of the three (eye, visible objects and eye-consciousness), there is contact (*sparśa*). Such an 'eye-contact' presents (lit. touches) only visible objects, and does not present the person. The person is not what is presented by 'eye-contact'. There are only visible objects, which are presented by 'eye-contact'. Therefore, the 'eye-contact' is not the contact of the person.

And conditioned by eye and visible objects, 'eye-consciousness' arises, and because of the connection of the three, there is contact. Conditioned by contact, sensation (*vedanā*) arises. Such a sensation originating from 'eye-contact' presents (lit. feels) only visible objects, and is not the person. The person is not what is presented by sensation originating from 'eye-contact'. There are only visible objects, which are presented by sensation originating from 'eye-consciousness'. Therefore, the sensation originating from 'eye-contact' is not the sensation originating from 'the person-contact'.

And conditioned by eye and visible objects, 'eye-consciousness' arises, and because of the connection of the three, there is contact. Conditioned by contact, perception (*saṃjñā*) arises. Such a perception originating from 'eye-contact' presents (lit. perceives) only visible objects, and is not the person. The person is not what is presented by perception originating from 'eye-contact'. There are only visible objects, which are presented by perception originating from 'eye-contact'. Therefore, the perception originating from 'eye-contact' is not the perception originating from 'the person-contact'.

And conditioned by eye and visible objects, 'eye-consciousness' arises, and because of the connection of the three, there is contact. Conditioned by contact, volition (*cetanā*) arises. Such a volition originating from 'eye-contact' presents (lit.wills) only visible objects, and is not the person. The person is not what is presented by volition originating from 'eye-contact'. There are only visible objects, which are presented by volition originating from 'eye-contact'. Therefore, the volition originating from 'eye-contact' is not the volition originating from 'the person-contact'.

Because the contact from which principles (*dharmas*) arise is the fifth *dharma* (of consciousness, contact, sensation, perception and volition, and there is no other *dharma* from which principles arise than contact), the person is not known, nor recognized and never exists actually and does not exist. Therefore, it is not the case that the person exists.

In the same way as 'eye-consciousness', the other five kinds of consciousness are also followed.

2. There are six kinds of consciousness, namely : 1. eye-consciousness, . . .and 6. mind-consciousness. Conditioned by eye and visible objects, 'eye-consciousness' arises. Eye, visible objects and eye-consciousness are not the person, and conditioned by only eye and visible objects, 'eye-consciousness' arises. And conditioned by eye and visible objects, 'eye-consciousness' arises, and because of the connection of the three (eye, visible objects and eye-consciousness), there is contact. Eye, visible objects, eye-consciousness and contact are not the person. Conditioned by only eye and visible objects, 'eye-consciousness' arises, and because of the connection of the three, there is contact.

And conditioned by eye and visible objects, 'eye-consciousness' arises, and because of the connection of the three, there is contact. Conditioned by contact, sensation arises. Eye, visible objects, eye-consciousness, eye-contact and sensation originating from 'eye-contact' are not the person. Conditioned by only eye and visible objects, 'eye-consciousness' arises. Because of the connection of the three, there is contact. Conditioned by contact, sensation arises.

And conditioned by eye and visible objects, 'eye-consciousness' arises, and because of the connection of the three, there is contact. Conditioned by contact, there is perception. Eye, visible objects, eye-consciousness, eye-contact and perception originating from 'eye-contact' are not the person. Conditioned by only eye and visible objects, 'eye-consciousness' arises, and because of the connection of the three, there is contact. Conditioned by contact, perception arises.

And conditioned by eye and visible objects, 'eye-consciousness' arises, and because of the connection of the three, there is contact. Conditioned by contact, volition arises. Eye, visible objects, eye-consciousness, eye-contact and volition originating from 'eye-contact' are not the person. Conditioned by only eye and visible objects, 'eye-consciousness' arises, and because of the connection of the three, there is contact. Conditioned by contact, volition arises.

Because the contact from which principles arise is the fifth *dharma* (of consciousness, contact, sensation, perception and volition, and there is no other *dharma* from which principles arise than contact), the person is not known, nor recognized, and never exists actually and does not exist. Therefore, it is not the case that the person exists.

In the same way as 'eye-consciousness', the other five kinds of consciousness are also followed.

3. There are six kinds of consciousness, namely : 1. eye-consciousness, . . .and 6. mind-consciousness. Conditioned by eye and visible objects, 'eye-consciousness' arises. It is impossible that eye and visible objects arise and 'eye-consciousness' does not arise. It is possible that eye and visible objects arise and 'eye-consciousness' also arises. It is impossible that eye and visible objects cease and 'eye-consciousness' does not cease. It is possible that eye and visible objects cease and 'eye-consciousness' also ceases.

And conditioned by eye and visible objects, 'eye-consciousness' arises, and because of the connection of the three, there is contact. It is impossible that eye, visible objects and 'eye-consciousness' arise and 'eye-contact' does not arise. It is possible that eye, visible objects and 'eye-consciousness' arise and 'eye-contact' also arises. It is impossible that eye, visible objects and 'eye-consciousness' cease and 'eye-contact' does not cease. It is possible that eye, visible objects and 'eye-consciousness' cease and 'eye-contact' also ceases, . . .The contact from which principles arise is the fifth *dharma*, and (the eighteen *dhātus* and the six contacts) arise simultaneously, and persist simultaneously, and cease simultaneously. When one of them arises, the other (principles) also arise; when one of them ceases, the other (principles) also cease. Because the contact from which principles arise is the fifth *dharma*, the person is not known, nor recognized, and never exists actually and does not exist. Therefore, it is not the case that the person exists.

4. There are six kinds of consciousness, namely : 1. eye-consciousness, . . .and 6. mind-consciousness. Conditioned by eye and visible objects, 'eye-consciousness' arises. Such an 'eye-consciousness' presents (lit. cognizes) visible objects, and is not contact nor sensation nor perception nor volition, because the characteristic (*lakṣaṇa*) of the activity of consciousness is 'eye-consciousness'.

And conditioned by eye and visible objects, 'eye-consciousness' arises, and because of the connection of the three, there is contact. Such an 'eye-contact' presents (lit. touches) visible objects, and is not sensation nor perception nor volition nor consciousness, because the characteristic of the activity of contact is 'eye-contact', . . .The contact from which principles arise is the fifth *dharma*, and (the eighteen *dhātus* and the six contacts) arise simultaneously, and persist simultaneously, and cease simultaneously. When one of them arises, the other (principles) also arise; when one of them ceases, the other (principles) also cease. Having arisen already, each of them functions properly and does not function as to what is unrelated to one another. Because the contact from which principles arise is the fifth *dharma*, the person is not known, nor recognized, and never exists actually and does not exist. Therefore, it is not the case that the person exists.

5. There are six kinds of consciousness, namely : 1. eye-consciousness, . . . and 6. mind-consciousness.

i. Ques. : What does 'eye-consciousness' distinguish (*vijñānāti*) ?

Ans. : It distinguishes visible objects.

Ques. : What does it not distinguish ?

Ans. : The other eleven *āyatanas* (spheres).

ii. Ques. : What does 'ear-consciousness' distinguish ?

Ans. : It distinguishes sounds.

Ques. : What does it not distinguish ?

Ans. : The other eleven *āyatanas*.

The six kinds of consciousness distinguish their own objects, and have the nature of distinguishing their own objects. It is not the case that (they) have not the nature of distinguishing their own objects. The person has not such a nature. Therefore it is not the case that the person exists.

6. There are twelve *āyatanas*, namely : 1. eye and 2. visible objects, 3. ear and 4. sound, 5. nose and 6. odour, 7. tongue and 8. taste, 9. body and 10. tangible object, 11. mind and 12. principles.

Ques. : By how many kinds of consciousness are visible objects presented (lit. cognized), . . .By how many kinds of consciousness are principles presented ?

Ans. : Visible objects are presented (lit. cognized) by two kinds of consciousness, that is, 'eye-consciousness' and 'mind-consciousness'. Sound is presented by two kinds of consciousness, that is, 'ear-consciousness' and 'mind-consciousness'. Odour is presented by two kinds of consciousness, that is, 'nose-consciousness' and 'mind-consciousness'. Taste is presented by two kinds of consciousness, that is, 'tongue-consciousness' and 'mind-consciousness'. Tangible object is presented by two kinds of consciousness, that is, 'body-consciousness' and 'mind-consciousness'. The other seven *āyatanas* (that is, eye, ear, nose, tongue, body, mind and principles) are presented by only 'mind-consciousness'. The twelve *āyatanas* are presented (lit. cognized) by one another, and have the nature of being presented by one another. It is not the case that (they) have not the nature of being presented by one another. The person has not such a nature. Therefore, it is not the case that the person exists.

7. There are six kinds of consciousness, namely : 1. eye-consciousness, . . .and 6. mind-consciousness. Conditioned by eye and visible objects, 'eye-consciousness' arises, and because of the connection of the three, there is contact. There is sensation, perception and volition, which arise simultaneously with contact. Because the contact from which principles arise is the fifth *dharma* (of consciousness, contact, sensation, perception and volition, and there is no other *dharma* from which principles arise than contact), the person is not known, nor recognized, and never exists actually and does not exist. Therefore, it is not the case that the person exists.

In the same way as 'eye-consciousness', the other five kinds of consciousness are also followed.

11.19 From chapter **11.11** up to chapter **11.18**, we have tried to translate the *pudgalaskandha* of the *Vijñānakāya* into English. It may be said that throughout the *pudgalaskandha* the Śūnyatāvādin (Sarvāstivādin) maintains the non-existence of the person and at the same time, the existence of *gatis*, because in each section the difference of *gatis* is emphasized by stating: "There are certainly five kinds of *gatis* and they are established as different, . . .," "If there are certainly eight types of person and they are established as different, then it must follow that one person becomes another person, which is unreasonable, . . ."

First of all, it must be noted that the Śūnyatāvādin begins by informing the Pudgala school of what was taught by the Buddha and tries to refute the Pudgala school by pointing out that the existence of the person maintained by the Pudgala school is inconsistent with what was taught by the Buddha. In the first section, for example, the Śūnyatāvādin asks as follows (see No. 1 of section 1 in chapter **11.11**):

> Is it true that the Buddha taught : "There are certainly five kinds of *gatis*, and they are established as different and are certainly different" ?

To this question, the Pudgala school answers "Yes." Then the Śūnyatāvādin asks as follows :

> Does the (same) person decease and is the (same) person born from *niraya* into *tiryagyoni* ?

Although the Pudgala school answers "Yes" to this question, the Śūnyatāvādin points out that in order to be consistent with what was taught by the Buddha, the answer to this question should be "No". In other words, the Śūnyatāvādin maintains the forms $p \supset -q$ and $q \supset -p$, whilst the Pudgala school maintains the form $p \supset q$. Such argument forms of the Śūnyatāvādin are also maintained in the beginning of the second and third sections (e.g. see No. 1 of section 2 in chapter **11.12**). It seems that the Śūnyatāvādin cites the Buddha's teachings to lend authority to his own statements.

Secondly, it is not a little remarkable to note that in demonstrating the non-existence of the person, the Śūnyatāvādin asks the Pudgala school if (1) the person is the same in the five *gatis*, or (2) he is different in them, or (3) he is neither the same nor different in them. Such questions are asked not only in the first section, but also in the second and third sections.

According to the Śūnyatāvādin, as far as the individuality of the five *gatis* is taught by the Buddha and also as far as the identity of the person is maintained by the Pudgala school, the person in one of the five *gatis* must be the same as the person in the other *gatis*. Therefore, the Śūnyatāvādin points out two matters :

> 1. If the person certainly deceases and is born from *niraya* into *tiryagyoni*, then you should say that this (person) is (the same as) that (person) (schematized by the form $p \supset q$).
>
> If you do not say that this (person) is (the same as) that (person), then you should not say that the person certainly deceases and is born from *niraya* into *tiryagyoni* (schematized

by the form $-q \supset -p$). (See No. 2. of section 1 in chapter **11.11**).[1]

2. If this (person) is (the same as) that (person), then you should say that the *niraya* is (the same as) the *tiryagyoni* (schematized by the form $p \supset q$).

If you do not say that the *niraya* is (the same as) the *tiryagyoni*, then you should not say that this (person) is (the same as) that (person) (schematized by the form $-q \supset -p$). (See No. 3 of section 1 in chapter **11.11**).[2]

On this point, the *Kathāvatthu* states as follows (p. 30):

If the same person transmigrates, without becoming different, when deceasing to another world, there will then be no death; the killing of life will cease to take place. There is a *karman*; there is its result; there is the result of *karman* done. But when good and bad *karmans* are maturing as results, you say that the same person transmigrates. This is wrong.

In the *pudgalaskandha*, the word '*karman*' itself is not used in explaining the transmigration from one *gati* into another, but what is emphasized here seems to be the same essentially in both the *puggalakathā* and the *pudgalaskandha*.

In the case that the proposition "the person is different in the five *gatis*" is stated by the Pudgala school, the identity of the person cannot be maintained. The Śūnyatāvādin stresses

---

1. What the Śūnyatāvādin points out in item 1 could be rephrased as follows: 1. If the person certainly deceases and is born from *niraya* into *tiryagyoni*, then you should say that this (person) is (the same as) that (person). 2. But it is not the case that this (person) is (the same as) that (person). 3. Therefore, it is not the case that the person certainly deceases and is born from *niraya* into *tiryagyoni*.

Symbolically:

1. $p \supset q$
2. $-q$
3. Therefore, $-p$

2. In the same way as in item 1 above, what the Śūnyatāvādin points out in item 2 could be schematized as follows:

1. $p \supset q$
2. $-q$
3. Therefore, $-p$

this point by asking : "Is this (person in *niraya*) annihilated and is that (person) born in *tiryagyoni* different ?" And also, since "to be annihilated" means here that the person becomes free from not only one *gati*, but also the other *gatis*, the Pudgala school cannot say "Yes" to the above question. Therefore, the Śūnyatāvādin skilfully defeats the Pudgala school.

It goes without saying that the third proposition "the person is neither the same nor different in the five *gatis*" is definitely irrational or unreasonable.

The last half sections are especially devoted to the demonstration of non-existence of the person by quoting the teaching of *anātman* (esp. section 6) and by explaining the relation of the eighteen *dhātus* and the six contacts (esp. section 9).

To speak more precisely, in sections 5 and 6, in order to maintain the existence of the person, the Pudgala school tries to express the person as *ātman*, *sattva*, *jīva*, *jantu*, *poṣa*, *puruṣa*, etc. and to explain that among *dharmas* (principles) seen, heard, sensed, cognized, what is obtained (or) sought for is pondered on by the mind. On the other hand, the Śūnyatāvādin asks the opponent if the Buddha taught the doctrine of *anātman* : "Whatever is seen, heard, sensed, cognized, obtained, sought for, pondered on by the mind is regarded as : 'this is not mine; I am not it; it is not my self'," and finally the Śūnyatāvādin argues down the Pudgala school. This may be compared in a sense with the discussion between the Sthaviravādin and the Pudgala school in the *puggalakathā* (see chapter **11.8**), in which there is the mixed hypothetical syllogism denying the consequent :

If the person exists in the real, ultimat sense, then everything is [inferred to be] of soul. $p \supset q$

It is not the case that all principles are of soul. $-q$

Hence, it is not the case that the person exists. Hence, $-p$

Although the mixed hypothetical syllogism denying the consequent is not used in the *pudgalaskandha*, the method of setting propositions is similar to that in the *puggalakathā*.

Then the Pudgala school tries to take up the problem of benevolence as an act of the person (section 7) and to disregard the doctrine of *anātman*. It is, however, pointed out by the Śūnyatāvādin that the 'being' is designated according to recognition and recognizing, and that there is benevolence through the continuance of the five *skandhas* (groups).

11.20 About each section of the *pudgalaskandha*, there is little need to talk at length. Our main discussion is to compare the forms of argument in the *puggalakathā* with those in the *pudgalaskandha*. A remarkable point here is that in the *pudgalaskandha* the form $p \supset q$ and the form $-q \supset -p$ are always used in their arguments.

As compared with the formulation of arguments in the *puggalakathā*, that of arguments in the *pudgalaskandha* is much simpler. But we see that the method of setting propositions side by side is similar to that in the *puggalakathā*. In other words, the *pudgalaskandha* looks like a simpler version of the debates in the *puggalakathā*. Logical techniques such as the distribution of terms and the relations between propositions are the same as those in the *puggalakathā*, though the distribution of terms in the *pudgalaskandha* can only very loosely be called a logical technique. But it seems that the Śūnyatāvāda school has picked out the essentials and recorded them in the *pudgalaskandha*, and that the forms such as $p \supset q$ and $-q \supset -p$ have developed with the relation of direct and reverse orders of the twelve *pratītyasamutpādas*, which are expressed in the words '*anuloma*' (normal) and '*paṭiloma*' (reverse).

On the whole, we would say that the *pudgalaskandha* is directed not only towards the demonstration of non-existence of the person, but also towards the existence of *dharmas* (esp. sections 7 and 9), in which there seems to be an embryonic anticipation of setting up the existence of the past, present and the future, especially in consideration of the first chapter named Maudgalyāyana.

The conclusion we arrived at is that the Śūnyatāvāda school as well as the Sthaviravāda school agreed on at least the following five points :

1. The structure of the Buddha's teachings.
2. The way of thinking of the early Buddhists.
3. The dialectic method of discussion.

4. How to constitute a valid proof.
5. Logical techniques.

In view of the fact that public debating was an ancient custom in India and that the Buddha stated the following words:

> You should respect the elders and should not be envious of them; you should know the time to look for teachings; you should know the instant when *dhammakathā* (talk on doctrine) begins; and you should listen to the goodly words with care (Sn. 325),

it may safely be said that in their discussions the Buddhists and afterwards the respective schools developed Buddhist philosophy by assimilating fully the five points mentioned above.

It would also appear that these logical techniques, etc., were understood at the time of the Pudgala schism (B.C. 286?[1]) and were consolidated in the Śūnyatā-Sthaviravāda school between that date and the Sarvāstivāda schism (B.C. 237?[2]). Subsequently we see some further clarifications in the Sthaviravāda school (*Kathāvatthu*, etc.).

1. On this, see A. K. Warder, *Indian Buddhism*, p. 240.
2. On this see A. K. Warder, Ibid., p. 273.

12

CONCLUSION

12.1. Since the *Nikāyas* as well as the *Āgamas* cover various fields of learning, they are required to be discussed from the viewpoints of dogmatics, philosophy, psychology, literature, linguistics, and the like. We have attempted to trace the development of the philosophical, and especially the logical aspects of Buddhist thought from the *Nikāyas* into the *Abhidhamma* texts.

12.2. In a sense, we could say that the Buddha teaches us the negative way of thinking, on which Buddhist thought is founded. The problem of negation in philosophy and logic has perplexed scholars of different ages. Apart from this scientifically intricate problem, it is certain that on the basis of the negative way of thinking, Buddhists searched for the humanism of the *Nikāyas*, they explored freedom, they formulated the social programme of non-violence, and they regarded everything with gentle tolerance. At this point, it seems that some Buddhists did not really understand the Buddha's negative way of thinking and others regarded the word 'negative' as meaning "characterized by the absence of distinguishing or marked qualities or features". Therefore, it was alleged by non-Buddhists that Buddhists maintain an uncertain attitude towards life.

For a certainty, the Buddha (as well as his disciples) avoided the expression of emphatic affirmative (or dogmatic) thinking; rather, he tried to give an expression of passivity by the practical use of the double negative, such as :

It is not the case that everything is not having the principle of change.

Such an expression is, however, not an expression arising from the Buddha's ambiguous thinking, but an expression originating from the result of seeking after the truth on the basis of his negative thinking. As we have already learned, the Buddha started with searching for what a human being is, and finally grasped the non-existence of the self, called *anattan.* In other words, the Buddha realized that a human being cannot be grasped without the absence of the self (*anattan*). This does not mean the mere "negation of the self", but means that he found 'not his own-ness' (i.e. the absence of the self) through the medium of his completely negative thinking. Therefore, he points out that ultimate truth cannot be directly expressed in affirmative words alone, and that at the stage of trying to explain what the ultimate truth is, there is no method of doing so other than using a negative phrase such as "this is not *A*", "not *B*", "not *C*", ..."not *X*". This negative phrase is denied by the use of the double negative; and is negated again by the practical use of the triple negative. In this sense, the recognition of *paññā* (understanding) originating from the real grasp of a human being is deeply rooted in the completely negative thinking, which could be formalized by :

("$-A$", "$--A$", "$---A$",...). ("$-B$", "$--B$", "$---B$",...). ... ("$-X$", "$--X$", "$---X$", ...)

Thus we understand the following words :

He who sees (*passati*) the truth (*dhamma*) sees me (the Buddha) ; he who sees me (the Buddha) sees the truth.

He who sees dependent origination (*paṭiccasamuppāda*) sees the truth; he who sees the truth sees dependent origination.

The verb *passati* (3rd person singular, present tense; the root of this is *pass*, and the meaning 'see') is used in the teaching of Buddhism in the meaning of "to have an insight into inner character or underlying truth through the medium of the completely negative thinking," so that "to see the truth" mentioned above is to grasp the absence of the self, and "to see dependent origination" is not only to have a scientific eye for understanding the law of cause and effect, but also to have the eye of truth (*dhammacakkhu*) to realize systematically the fact that all phenomena are composed of involved relations. In this respect, the twelve *paccayākāras* (aspects of condition) in direct and reverse orders teach us the real logic of relations.

12.3 Throughout the whole of Buddhism, we cannot disregard the relation of *sacca*, *paññā*, *anattan*, *paṭiccasamuppāda*, and other principles. These are closely connected with the negative thinking. If we overlook it, we fail to seize the characteristics of all the principles in Buddhism. The reason why the Buddhists' uncertain attitude towards life was alleged by non-Buddhists was, we may say, that Buddhists were far from following the Buddha's completely negative thinking and made an effort only to put constructions upon philosophical terms in Buddhism. In this sense, we must get back to the Buddha. To get back to the Buddha is to look at again the Buddha's way of thinking. This is the only way to trace accurately the development of Buddhist thought.

WORKS CITED

Andersen, D. and Smith, H. ed. *Suttanipāta*. PTS, London, 1913.

Angell, R. B. *Reasoning and Logic*. New York, 1964.

Aung, S. Z. and Rhys Davids, C. A. F. tr. *Points of Controversy* (*Kathāvatthu*), PTS, 1915.

Bally, C. "L' Arbitraire du signe," *Le Francais Moderne*, 8, 1940, pp. 193-206.

Banerjee, A. C. *Sarvāstivāda Literature*. Calcutta, 1957.

Bareau, A. "Les origines du *Śāriputrābhidharmaśāstra*," *Le Muséon*, t. LXIII, 1-2. Louvain, 1950, pp. 69-95.

Basham, A. L. *History and Doctrines of the Ājivakas*. London, 1951 MLBD (Reprint) 1981.

Bloomfield, L. *Language*. MLBD (Reprint) 1980.

Bosanquet, B. *The Essentials of Logic*. London, 1895.

Buddhadatta, A. P. and Warder, A. K. ed. *Mohavicchedanī Abhidhamma-mātikatthavaṇṇanā*. PTS, 1961.

Buddhaghosa, *Sumangalavilāsinī*, ed. Rhys Davids, T. W. Carpenter, J. E. and Stede, W. 3 vols., PTS, 1886-1932.

——— *Atthasālinī*, ed Müller, E. PTS, 1897.

——— *Samantapāsādikā*, ed. Takakusu, J., Nagai, M. and Mizuno, K. 7 vols., PTS, 1924-1947.

Carnap, R. *The Logical Syntax of Language*. London, 1937.

Carpenter, J. E., Rhys Davids, T. W. and Stede, W. ed. *Sumangalavilāsinī* by Buddhaghosa. 3 vols., PTS, 1886-1932.

——— and Rhys Davids, T. W. ed. *Dīgha nikāya*. 3 vols., PTS. 1889-1910.

Chalmers, R., Trenckner, V. and Rhys Davids, C. A. F. ed. *Majjhima nikāya*. 4 vols., PTS, 1887-1925.

Chomsky, N. *Syntactic Structures*. Paris, 1957.

Feer, L. and Rhys Davids, C. A. F. ed. *Saṁyutta nikāya*. 6 vols., PTS, 1884-1904.

Geiger, M. & W. *Pāli Dhamma*. Munich, 1921.

Geiger, W. *Pāli Literature and Language*. English translation, Calcutta University, 1943.

Gnoli, R. ed. *The Gilgit Manuscript of the Saṅghabhedavastu*—Being the 17th and Last Section of the Vinaya of the Mūlasarvāstivādin, Part II. Instituto Italiano per il Medio ed Estremo Oriente, Roma, 1978.

Hardy, E. and Morris, R. ed. *Aṅguttara nikāya*. 6 vols., PTS, 1885-1910.

Hare, E. M. and Woodward, F. L. tr. *The Book of Gradual Sayings* (*Aṅguttara nikāya*). 5 vols., PTS, 1932-1936.

Hiriyanna, M. *The Essentials of Indian Philosophy*. London 1956.

Horner, I. B., Woods, J. H. and Kosambi, D. ed. *Papañcasūdanī: Majjhima Aṭṭhakathā*. 5 vols., PTS, 1922-1938.

——— tr. *The Book of the Discipline* (*Vinaya Piṭaka*). 5 vols., SBB, 1938-1952.

——— "*Abhidhamma, Abhivinaya* in the First Two *Piṭakas* of the Pāli Canon," IHQ, Vol. XVIII, No. 3, September 1941, pp. 219-310.

——— tr. *Middle Length Sayings* (*Majjhima nikāya*). 3 vols., PTS, 1954-1959.

——— tr. *Milinda's Questions* (*Milindapañha*). 2 vols., PTS, 1963-1964.

Jaini, P. S. ed, *Milinda-Ṭīkā*. PTS, 1961.

Jayatilleke, K. N. *Early Buddhist Theory of Knowledge*. London, 1963. MLBD (Reprint) 1981.

Kajiyama, Y. "An Introduction to Buddhist Philosophy : An Annotated Translation of the *Tarkabhāṣā* of Mokṣākaragupta," *Memoirs of the Faculty of Letters*. Kyoto University, No. 10, 1966, pp. 1-173.

Kimura, T. *A Study of Abhidhamma Texts* (*Abhidhamma*-ron no Kenkyu). Tokyo, 1937.

Kopp, H. and Walleser, M. ed. *Manorathapūraṇī : Aṅguttara Aṭṭhakathā*. 5 vols., PTS, 1924-1957.

Kosambi, D., Woods, J. H. and Horner, I. B. ed. *Papañcasūdanī: Majjhima Aṭṭhakathā*. 5 vols., PTS, 1922-1938.

Lamotte, E. *Histoire de Bouddhisme Indien.* Louvain, Muséon, 1958.

La Vallée Poussin, L. de and Thomas, E. J. ed. *Mahāniddesa.* 2 vols., PTS, 1916-1917.

——— "La Controverse du Temps et du Pudgala dans le *Vijñānakāya,*" *Études Asiatiques.* Publications de L'École Francaise d' Extreme-Orient, T. I. 1925, pp. 343-376.

Linsky, L. ed. *Semantics and the Philosophy of Language.* The University of Illinois Press, 1952.

Matilal, B. K. *The Navya-nyāya Doctrine of Negation.* Harvard Oriental Series 46. Harvard University Press, 1968.

Mayeda, E. *A History of the Form of Original Buddhist Texts.* Tokyo, 1964.

Meillet, A. *Linguistique historique et linguistique générale.* New ed., 2 vols., Paris, 1948-1952.

Minayeff, J. ed. *Kathāvatthu Commentary.* JPTS, 1889.

Misra, G. S. P. "Logical and Scientific Method in Early Buddhist Texts," JRAS, parts 1 and 2, 1968, pp. 54-64.

Mizuno, K., Takakusu, J. and Nagai, M. *Samantapāsādikā.* 7 vols., PTS, 1924-1947.

Morris, R. and Hardy, E. ed. *Aṅguttara nikāya.* 6 vols., PTS, 1885-1910.

Müller, E. ed. *Dhammasaṅgaṇi.* PTS, 1885.

——— ed. *Atthasālini.* PTS, 1897.

Murti, T. R. V. *The Central Philosophy of Buddhism.* London, 1955.

Nagai, M., Takakusu, J. and Mizuno, K. ed. *Samantapāsādikā.* 7 vols., PTS, 1924-1947.

Nakamura, H. *Ways of thinking of Eastern Peoples.* East-West Center Press, Honolulu, 1964.

Nyanatiloka, *Buddhist Dictionary.* Colombo, 1956.

——— *Guide through the Abhidhamma-Piṭaka.* Colombo, 1957.

Ogden, C. K. and Richards, I. A. *The Meaning of Meaning.* London, 1923.

Oldenberg, H. ed. *Dipavaṃsa.* London : Williams and Norgate, 1879.

——— ed. *Vinaya Piṭaka.* 5 vols., PTS, 1879-1883.

——— and Pischel, R. ed. *Thera-theri-gathā.* PTS, 1883.

Pischel, R. and Oldenberg, H. ed. *Thera-therī-gāthā*. PTS, 1883.

Pradhan, P. ed. *Abhidharma-koshabhāṣya of Vasubandhu*. Tibetan Sanskrit Works Series, Vol. VIII, K. P. Jayaswal Research Institute, Patna, 1967.

Quine, W. V. O. *Methods of Logic*. Revised edition. New York, 1959.

——— *Elementary Logic*. Revised edition. New York, 1965

Rhys Davids, C. A. F. and Feer, L. ed. *Saṁyutta nikāya*. 6 vols., PTS, 1884-1904.

———, Trenckner, V. and Chalmers, R. ed. *Majjhima nikāya*. 4 vols., PTS, 1887-1925.

——— tr. *Dialogues of the Buddha* (*Digha nikāya*). 3 vols., PTS, 1899-1921.

——— ed. *Vibhaṅga*. PTS, 1904.

——— and Aung, S. Z. tr. *Points of Controversy* (*Kathāvatthu*). PTS, 1915.

——— and Woodward, F. L. tr. *The Kindred Sayings* (*Saṁyutta nikāya*). 5 vols., PTS, 1917-1930.

——— tr. *A Buddhist Manual of Psychological Ethics* (*Dhammasaṅgaṇi*) RAS, 1923.

——— *The Birth of Indian Psychology and its Development in Buddhism*. London, 1936.

Rhys Davids, T. W. ed. *Abhidhammatha-saṅgaha*. JPTS, 1884.

———, Carpenter, J. E. and Stede, W. ed. *Sumaṅgalavilāsinī*. 3 vols., PTS, 1886-1932.

——— and Carpenter, J. E. ed. *Dīgha nikāya*. 3 vols., PTS, 1889-1910.

——— tr. *Dialogues of the Buddha* (*Dīgha nikāya*). 3 vols., PTS, 1899-1921.

——— and Stede, W. ed. *Pāli-English Dictionary*. PTS, 1921-1925.

Richards, I. A. and Ogden, C. K. *The Meaning of Meaning*. London, 1923.

——— *The Philosophy of Rhetoric*. Oxford University Press, 1965.

Rudskoger, A. 'Fair, Foul, Nice, Proper' : *A Contribution to the Study of Polysemy*. Stockholm, 1952.

Saddhatissa, H. ed. *Upāsakajanālaṅkāra*. PTS, 1965.

Sakurabe, H. *A Study of the Abhidharmakośabhāṣya* (*Abhidharmakośabhāṣya* no Kenkyu). Kyoto, 1969.

Saussure, Ferdinand de, *Cours de linguistique générale*. 5th ed. Paris, 1955.

Smith, H. and Andersen, D. ed. *Suttanipāta*. PTS, 1913.

Stache-Rosen, Valentina, ed. *Das Saṅgitisūtra und Kommentar Saṅgitiparyāya*. (*Dogmatische Begriffsreihen im älteren Buddhismus*. II, Berlin, DAWB), 1968.

Stcherbatsky, Th. *The Central Conception of Buddhism and the Meaning af the Word "Dharma"*. RAS, 1923. MLBD (Reprint) 1980.

Stede, W., Rhys Davids, T. W. and Carpenter, J. E. ed. *Sumaṅgalavilāsinī*. 3 vols., PTS, 1886-1932.

——— ed. *Niddesa, Cūḷa*. PTS, 1918.

——— and Rhys Davids, T. W. ed. *Pāli-English Dictionary*. PTS, 1921-1925.

Steinthal, P. ed. *Udāna*. PTS, 1885.

Sumaṅgala, S. ed. *Dhammapada*. PTS, 1914.

Takakusu, J. and Watanabe, K. ed. *Taisho Shinshu Daizokyo*. 55 vols., Tokyo, 1924-1929.

———, Nagai, M. and Mizuno, K. ed. *Samantapāsādikā*. 7 vols., PTS, 1924-1947.

Taylor, A. C. ed. *Paṭisambhidāmagga*. 2 vols., PTS, 1905-1907.

Thomas, E. J. and La Vallée Poussin, L. de, ed. *Mahāniddesa*. 2 vols., PTS, 1916-1917.

Tin, P. M. tr. *The Expositor* (*Atthasālinī*). 2 vols., PTS, 1920-1921.

Trenckner, V. ed. *Milindapañha*. PTS, 1880.

———, Chalmers, R. and Rhys Davids, C. A. F. ed. *Majjhima nikāya*. 4 vols., PTS, 1887-1925.

Tripāṭhī, C. ed. *Fünfundzwanzig Sūtras des Nidānasaṃyukta*. (Sanskrit texte aus den Trufanfunden VIII) DAWB, Institut für Orientforschung, 1962.

Ullmann, S. *The Principles of Semantics*. Oxford, 1951.

——— *Semantics : An Introduction to the Science of Meaning*. Oxford, 1962.

Venkatacharya, T. ed. *The Gilgit Manuscript of the Saṅghabhedavastu*—Being the 17th and Last Section of the Vinaya of the Mūlasarvāstivādin, Part II. Instituto Italiano per il Medio ed Estremo Oriente, Roma, 1978.

Vidyabhusana, S. C. *History of the Mediaeval School of Indian Logic*. Calcutta, 1921.

Waldschmidt, E. ed. "Beitrage zur Textgeschichte des *Mahāparinirvāṇasūtra*," Nachrichten GWG, Fachgr. 3, Bd. 2, Hr. 3, 1939, ss. 55-94.

——— ed. Das *Mahāparinirvāṇasūtra*—text in Sanskrit und Tibetisch, verglichen mit dem Pāli nebst einer übersetzung der Chinesischen entsprechung im *Vinaya* der Mūlasarvāstivādins, Abhandlungen DAWB, Klasse für Sprachen, Literatur und Kunst, 2 parts, 1950 and 1951.

——— "Die Einleitung des *Saṅgītisūtra*," ZDMG, 1956, pp. 298-318.

Walleser, M. and Kopp, H ed. *Manorathapūraṇī : Aṅguttara Aṭṭhakathā*. 5 vols., PTS, 1924-1957.

Warder, A. K. and Buddhadatta, A. P. ed. *Mohavicchedanī Abhidhammamātikatthavaṇṇanā*. PTS, 1961.

——— "The Earliest Indian Logic," *Proceedings of the 25th International Congress of Orientalists*. vol. 4, Moscow, 1963, pp. 56-68.

——— *Introduction to Pālı*. PTS, 1963.

——— *Pāli Metre*. PTS, 1967.

——— *Indian Buddhism*. First Edition, Delhi, 1970; Second Edition, Delhi, 1980 .(MLBD)

——— *Outline of Indian Philosophy*. Delhi, 1971. (MLBD)

——— "Dharmas and Data," *Journal of Indian Philosophy*. Vol. 1, No. 3, D. Reidel Publishing Company / Dordrecht-Holland, November 1971, pp. 272-295.

——— "The Concept of a Concept," *Journal of Indian philosophy*. Vol. 1, No.2, D. Reidel Publishing Company / Dordrecht-Holland, March 1971, pp.181-196.

Watanabe, K. and Takakusu, J. ed. *Taisho Śhinshu Daizokyo*. 55 vols., Tokyo, 1924-1929.

Windisch, E. ed. *Itivuttaka*. PTS, 1890.

Woods, J. H., Kosambi, D. and Horner, I. B. ed. *Papañcasūdanī: Majjhima Aṭṭhakathā*. PTS, 1922-1938.

Woodward, F. L. and Rhys Davids, C. A. F. tr. *The Kindred Sayings* (*Saṁyutta nikāya*). 5 vols., PTS, 1917-1930.

——— ed. *Sāratthappakāsinī* : *Saṁyutta Aṭṭhakathā*. 3 vols., PTS, 1927-1937.

——— and Hare, E. M. tr. *The Book of Gradual Sayings* (*Aṅguttara nikāya*). 5 vols., PTS, 1932-1936.

INDEX

B

Q

U